Conditions for Second Language Learning

Introduction to a general theory

Bernard Spolsky

Oxford University Press

Oxford University Press
Walton Street, Oxford OX2 6DP

Oxford   New York   Toronto
Delhi   Bombay   Calcutta   Madras   Karachi
Petaling Jaya   Singapore   Hong Kong   Tokyo
Nairobi   Dar es Salaam   Cape Town
Melbourne   Auckland

and associated companies in
Berlin   Ibadan

Oxford and *Oxford English* are trade marks of
Oxford University Press

ISBN 0 19 437063 1

Typeset by Pentacor Ltd, High Wycombe, Bucks.
Printed in Hong Kong.

For Ellen

פיה פתחה בחכמה

Acknowledgements

The author and publishers would like to thank the following for permission to reproduce the material below:

Edward Arnold for the extract from R. C. Gardner: *Social Psychology and Second Language Learning: the Role of Attitudes and Motivation*

Professor James J. Asher and the Annals of the New York Academy of Sciences for the extract from 'The total physical response (TPR): Theory and practice' in H. Winitz (ed.): *Native and Foreign Language Acquisition*

Professor Leslie Beebe and Professor Howard Giles for the extract from 'Speech accommodation theories: a discussion in terms of second-language acquisition' in *International Journal of the Sociology of Language* 46

Cambridge University Press for extracts from A. Bell: 'Language style as audience design' in *Language in Society* 13

Professor R. L. Cooper and Professor C. W. Greenbaum for extracts from their unpublished manuscript: 'Accommodation as a framework for the study of simplified registers'

The Economist for the extract on Parallel Distributed Processing published in the issue of 26 December 1987

Professor Sascha W. Felix for extracts from 'The effect of formal instruction on second language acquisition' in *Language Learning* 31

The authors for extracts from R. C. Gardner, P. C. Smythe, and G. R. Brunet: 'Intensive second language study: effects on attitudes, motivation, and French achievement' in *Language Learning* 27

Harper & Row, Publishers, Inc. for extracts from S. Krashen: 'The theoretical and practical relevance of simple codes in second language acquisition' in R. C. Scarcella and S. D. Krashen (eds.): *Research in Second Language Acquisition*

The MIT Press for extracts from R. Jackendoff: *Semantics and Cognition*

Professor John H. Schumann for the extract from 'Second language acquisition: the pidginization hypothesis' in *Language Learning* 26

Simon and Schuster for extracts from M. L. Kean: 'Core issues in transfer' in E. Kellerman and M. Sharwood Smith (eds.): *Crosslinguistic Influences in Second Language Acquisition*

Professor Peter Strevens for the extract from 'Learning English better through more effective teaching: six postulates for a model of language learning/teaching' in *World Englishes* 7/1

Professor Merrill Swain for the extract from 'Time and timing in bilingual education' in *Language Learning* 31

Contents

Preface

It is more than a little humbling to find that a book one has spent much of one's professional career trying to write can claim to be no more than an introduction. The ideas in it have developed over twenty years. Whenever I can, I have said where they come from, but I am certain that there will be many sources that I do not recall, notions and phrases I have absorbed from reading and teaching and listening, and that I pass on into the public domain of knowledge. I take this opportunity to thank my teachers, colleagues, and students.

Apart from the longish incubation period, the writing of this book took a number of years. An unexpected gap in a teaching programme gave me the opportunity to prepare a dozen or so lectures on current theories of second language learning; this later formed the basis for a paper I was invited to give at the University of Wisconsin-Milwaukee conference in 1985. From these initial notes, the book started to take shape, but the bulk of the work of writing waited for a year's leave from Bar-Ilan University; without the sabbatical, I doubt that it would have been finished.

I am grateful therefore to Bar-Ilan University for the time to write the book, to the University of London Institute of Education, which made me a research fellow while I was writing, and to Carmel College, which provided me with an ideal setting for scholarly work. In particular, I must thank my colleagues at Bar-Ilan, who allowed me a year free from departmental responsibility; Henry Widdowson, who took a deep interest in the book and whose questions I have tried to answer, often unsuccessfully, but always feeling it was worth trying; Peter Skehan, who provided access to computers and—even more important—a fund of useful information and a continuing availability for discussion; and the Headmaster, Phillip Skelker, of Carmel College, its staff, and pupils, who encouraged and suffered and shared in the case study. I also want to thank a number of universities in Britain, Japan, the Netherlands, and New Zealand, which during the year I was on sabbatical leave gave me the opportunity to try out some of the formulations on captive audiences; questions raised in those lectures led to much necessary rethinking.

I should like also to thank Raphael Nir for discussions and collaboration on a larger Hebrew language study, part of which is reported here; Robert Cooper for providing a critical and friendly ear over the years; Ellen Bialystok, whose wise comments on the draft manuscript helped solve some problems and raised others I am unable (or unwilling) to answer; and Cristina Whitecross, Anne Conybeare, and others at the Oxford University Press, who have encouraged me and helped me prepare the book for publication.

The dedication recognizes a quarter-century of love, companionship, stimulation, and the sharing, among other things, of conditions for second language learning, preference rules, computers, and our two children, whose characters and actions honour their mother and delight their father.

Jerusalem
February 1988

Introduction
The need for a general theory

The task of a general theory

Like many other workers faced with difficult and often unrewarding tasks, language teachers long for someone to offer them a simple and effective method that will suit all kinds of learners. Responding to this demand, scholars who have built theories of second language learning have often set as their main criterion not the elegant parsimony expected of a scientific theory but the stark appeal of a crisp advertising slogan. Translatability (even translation) into a teaching method rather than accounting for the empirical facts has been the goal pursued by many theory builders.

With the toppling of the Audio-Lingual Method from its throne, however, it seemed for a while that a general acceptance of eclecticism in language teaching would relax pressure on theorists and let them get on with their own particular job. All indications were, Stern (1985) remarked, that the profession would get over the 'century-old obsession' with finding a panacea and that 'a more sophisticated analysis of pedagogy would no longer be satisfied with the global and ill-defined method concept'. We might even have hoped that the sound notion of informed language teaching described by Strevens (1985) would come to hold sway, but the seventies and eighties have continued the search for the pot of gold, and there has been a new method boom. Where once they were faced with Berlitz Methods, and Army Methods, and Ollendorf Methods, and Direct Methods, and Series Methods, language teachers are now offered the Total Physical Response, Community Counselling, and Suggestopedia. Even scholars who started in solid theoretical research have caught the methods fever, as Oller and Richard-Amato (1983) published *Methods that Work* and Stephen Krashen, who made an important attempt to assemble current research into an integrated theory, latched on to the Natural Approach[1] and went from theorizing to promotion.

There are two points that I want to make: the first is that there are serious weaknesses with the theoretical bases of these various methods, not excluding Krashen's method and the theory it is based on;[2] the second is the more general point that any theory of second language learning that leads to a single method is obviously wrong. If you look at the complexity of the circumstances under which second languages are learned, or fail to be learned, you immediately see that a theory must not only be equally complex but must also be able to account for the success and failures of the many different methods that have been and are used throughout the language teaching world.

The goal of this book then is certainly not to propose a new method but rather to explore the requirements for a general theory of second language learning by examining the conditions under which languages are learned, and to consider the relevance of such a theory for language teaching. I describe the theory as *general* to distinguish it from theories of formal classroom learning,[3] or of informal natural learning,[4] or the learning of one part of a language, such as sentence-level syntax.[5] I use the term *theory*[6] to mean a hypothesis or set of hypotheses[7] that has been or can be verified empirically.[8] I use the term *second language learning* to refer to the acquisition of a language once a first language has been learned, say after the age of two,[9] without any technical definition or jargon or in-group implication for the words *learning* or *acquisition*.[10] Within these definitions, I see the task of a theory of second language learning as being to account both for the fact that people can learn more than one language, and for the generalizable individual differences that occur in such learning.

> First, it is always the case that some individuals are more successful than others in mastering the language, even though the language experience has in all cases been ostensibly identical. Second, for a particular individual, some aspects of language learning are mastered more easily than are others. (Bialystok 1978:69)

This makes the task similar in many ways to that of understanding first language learning at more advanced stages, although it must be pointed out that current psycholinguistic interest in first language acquisition has focused on the initial stages of learning and on the universal acquisition of language rather than on the individual variations in ultimate accomplishment.

A general theory of second language learning such as I am seeking to develop will need to relate in significant ways to a theory of first language learning. Ideally, rather than seeking separate theories of first and second language learning, I should perhaps be pursuing a unified theory of language learning (Carroll 1981), which would, within itself, distinguish between first and second language learning,[11] including, for instance, the fact that in the case of second language learning, learners have already succeeded in such crucial issues as distinguishing the sounds of language from the noise around them, and recognizing the basic working of speech acts. Omitting this initial stage of first language acquisition, much of what I propose here can easily and usefully be applied to mother tongue learning, to the learning of additional dialects and registers, to the development of control of standardized and classical varieties of one's first language, and to the complex variation of individual achievement in all language learning.

In spite of the attractiveness of this challenge, I have chosen at this stage to accept the constraint of working to develop a theory of second language learning independently, accepting the common scientific practice when dealing with complex systems of attempting to deal with one definable part at a time. But, as is clear in the use of the term 'general' and will be shown in more detail, it is an essential part of my approach to consider all kinds of second language learning together, calling on the model (and not some a priori limitation of scope) to show the differences proposed between, for example, second and foreign language learning and formal and informal learning.

If I may use a rhetorical form that is favoured by Joshua Fishman, the critical issues to be dealt with may be set out in the following question:

Who learns how much of what language under what conditions?

Using this as a mnemonic, a theory of second language learning must account for:

who: differences in the learner. This includes such factors as age, ability, intelligence, specific abilities (for example, hearing acuity), special aptitudes, attitudes (to learning, to a language, and to its speakers), motivation, choice among strategies, personality. These factors form a continuum from permanence (for example, those that are biologically given) to modifiability (under various controls).

learns: the process itself. How many kinds of learning are there? What is already there, preprogrammed in some way? What is the difference between conscious (explicit) and unconscious (implicit) knowledge? Between knowing and being able to? Between learning a single item and gaining control of functional skill? How does transfer work? How does learning vary individually and culturally?

how much of: What is the criterion for having learned? What part of language is learned (for example, phonology versus grammar versus semantics versus culture)? How does one account for learning single items? How different is the development of functional proficiency?

what language or variety, or mode, or dialect. And what about culture?

under what conditions: Is it amount or kind of exposure that makes the difference? How does exposure lead to learning? Who is the best person to learn from?

And how does each of these factors interact with the others? What kind of person prefers what kind of strategy? Who learns best under what conditions? What kind of person learns what parts of language? What variety of language is best learned by what kind of learner under what kind of circumstances?

This brief analysis helps us see the complexity of the question and suggests something about the nature of the model that might provide a satisfying solution to it. It is most unlikely to be a simple basic principle such as those proposed by any of the New Key Methods,[12] or even a more sophisticated combination of half a dozen hypotheses such as Stephen Krashen has proposed. The claims behind these method-supporting theories of course all have a modicum of truth; they are 'correct' with certain interpretations under certain conditions; they capture certain facts; but they are either so loosely worded as to be meaningless, or when they are made precise, they are wrong. Rather, as I will try to show in this book, a general theory of second language learning is best expressed as a complex collection of typical and categorical rules or conditions. As I will suggest in Chapter 1, it can be most appropriately stated in terms similar to the preference model in linguistics proposed by Jackendoff (1983), and not by models consisting only of well-formedness conditions nor certainly by single factor or simple models. Language learning results, the theory will claim, from the interaction and integration of a large number of factors and not from any single factor.

Two preliminary questions arise. First, one might ask how theory relates to practice. A theory of second language learning will need to explain (that is to say, it will be testable against) any kind of example of second language learning; it will not be useful to have, for instance, a separate theory of adult second language learning, or of immersion learning, but at the same time, a theory will be expected to explain differences observable between these various kinds of learning. A complete theory will thus be a heuristic for studying the effect of various modifications of teaching goals, situations and approaches rather than a prescription for how to teach. Teaching practice will in essence serve as a method of testing a theory empirically, rather than being its direct outcome. A theory of second language learning, then, will have implications for teaching and not direct applications.[13] It will be relevant to any model of language teaching, but will not be its only component. In other words, it will need to avoid both the Scylla of imperialistic application and the Charybdis of scholarly irresponsibility: both theory and practice must work in mutual respect, for, as Widdowson (1984a:36) summed it up, 'The effectiveness of practice depends on relevant theory; the relevance of theory depends on effective practice.' One of my main tasks in this book is to try to clarify the notions of relevance and effectiveness.

A second important question is whether or not a theory of second language learning needs to be a processing model, proposing a working model of exactly how language learning takes place. I think the answer is, not yet. While there is some value in the metaphors provided by building models that simulate the process of language use or learning, there is also a cost, for a metaphor, once it has been created, tends to dominate our thought. Having made up a name like a 'language acquisition device' or a 'monitor' or an 'affective filter', or having drawn a 'model' with labelled boxes, it is easy to fall into the trap of believing that this now accounts for the process. If it is to be productive, a metaphor or model may serve us only as a starting point, for the challenge remains to specify exactly how such a model could work in the human brain as we know it. And, as I shall argue later, it is too early to do this with any feeling of certainty.

My goal in this book, then, will not be to establish a model of how language is learned, but rather to explore how to specify, as exactly as possible, the conditions under which learning takes place. As such, while this study will set out specifications that must be met by a processing model and while it aims to be consistent with what little is known about language in the brain, it will make no claims as to the nature of such processing nor rely on any guesses from neurophysiology. In the last chapter, however, I will speculate on more process-oriented approaches, when I consider the possible application of expert systems, or, more challenging, the revolutionary implications of research on Parallel Distributed Processing.

Other models

In the light of the discussion so far, it is understandable that there are very few adequate candidates for the title of a general theory (although there is a great deal of evidence and theorizing that needs to be taken into account in developing such a theory). The most vigorous is probably Krashen's Monitor Model, which with all its fundamental weaknesses makes the best attempt at a comprehensive theory accounting for current research in second language learning. In critical ways that I have discussed elsewhere (Spolsky 1985c), Krashen's model is too vague for our purposes.

The closest models in spirit and completeness to my approach are the informal presentation of second language learning theory in Stern (1982–3) and the socio-educational model proposed by Gardner (1983, 1985). Stern sets out a balanced description of the state of the art, cautioning where he sees uncertainty. As will become clear, I not only accept this uncertainty but attempt to integrate it into the theory by using the insights of Preference Linguistics. Gardner builds on Lambert's and his own earlier work with attitudes and motivations to develop a causal model that can be empirically tested. My differences from him are partly in details of the theory and partly in the implications of the preference model. I will also attempt to make clear my relations to current views of language learning called Second Language Acquisition theory and ably summarized by Ellis (1985)[14] and Klein (1986). While my approach is what Strevens (1985) would have to label a 'theory-dominated paradigm' because it is interested in theory, it attempts to avoid the constraints Strevens sees in the paradigm's lack of interest in practice.

The failure of models like Krashen's to stand up to detailed scrutiny has discouraged many scholars from expecting any kind of useful results from theorizing, and many others from expecting that theory will have any practical relevance. The most extreme view is perhaps that restated by Hughes (1983:1–2): 'It must be said at the outset that it is not at all certain that at the present time there are any clear implications for language teaching to be drawn from the study of second language learning.' Similar concern is expressed by many others. It is not easy at this time even to be clear on the nature of the model that will succeed. As Wode concludes in his excellent review of issues in second language learning, a comprehensive view is necessary but 'No neurophysiological model of the functioning of the human brain, no linguistic theory, and no psychological learning theory—whether behaviouristic, cognitive, or other—is presently available which seems suited to describe the facts empirically observable when human beings learn language' (Wode 1981:8).

But if we are to persist in our search for a general theory, where can we look? One strategy is always to guess that someone else might have the answer. This is essentially what happens with those of our colleagues who go to neurophysiology, but the answers they receive are far from conclusive. In an introduction to the field of psycholinguistics from the point of view of second language learning, Hatch describes the neurolinguistic basis of language as something still to be established: 'Where messages go and what happens to them are two of our most intriguing unanswered questions. We do, of course, know a great deal about the brain, but although we have learned to name all the parts, we still do not truly understand what happens to language input or how language output is formed' (Hatch 1983:198). The black box in other words remains opaque, but there are a number of more or less informed and more or less plausible guesses about how it might work, and some rather imaginative guesses about the implication of these guesses for second language learning. In spite of the optimism of scholars like Lamendella (1977), there seem to be more solid grounds for the caution expressed by people who have looked at implications of neurophysiology for second language learning; I refer readers in particular to Hatch, Galloway (1981), Cohen (1982), Seliger (1982), Genesee (1982), and Scovel (1982).

If we eschew neurophysiology, there are alternative approaches. One is to start with our own knowledge, as linguists or language teachers, and set out to build a learning theory that fits that knowledge. This is what Lado (1985) does, describing in more or less linguistic terms his observations of the complexity of first language learning. It is salutary, for instance, to be reminded that children have as hard a job learning their first as any subsequent language. Lado's four stages are interesting to look at in the light of Krashen's very different hypotheses; Lado too sees the importance of meaning for 'completion of the communication cycle' which is the first stage of learning; he adds an important role for conscious knowledge in the second stage of 'assimilation'; he recognizes the place of practice in the 'development of facility' (something that Krashen seems to omit completely); and adds a further stage of going beyond language learning to language use, which seems to suggest that any use in the first stages is limited. It would be interesting to see these ideas developed into a full blown-theory of second language learning.

Another complete model that deserves attention is that proposed by Gloria Sampson (1982) who, in an intriguing paper, starts with a baker's dozen of facts, some controversial but many fair statements of current consensuses, goes on to note that one of the main problems in language learning is to explain how quantitative changes (for example, in the ratio of incorrect to correct forms) lead to qualitative changes (the move from one system to a new one), and proposes as a solution a dialectical model of function and form. What is especially important is that Sampson tries to deal with the social influence on the biological unfolding of language. Like all dichotomous models, hers is a powerful one, enabling her to explain away for instance the morpheme-ordering studies by the fact that they were all done with students taught in classrooms with similarly restricted functions, and providing socio-political support for evidence of fossilization in the second language learning of the underprivileged classes. This last point fits in very interestingly with Schumann's (and others') observations about second language learning and pidginization.[15]

Another field has claim to attention. As linguists often tend to forget, learning theory is the special province of psychology. Lulled by the belief that Chomsky overthrew Skinner who had earlier cast aside Pavlov, we have been trying to build our own models of learning, and the results of amateur work show up. But it is surely to be expected that there would be psychologists who have tried not to abandon but, in the traditional way of all good paradigms, to patch up old models by seeing what they can incorporate of the new. We have been fortunate (although we have not taken full enough advantage of this) to have John Carroll who in his long and productive career has worked to convince both psychology and linguistics of the relevance of the other field, and has constantly been willing to consider the practical implications of each field for language teaching or testing. I cannot do justice to one of his most recent (1981) attempts at sketching what he calls a unified theory of language learning—it aims to include first as well as second language learning, postulating a way to distinguish between them. As he describes it, his model starts with a traditional learning theory of the Thorndikian or Skinnerian variety but varies from that theory in a number of ways: most fundamentally, it allows conscious response selection, which makes it a cognitive theory; it also allows for antecedent effects (explaining how it is possible to recognize a stimulus as of a specific type); and it distinguishes between controlled and automatic processes. It further includes a kind of 'performance grammar' (Carroll's own term, but similar, he points out, to models proposed by Halliday and Schlesinger). His model will, I hope, be further explained and developed; it deserves very careful attention as one possible map to follow.

One of the key problems with reconciling current theories of second language learning is the lack of clarity over the level of focus of their application. A theory of second language learning may try to account for an individual learning a single item: to predict or explain the learning of, for instance, a particular grammatical, phonological, or lexical item.[16] The task given to the theory may be made more complicated in various ways: it may be asked to account for more than one individual (or to distinguish among individuals or groups), or for more than one kind of learning, or for learning to more than one kind of criterion level; or it may be applied to various parts of the language or various clusters of functions and uses. Further, it may be called on to deal with various levels of this complication. Some studies, then, are concerned with a small group of individuals developing sufficient control of a few selected defined items to pass a test on them:[17] others aim to make generalizations about the degree of second language proficiency attained by a certain national population.

Once the enormous variation (as well as complexity) involved has been recognized, it is possible to understand both the difficulty of reaching valid and supportable generalizations and the fascination and appeal of such simplified claims as are regularly made in simple powerful models. The constant cries of developers hawking new methods of teaching second languages is the best evidence one can have of the complexity of the practical problems faced by those who would teach or learn. At the same time, the dissatisfaction continually expressed with new proposals that try to account for the nature of language learning confirms that the problem is theoretical as well as practical. There is an attraction in attempts to simplify, and one can appreciate Krashen's urge to fit the large body of facts he has mastered into a easily communicable five-point model. In doing this, he has done a major service in providing a worthwhile target, reminded us of the value of comprehensive models and challenged others to develop their own. But comprehensive models must be, I believe, more complex than his if they are to account not just for the material he covers but for the full complexity of the ways in which people develop the complex ability to use more than one language. Such a model will be explored in the rest of this book.

Notes

1 The Natural Approach is set out in Krashen and Terrell (1983); a review by Krahnke (1985) shows the dangers of the presentation of an absolutist set of claims, many of them sensible, that appears to justify just about any method of instruction.
2 See for detailed discussion McLaughlin (1978, 1987), Gregg (1984), and Spolsky (1985b, 1985c). Klein (1986:29) points out also that Krashen's Monitor Model is 'not a model of language acquisition in general' but an attempt to explain how acquisition might be 'influenced by conscious awareness'.
3 For example, that proposed by Robert Gardner, although Gardner now concedes that his theory might be more general than he originally proposed.
4 For example, John Schumann's acculturation model, although Schumann has now been persuaded that it might be relevant to classroom learning too.
5 For example, Second Language Acquisition (SLA) is generally restricted to this level.
6 For a discussion of various uses in language learning of the term *theory*, see Stern (1983:25ff).
7 The major hypothesis of the book is that second language learning can be accounted for by a set of hypotheses that will be stated informally as conditions for learning.
8 Given the complexity of studies involving human beings, not all hypotheses can be formally tested, but one should expect to be shown how they might be falsified.
9 Klein (1986:15) would set this age a little higher: 'at the age of 3 or 4'. He draws attention to the fine distinctions that occur when two languages are acquired early between 'second language learning' and 'bilingual first language acquisition'. Dodson (1985) points out that even if two languages are acquired as first languages, one is generally preferred for each area of experience.
10 As will become clearer, the post-Chomskyan distinction between these two, carried to its ultimate in Krashen's first hypothesis, turns out to be confusing and unnecessary.
11 A general model of this kind is sketched out in Titone (1982) and Titone and Danesi (1985).
12 Gouin, Lozanov, Gattegno, and Asher all surely have made important contributions, but none of their panaceas can be said to fill the need for an overall theory.

13 Compare Spolsky (1969b). Similar approaches are accepted in Titone and Danesi (1985); see also Widdowson (1984a:28–36) and Lightbown (1985).

14 The eleven hypotheses with which Ellis (1985:278–80) concludes are not proposed as a single or necessarily consistent theory, but are an excellent summary of the present state of knowledge of the learning of some important features of the grammar of a second language.

15 See Cazden, Cancino, Rosansky, and Schumann (1975), Corder (1975), Schumann (1978a, 1978b), Stauble (1978).

16 Of course it is far from simple to define in any precise way what is meant by a single item.

17 Researchers in the Second Language Acquisition (SLA) tradition tend, as Ellis (1985) regularly and wisely points out, to concentrate their attention on studies of learning a restricted number of morphological and syntactic items.

1 A general theory of second language learning

Features of a general theory

The model that I am proposing in this book derives its strength from five features. The first of these is its unabashed immodesty in attempting to be general, to combine in a single theory all aspects of second language learning. Its very generality makes it possible to consider within one model (and so to attempt to understand and describe the relevant differences that exist between) second and foreign language learning, learning for general and specific purposes, formal and informal learning, developing knowledge and skills, to mention just a few of the ways theories are sometimes specialized.

While general, the theory is restricted to second language learning. As I said in the Introduction, this avoids the challenge of dealing with the special problems of first language acquisition. It leaves out, in other words, the important but distinct problems of how a child differentiates language from noise, the critical role of innate mechanisms in developing a grammar for the first language, the problem of how children come to acquire the grammatical, semantic, and pragmatic rules that they do with their first language. The restriction to second language learning permits a concentration not on the universality that is the concern of first language acquisition study but on the explanation of individual differences that is the focus of second language learning research. The examples that I cite are in the main selected from second and foreign language learning, but the principles are, I believe, equally applicable to the issues of second or standard dialect learning and the development of more sophisticated skills and knowledge in the mother tongue.

There is a danger, as McLaughlin (1987:157) remarks, in a general theory becoming too broad, and so blurring the details. A necessary result of this broadness of coverage, then, is the second feature of my approach, the emphasis on the fundamental need to be precise and clear on the nature of the goals and outcomes of learning. The theory requires us to recognize the complexity of the concept 'knowing a second language', which can vary almost without restriction in both kind and amount. There is no simple and single criterion according to which one can be said to know a language. There are varying criteria for successful learning that can be described in terms of linguistic knowledge (as the items of a grammar or a lexicon, for instance); in terms of generalized skills (reading, writing, speaking, listening); in terms of pragmatic or communicative functions (persuading, asking, apologizing, etc.); in terms of topic (for example, 'He knows enough French to read a sports page', 'She can give a lecture in Japanese on nuclear physics'), situation (for example, 'He knows kitchen French'), or interlocutor (for example, 'She knows enough German to talk to a Swiss banker'); or in terms of ability to perform a described task, usually a test (for example, 'He scored 625 on TOEFL, but the students in his section still cannot understand him'). A general theory of second language learning must not only be able to define all these possible outcomes, but it will also need to show how various combinations of conditions will be most likely to lead to each of them. Thus, a general theory of second language learning must allow for all the complexity of what it means to know and use a language. In doing this, it will need in particular to account both for the macrolevel of various kinds of functional proficiency and the microlevel of specific items and structures.

The third important feature of the model is that it is integrated and interactive: it assumes that all or many parts of it apply to any specific kind of learning, and that there is close interaction among the various parts of the model. In some cases, some of the components of the theory may not be relevant but all are potentially so, and when they work, they work together. For example, the theory will attempt to show not just how motivation affects learning, but how a particular strength and kind of motivation, with a particular kind of learning, leads to specific kinds of learning of certain parts of language in certain circumstances. Its generality requires that all potential connections be tested.[1]

The fourth feature of the model, and a major innovation in second language learning theory, is the use of an approach that includes a formally valued eclecticism. This is achieved through a model which recognizes that the various conditions for language learning are not all of them necessary conditions, without which learning will not take place; many of them are graded conditions (the more something is true, the more its consequence is likely to occur) and others are typicality conditions (that apply typically but not necessarily).[2] Many readers will recognize that I am drawing here on the preference model proposed by Ray Jackendoff and applied to semantics (Jackendoff 1983) and music (Lerdahl and Jackendoff 1983) and to literary interpretation (Schauber and E. Spolsky 1986). For those to whom the preference model is unknown, a brief summary will be useful.

Jackendoff sets out his argument for the power and ubiquity of preference rules in Chapter 8 of his book on semantics (1983). He distinguishes between well-formedness or necessary conditions on the one hand and typicality or preference conditions on the other, tracing his work to problems tackled by Gestalt psychologists such as Wertheimer (1923) in their attempts to deal with problems of grouping. The key point of this work was to establish the notion of stronger and weaker judgements that result from the convergence or the conflict of competing criteria. Lerdahl and Jackendoff (1983) show how these and similar principles apply to groupings in music. Jackendoff (1983) demonstrates the principle as it applies to word meanings; it provides in particular formal properties that will account for:

> . . . the gradation of judgements and . . . . the existence of exceptions to many apparently defining conditions. We can thus include in word meanings all those conditions that people seem to consider crucial, such as stripedness in tigers, two-leggedness in humans, and competition in games; they are simply marked as typicality conditions rather than as necessary conditions. (Jackendoff 1983:139)

After a number of examples relevant to semantics, Jackendoff concludes with the argument that preference rules are to be found throughout the range of human psychological processes.

> I see a preference rule system as a way to accomplish what psychological systems do well but computers do very badly: deriving a quasi-determinative result from unreliable data. In a preference rule system there are multiple converging sources of evidence for a judgement. In the ideal (stereotypical) case these sources are redundant; but no single one of the sources is essential, and in the worst case the system can make do with any one alone. Used as default values, the rules are invaluable in setting a course of action in the face of insufficient evidence. At higher levels of organization, they are a source of great flexibility and adaptivity in the overall conceptual system. (op.cit.:157)

As will become evident, I find Jackendoff's proposal to be of importance in two ways: first, it suggests important characterizations about the nature of language, and thus sets some of the parameters involved in learning a second language. To the extent that it is true of some aspects of language competence, it must be accounted for in a general theory of second language learning. Second, it makes important claims about the nature of learning itself, and so provides a model for the form of the theory of second language learning. Ellen Spolsky (1985) has shown that a preference model, with its rejection of purely binary logic, is consistent with current knowledge of the physiology of the brain. The preference model, while still at a level of gross generalization, is a further step towards the complexity of a model like that envisaged in Parallel Distributed Processing, as will be discussed in the last chapter.

The fifth feature of the model proposed in this book is its acceptance of the need to establish a general theory of second language learning firmly and clearly in a social context. Language learning is individual, but occurs in society, and while the social factors are not necessarily direct in their influence, they have strong and traceable indirect effects on the model at several critical instances.

Conditions for second language learning

Using the preference model as my base, then, I propose a first form of a general theory of second language learning as follows. The achievement of the various possible outcomes in second language learning depends on meeting a number of conditions. Some of these are necessary conditions,[3] without which learning is impossible; many are graded conditions, in which there is a relation between the amount or extent to which a condition is met and the nature of the outcome; others again are typicality conditions, that apply typically but not necessarily. All this allows, therefore, for the existence of a varied but limited set of alternative paths to the various possible outcomes.

Having mentioned what I consider strengths of the model, it is only fair to acknowledge weaknesses, ways in which I recognize that what I am proposing constitutes the prolegomena to a general theory rather than the theory itself. First, the fully developed model will need not just to be internally consistent but to make verifiable claims. While the enormous complexity of any studies of human beings means that verification in practice might be difficult or even impossible, the theory must make clear what kind of evidence will show that its claims are wrong. As will be argued in more detail in Chapter 13, falsifying a necessary condition is relatively simple, for one needs only to present counter-evidence. Typicality conditions are more of a problem; they can be shown to be necessary if there are no cases where they do not apply, but it is more difficult to pin down empirically claims that rules sometimes apply and sometimes do not. Larger arrays of preference rules may perhaps be falsifiable by statistical techniques (for example, if it is shown that the proposed condition is not a relevant factor in accounting for outcomes) and by being shown to be irrelevant to expert systems. But I am fully aware of the informality with which the conditions set out later in this chapter are expressed, looking in many cases much more like postulates or premises than the formal rules of linguists or the precise hypotheses of experimental psychologists.

There is a second problem. If I have risked upsetting the theorists by my lack of formalization, I may at the same time disappoint language teachers who are looking for a clear set of guidelines to their practice. Because the model shows that there are in fact multiple paths to a complex set of outcomes, it is likely to have been oversimplified if it seems to have direct applications or lead to a single approach to language teaching. Any intelligent and disinterested observer knows that there are many ways to learn languages and many ways to teach them,[4] that some ways work with some students in some circumstances and fail with others. This is why good language teachers are and always have been eclectic: they are open to new proposals, and flexible to the needs of their students and the changing goals of their course. At best, the theory will aim to explain these variable successes; at the same time, it might suggest the possibility of modifications in practice, and the evaluation of methods that are most appropriate, for given kinds of students with certain kinds of motivation, to achieve certain defined kinds of second language knowledge and skills.

As an overview, one way of attempting to present a model of second language learning, a formalization that will permit empirical testing, is in the form of an underspecified mathematical formula. In later parts of the book I will try to show the nature of the underspecification and consider how the formula might be refined and made more sophisticated.

Let us call the linguistic outcome in which we are interested K, a symbol standing for the knowledge and skills in the second language of the learner. We can then say that K_f (knowledge and skills at some future time) is a result of four groups of factors: K_p (knowledge and skills at the moment including general knowledge of the learner's first and any other languages), A (a symbol intended to represent various components of ability including physiological, biological, intellectual, and cognitive skills), M (a symbol to include various affective factors such as personality, attitudes, motivation, and anxiety), and O (or opportunity for learning the language, consisting of time multiplied by kind, the latter covering the range of formal and informal situations in which the learner is exposed to the language).[5]

Simply stated, the formula $K_f = K_p + A + M + O$ is then a claim that each of the parts will make a difference to the result: if any one is absent, there can be no learning, and the greater any one is, the greater the amount of learning. In this form, it encompasses such cases as the specially able or the highly motivated learner who takes advantage of minimal opportunity, or the critical importance of amount of opportunity (time) in accounting for success. It will receive greater specification, so that we will see not just the composition and contribution of each of the factors, but the degree to which differentiation in one element can lead to different results. In its initial simplicity, then, it invites the elaboration that will capture the complexity of the phenomenon being studied.[6]

The special interest of the formula is that it is applicable not just to the macrolevel, the development of larger levels of proficiency especially dealt with by the descriptive model, but also to the microlevel, the learning of single items. For learning a language involves learning one item—sound, word, structure, speech formula, usage, whatever—at a time (although it must be noted that adding an element can often lead to the restructuring of what is already there into new larger units): the larger proficiencies are made up of the smaller particles. At the macrolevel, the elements of the formula are complex, but in the learning of single items, they are necessarily more simple and compressed effects of other factors. Thus, whereas the conditions making up M in developing a general proficiency have a strong enough effect to vary according to the kind as well as strength of motivation, M in learning a single item is more likely to be a single measure of willingness to persist in the effort to understand, memorize or practise the item. It is here that one might look for the connection between microlevel and macrolevel.

The additive model suggested by the formula is a useful starting point, and forms the basis for some of the statistical models used in the case study discussed in Chapter 13. But it does not go far enough in capturing the complex interaction or all the interlocking influences that a preference model will demonstrate.

The preference model involves the interaction of several clusters of interrelated conditions. In this chapter I shall give with minimum comment a list of 74 conditions which I propose are relevant to second language learning. These conditions will be further discussed in the rest of the book where they will be shown to be the natural and logical conclusion of current research in second language learning. They form, in other words, a statement of the 'state of the art', but it must be stressed that they are not presented as novel or original (although there will be some where it is clear that my position is different from that of other scholars); the originality is in the claim that they all interact to form a general theory.

The first argument that will be presented is the need for precise specification of the linguistic knowledge that is the outcome of second language learning. In Chapter 2 I deal with what it means to know a language, and propose that the best summary of our present under-standing of the nature of language knowledge and how to measure it is provided by the following conditions:

Condition 1
Language as System condition (necessary): A second language learner's knowledge of a second language forms a systematic whole.

Condition 2
Native Speaker Target condition (typical, graded): Second language learner language aims to approximate native speaker language.

Condition 3
Variability condition (necessary): Like first language knowledge, second language knowledge is marked by variability.

Condition 4
Unanalysed Knowledge condition (necessary, graded): Unanalysed knowledge (memorized chunks of the second language) may be used by second language learners, but unanalysed knowledge by itself provides for very restricted, language-like behaviour.

Condition 5
Analysed Knowledge condition (necessary, graded): As linguistic knowledge is analysed into its constituent parts, it becomes available for recombination; this creative language use may be enriched with unanalysed knowledge.

Condition 6
Specific Variety condition (necessary): When one learns a second language, one learns one or more varieties of that language. As a corollary, goals for a formal course of instruction need to specify the variety or varieties of language being taught.

Condition 7
Academic Skills condition (typical, graded): Learning of a second language may be associated to varying degrees with the development of academic language skills.

In Chapter 3 the importance of language use is stressed, and the following conditions are introduced:

Condition 8
Productive/Receptive Skills condition (necessary, graded): Individual language learners vary in their productive and receptive skills.

Condition 9
Receptive Skills stronger than Productive condition (typical, graded): Receptive language skills (understanding speech or written text) usually develop before productive skills (speaking, writing) and usually develop to a higher level.

Condition 10
Implicit Knowledge condition (typical, graded): Language knowledge, analysed and so available for recombination, may be intuitive and so not be consciously available to the learner.

Condition 11
Explicit Knowledge condition (typical, graded): Analysed language knowledge may be consciously available to the speaker who is able to state a rule or explain the reason for a decision to use a certain form.

Condition 12
Automaticity condition (necessary, graded): Ability to use language knowledge varies in automaticity; this is shown by the fluency with which a person speaks.

Condition 13
Accuracy condition (necessary, graded): Ability to use language knowledge varies in accuracy.

Condition 14
Dual Knowledge condition (necessary): When one learns a second language, one develops both knowledge and skills in using that knowledge. As a corollary, goals for a formal course of instruction or tests of proficiency need to distinguish between knowledge and use, as well as between various levels of automaticity and accuracy in use.

Condition 15
Communicative Goal condition (typical, graded): Language learners may aim to achieve various degrees of control of a language for communicative purposes.

Chapter 4 begins a consideration of the measurement of language knowledge and skills, and discusses the functional and structural aspects of testing. From this discussion, the following conditions are derived:

Condition 16
Discrete Item condition (necessary): Knowing a language involves knowing a number of the discrete structural items (sounds, words, structures, etc.) that make it up.

Condition 17
Integrated Function condition (necessary): Knowledge of a language involves control of one or more integrated functional skills.

Condition 18
Integrated Skills Weighting/Ordering condition (typical, graded): The weighting (relative importance) and ordering of integrated skills are dependent on individually or socially determined goals for learning the language.

In Chapter 5 the implication of overall proficiency is considered, and a general summarizing condition for second language knowledge and skills is proposed:

Condition 19
Overall Proficiency condition (necessary): As a result of its systematicity, the existence of redundancy, and the overlap in the usefulness of structural items, knowledge of a language may be characterized as a general proficiency and measured.

Condition 20
Linguistic Outcome condition (typical, graded): Prefer to say that someone knows a second language if one or more criteria (to be specified) are met. The criteria are specifiable:

(a) as underlying knowledge or skills (Dual Knowledge condition)
(b) analysed or unanalysed (Analysed Knowledge condition; Unanalysed Knowledge condition)
(c) implicit or explicit (Implicit Knowledge condition; Explicit Knowledge condition)
(d) of individual structural items (sounds, lexical items, grammatical structures) (Discrete Item condition)
(e) which integrate into larger units (Language as System condition)
(f) such as functional skills (Integrated Function condition)
(g) for specified purposes (see, for instance, Academic Skills condition, Communicative Goal condition)
(h) or as overall proficiency (Overall Proficiency condition)
(i) productive or receptive (Productive/Receptive Skills condition)
(j) with a specified degree of accuracy (Variability condition; Accuracy condition)
(k) with a specified degree of fluency (Automaticity condition)
(l) and with a specified approximation to native speaker usage (Native Speaker Target condition)
(m) of one or more specified varieties of language (Specific Variety condition).

In Chapter 6 I start to look at individual factors that affect learning, and set out the psycholinguistic basis for second language learning. The following conditions derived from the overview of present knowledge are proposed and discussed:

Condition 21
Human Learner condition (necessary, postulate): A general theory of second language learning deals with the learning of a second or later language by a human being who has already learned a first language.

Condition 22
Physiological Normality condition (necessary): Any physiological or biological limitations that block the learning of a first language will similarly block the learning of a second language.

Condition 23
Native Pronunciation condition (typical, graded): The younger one starts to learn a second language, the better chance one has to develop a native-like pronunciation.

Condition 24
Abstract Skills condition (typical, graded): Formal classroom learning of a second language is favoured by the development of skills of abstraction and analysis.

Condition 25
Child's Openness condition (typical, graded): The greater openness to

external influence of a child favours the learning of a second language in informal situations.

Condition 26
Child's Dependence condition (typical, graded): The social situation faced by a child in a second language environment favours second language learning.

Chapter 7 looks at individual differences in ability and in personality. These conditions are identified:

Condition 27
Intelligence condition (typical, graded): The ability to perform well in standard intelligence tests correlates highly with school-related second language learning (i.e. in functional terms, such tasks as reading and writing of academic material in formal language, and as performing abstract tests of structural knowledge) but is unrelated to the learning of a second language for informal and social functions, except perhaps in the case of older learners.

Condition 28
Sound Discrimination condition (necessary, graded): The better a learner can discriminate between the sounds of the language and recognize the constituent parts, the more successful his or her learning of speaking and understanding a second language will be.

Condition 29
Memory condition (necessary, graded): In learning a new language, the better the learner's memory, the faster he or she will learn new items and the larger his or her vocabulary will be. This ability may vary for learning words aurally and visually.

Condition 30
Grammatical Sensitivity condition (necessary, graded): Beyond the necessary minimum ability to 'derive a grammar' implicitly, the better a learner's ability to recognize constituents and develop or understand generalizations about recombination and meaning (whether from explicit or implicit generalizations, in whatever forms), the faster he or she will develop control of the grammatical (and pragmatic) structure of a second language.

Condition 31
Learning Style Preference condition (typical, graded): Learners vary (both individually and according to such characteristics as age, level, and cultural origin) in their preference for learning style (visual, auditory, kinaesthetic, and tactile) and mode (group or individual); as a result, learning is best when the learning opportunity matches the learner's preference.

Condition 32
Expectations condition (typical, graded): A learner's expectations of the outcome of language learning interact with the learner's personality to control the selection of preferred learning strategies.

Condition 33
Second Language Learning Anxiety condition (typical, graded): Some learners, typically those with low initial proficiency, low motivation, and high general anxiety, develop levels of anxiety in learning and using a second language that interfere with the learning.

In Chapter 8 a discussion of the linguistic basis for second language provides the following conditions:

Condition 34
Language Distance condition (necessary, graded): The closer two languages are to each other genetically and typologically, the quicker a speaker of one will learn the other.

Condition 35
Shared Feature condition (necessary, graded): When two languages share a feature, learning is facilitated.

Condition 36
Contrastive Feature condition (necessary, graded): Differences between two languages interfere when speakers of one set out to learn the other.

Condition 37
Markedness Differential condition (necessary, graded): Marked features are more difficult to learn than unmarked.

Condition 38
Shared Parameter condition (necessary): When both native and target language have the same setting for some parameter of Universal Grammar (= have the same rule), minimal experience will be needed to trigger the correct form of the grammar.

Condition 39
Unmarked Parameter condition (typical): Prefer to use the unmarked (core, Universal Grammar) setting of the parameter.

Condition 40
Native Language Parameter condition (typical): Prefer to use the native language setting of the parameter.

Condition 41
Most Frequent Parameter condition (typical, graded): Prefer to use the most frequent setting of the parameter.

Chapter 9 turns to the social context in which second language learning takes place, and conditions are proposed that affect attitudes to and opportunities for learning:

Condition 42
Number of Speakers condition (typical, graded): The number of people who speak a language as a first or second language influences the desire of others to learn it.

Condition 43
Standard Language condition (necessary): Formal teaching situations are possible only with standardized languages.

Condition 44
Vitality condition (necessary): Informal learning situations are possible only with languages with vitality.

Condition 45
Official Use condition (typical, graded): Prefer to teach or learn a language which is officially used or recognized.

Condition 46
Modernized Language condition (typical, graded): Prefer to teach or learn a language which is standardized and which has been modernized.

Condition 47
Great Tradition condition (typical, graded): Prefer to teach or learn a language which has a desirable Great Tradition (including a religion) associated with it.

Condition 48
Linguistic Convergence condition (typical, graded): Prefer to learn a language when

(a) you desire the social approval of its speakers, and/or
(b) you see strong value in being able to communicate with its speakers, and/or
(c) there are no social norms providing other methods of communicating with speakers of that language, and/or
(d) your learning is reinforced or encouraged by speakers of the language.

Condition 49
Linguistic Divergence condition (typical, graded): Prefer not to learn a language if

(a) you wish to stress your continued membership of your own language community, and/or
(b) you wish to stress your dissociation from speakers of the language, and/or
(c) you wish speakers of that language to learn your language.

Against this social background, Chapter 10 proposes conditions relating to attitudes and motivation of the second language learner:

Condition 50
Aptitude condition (typical, graded): The greater a learner's aptitude, the faster he or she will learn all parts of the second language.

Condition 51
Exposure condition (necessary, graded): The more time spent learning any aspect of a second language, the more will be learned.

Condition 52
Motivation condition (typical, graded): The more motivation a learner has, the more time he or she will spend learning an aspect of a second language.

Condition 53
Attitude condition (typical, graded): A learner's attitudes affect the development of motivation.

Condition 54
Integrative Motivation condition (typical, graded): Integrative orientation, a cluster of favourable attitudes to the speakers of the target language, has a positive effect on the learning of a second language, and in particular on the development of a native-like pronunciation and semantic system.

Condition 55
Instrumental Language Learning or Teaching condition (typical, graded): If you need to speak to someone who does not know your language, you can learn that person's language or help that person to learn your language.

Condition 56
Language Values condition (graded, typical): The social and individual values which underlie language choice also determine the value an individual assigns to the learning of a specific language.

Chapter 11 begins the discussion of conditions to be met by learning opportunities:

Condition 57
Opportunity for Analysis condition (necessary, graded): Learning a language involves an opportunity to analyse it, consciously or unconsciously, into its constituent parts.

Condition 58
Opportunity for Synthesis condition (necessary, graded): Learning a language involves an opportunity to learn how its constituent parts are recombinable grammatically into larger units.

Condition 59
Opportunity for Contextual Embedding condition (necessary, graded): Learning a language involves an opportunity to learn how its elements are embedded in linguistic and non-linguistic contexts.

Condition 60
Opportunity for Matching condition (necessary, graded): Learning a language involves an opportunity for the learner to match his or her own knowledge with that of native speakers or other targets.

Condition 61
Opportunity for Remembering condition (necessary, graded): Learning a language involves an opportunity for new items to be remembered.

Condition 62
Opportunity for Practice condition (necessary, graded): Learning a language involves an opportunity for the new skills to be practised; the result is fluency.

Condition 63
Communication condition (typical of natural learning, graded): The language is being used for communication.

Condition 64
Learning Goal condition (typical of formal learning, graded): The language is being used so that it can be learned.

Condition 65
Fluent Speakers condition (typical of natural learning, graded): Many speakers in the environment are fluent and native.

Condition 66
Teacher Model condition (typical of formal learning, graded): Only one speaker (the teacher) is fluent; the majority in the environment (classroom) are not.

Condition 67
Open Area condition (typical of natural learning, graded): The learning takes place in the open or in unconstrained areas.

Condition 68
Classroom condition (typical of formal learning, graded): The learning takes place in a closed physical space, a single classroom.

Condition 69
Uncontrolled Language condition (typical of natural learning, graded): The language is normal and uncontrolled.

Condition 70
Simplified Language condition (typical of formal learning, graded): The language is simplified and controlled.

Condition 71
Comprehensible Input condition (typical of natural learning, graded): The learner is expected to understand; therefore the speaker makes an effort to see that language is comprehensible.

Condition 72
Drill Input condition (typical of formal learning, graded): The learner is expected to learn; therefore ample practice is given to develop automatic control.

Condition 73
Foreigner Talk condition (typical, graded): Conditions of speech addressed by native speakers to non-natives (foreigner talk) lead to modification in the structures and frequency of language that form the basis for input in natural learning situations.

Chapter 12 looks at some of these conditions in more detail and adds a general condition on formal instruction:

Condition 74
Formal Language Learning-Teaching condition (typical, graded): In formal language learning situations, multiple opportunities to observe and practise the new language can be provided. The more these match other relevant conditions (the learner, the goals, the situation), the more efficient the learning will be.

The conditions listed above have generally been stated informally. A more precise statement, looking more like a rule (Schauber and E. Spolsky 1986:22), would be in the form:

If (a specified condition) is met, then (a specified linguistic outcome) is true.

In the case of graded conditions, the form of the statement would be:

To the extent that (a specified condition) is met, then it is more likely that (a specified outcome) is true.

The conditions are also translatable (but not translated here) into hypotheses which might be tested empirically.

An overview

Because the model is interactive, it is useful at this point to sketch roughly how its parts go together.[7] Second language learning of any kind takes place in a social context, which makes up the first cluster of conditions. The social contexts of both the family or home, and the community, city, and state are relevant. The social context includes components such as the sociolinguistic situation, the general exposure of learners to other languages, the roles of the target language and other languages in the outside community and in the home, and the general perception of values of the target language and of bilingualism. It is expressed formally in language policies of various kinds: at the state level these may be laws or provision of language education;[8] at the home level these include decisions to speak a certain language or to encourage or discourage language learning.

The conditions described for the social context influence language learning in two ways: first, they lead to a learner's attitudes which are divisible, following Gardner (1979) and Gardner and his colleagues (1983), into those towards the community speaking the target language (integrativeness) and into those towards the learning situation. In this latter set I would want to include the learner's expectations and perceptions of the learning task and its possible outcomes. These two kinds of attitude and specific learning goals lead to the development of motivation on the part of the learner.

The second influence of the social context is in the provision of opportunities for language learning; these may be grouped roughly into formal and informal situations. Formal situations are the various institutionalized educational opportunities provided by a society for language learning. The availability of formal or informal learning opportunities (ranging from formal instruction to exposure to the language in use) itself also depends on the social context. More precisely, when there is formal instruction in a school, the social context and various parent factors (their education, their level of religious or ethnic or national allegiance, their socio-economic status, their place of birth, their knowledge of languages) determine parents' rationales, goals, and priorities. The social context (including any political expression of it) together with parents' rationales, goals and priorities, modified (or replaced) by any independent ideology of the school offering the programme determine the school's rationales, goals, and priorities. The school's rationales, goals, and priorities account for formal learning opportunities. It is also the social context that is the source of informal opportunities for language use and learning. Informal situations are available in different kinds and amount according to social conditions which determine the potential opportunities for a learner to interact with speakers and writers of the target language. Thus, the social context determines the actual nature of possibilities for social intercourse and other communicative transactions.

The second cluster comprises conditions of the learner: the language learner brings to the language learning task, besides the motivation already referred to, a number of capabilities and a body of previous knowledge and experience. Some of these capabilities are universal, such as an innate capability for deriving a grammar, an innate or learned capability for inferring interpretation from speech acts, and presuppositions about the uses of language. While these universal capabilities are basic in that they set necessary conditions for any learning, they are not of special interest in explaining variation in the outcomes, for they are theoretically available in all learners: they are as characteristic of human learners as are arms and legs. Others are specific to each learner's own background, whether linguistic or non-linguistic. Of particular import-ance among these personal learner characteristics are previous knowl-edge (of the first or other languages); age; language learning aptitude (especially important in formal learning situations); learning style and strategies; and personality factors, of which anxiety is the most clearly relevant. The combination of these learner factors accounts for the use the learner makes, consciously or unconsciously, of the socially provided formal or informal learning opportunities.

The interplay between language learner and learning opportunity (and in particular language addressed to the second language learner as modified by communication and performance strategies of learner and source) determines the learner's success in achieving the linguistic outcomes (linguistic and communicative competence of a variable nature) and non-linguistic outcomes (including changes of attitude) that have been determined personally (by the learner) or socially (by home, school, state, etc.). As a result of the interaction of 'strategies' used by the potential learner and by the teacher (or any other source of the target language), various outcomes occur, which may be linguistic or non-linguistic. I have already mentioned the complexity of linguistic outcomes, and will look at them in considerably more detail in the next chapters; non-linguistic outcomes include changes in attitude and satisfaction or frustration of personal learning goals.

The model so far described may be presented schematically as in Figure 1.1 (overleaf). This schematic layout is no more than a rough representation: the critical claim being made is that the preference model offers a method for formalizing what is left unspecified.

Given its fundamental importance to the theory, we will start to look in the next chapters at the nature of linguistic outcomes of second language learning, first (in Chapters 2 and 3) from the point of view of theory (What does it mean to know a language and to know how to use it?), and then (in Chapters 4 and 5) from the point of view of language testing (How do you get someone to perform their competence?). Chapter 6 will investigate capabilities and describe the general psycho-linguistic basis for learning a second language, looking at biological and neurophysiological aspects and the question of age as a factor. The following chapter will deal with individual differences in cognitive capacities and personality. In Chapter 8 I will discuss previous knowledge and in particular the linguistic basis (knowledge of the first language) and the way it may be seen as setting conditions for second language learning. In Chapters 9 and 10 I will set out the social context in which second languages are learned and explore the relation between social context and individual psychology as expressed in the develop-

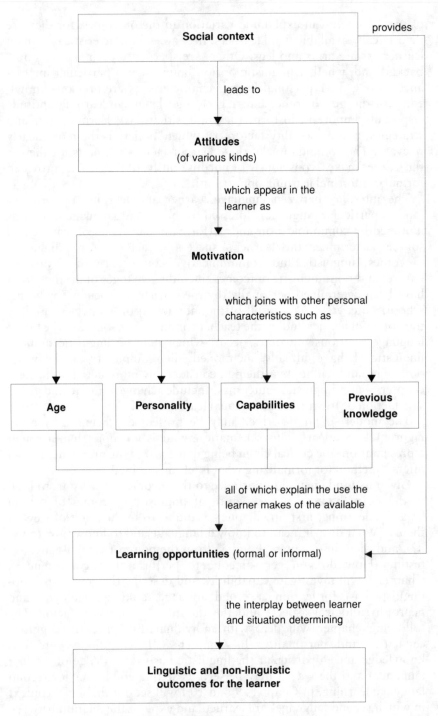

Figure 1.1   A model of second language learning

ment of attitudes and motivation. Chapters 11 and 12 will then look at conditions for language learning in, respectively, informal and formal language learning situations. Chapter 13 will discuss a single case study carried out to test the model; more data from the study are given in the Appendix. Finally, Chapter 14 will summarize the model and discuss the implications of an expert system as a method of setting it out and testing it and of other formal models including the implications of recent research on Parallel Distributed Processing.

Notes

1 The problem of dealing with complex causal models is discussed in Chapters 13 and 14.
2 Graded conditions are similar in many ways to the probability statements on linguistic variables that Labov proposes; typicality conditions are similar to the approach of prototypical semantics.
3 Schauber and E. Spolsky (1986:22) make a useful distinction between rules and conditions which I have not attempted to apply in this book.
4 Ellis (1985:297) recognizes this possibility when he says that 'It is also possible that a single phenomenon is the result of more than one cause.'
5 The formula proposed here is based on John Carroll's model for instruction; see Carroll (1962).
6 As will become clear, the use of addition is possibly misleading. A more precise formulation is suggested in Chapter 13.
7 The way the model works as a whole is illustrated in Chapter 13 and discussed in Chapter 14.
8 For a detailed consideration of the relation of the community to second language teaching, see Ashworth (1985).

2 Knowing a language

Interlanguage

To be able to discuss intelligently the conditions that lead to second language learning requires a clear and precise definition of what it means to know a second language. The first task, then, is to investigate and establish the nature of K, the symbol for the outcome proposed at the end of the last chapter.

One of the most severe criticisms that can be fairly levelled against the presentation of many existing methods and attempts at theories is that they talk about learning a language as a general goal and do not specify exactly what kind of learning of what aspects of language they are trying to account for, or what criterion they set for achievement. For example, on close examination, Krashen's model turns out to be a theory of learning sentences in a second language. Although this is arguably a basic component of language knowledge, it is an unacceptably restricted goal for the vast majority of second language teaching programmes. Similarly, as Ellis is quick to admit, current work in what is called Second Language Acquisition[1] is largely restricted to some features of syntax and morphology: research in this tradition 'has tended to ignore the other levels of language' (Ellis 1985:5). As Gass (1986) remarks, many studies are further limited not just to single sentences but to a single grammatical component: phonology, syntax, semantics, or pragmatics.

In much the same way, it is often difficult to evaluate and compare theoretical claims, and the empirical studies that are intended to validate them, because their proponents use completely different criteria as measures of success. The Audio-Lingual Method involved a change in goal as much as in method. In contrast to the traditional teaching that it was intended to replace in American schools, it set a new goal of oral proficiency and resulted in the teaching of a number of pattern sentences with good pronunciation. From the first major study intended to investigate the effectiveness of the Audio-Lingual Method (Scherer and Wertheimer 1964), this confusion in the comparison of methods with different goals is apparent. The Audio-Lingual Method was in its turn to be blamed for not developing in students the ability to carry on spontaneous conversations, a goal it had not originally recognized.

A necessary first task, then, in developing a general theory of second language learning must be to deal with the fundamental question of what it means to know a language, to recognize its complexity and suggest a way of setting criteria. Only in the light of an answer to this question can one investigate the conditions in which this knowledge can be achieved, for, clearly, different aspects of knowledge and ability will be developed according to the learning conditions. Learner characteristics, circumstances, kind of exposure, ideology, and goals will all lead to different levels of mastery of the various language skills.

At various periods second language theorists have offered contrasting and conflicting views of the concept of knowledge of language. In the early 1950s most scholars would have assumed that knowing a language involved knowing a number of items and their potential arrangements; this item and arrangement grammar was just starting to be challenged by a notion of items and processes (rules). The second language learner was seen as having an imperfect knowledge of the items and arrangements of the language he or she was learning; the gaps waited to be filled by learning.

The major innovation of the American school of contrastive analysis, following the work of Charles Fries and Robert Lado, was to propose that the gaps were generally filled, and some of the correct knowledge was replaced or confused, by the grammar of the learner's first language. Thus, a second language learner's knowledge of a second language was subject to interference from his or her knowledge of the first.

While this notion is still held to be important (it will be discussed in much more detail in Chapter 8), the most widespread set of views at the present time has a somewhat different approach. Though, as we shall see, not constituting an organized and consistent body of theory, the most common approach is probably that loosely grouped under the rubric 'interlanguage', a term that in its various uses can perhaps be best glossed as 'a second language learner's knowledge of the target language'. Ellis (1985) regularly replaces it by the admittedly awkward but more accurate term 'language-learner language'.

The notion of interlanguage first appeared in the mid–1960s. One of its principal contributions was its underlying claim that the learner's knowledge is to be seen as a unified whole, in which new knowledge is integrated and systematically reorganized with previous knowledge of the native language. In this view, there are not gaps waiting to be filled by the first language, or even two competing language systems struggling for control, but rather the second language learner's knowledge is a complete whole, critically different from that of the first language learner. The principle may be summed up as a necessary condition:

Condition 1
Language as System condition (necessary): A second language learner's knowledge of a second language forms a systematic whole.

The earliest formulation of the notion was that proposed by S. Pit Corder (1967). Corder was influenced by the research in first language learning (for example, McNeill 1966) which was starting to show how the study of children's developing linguistic competence could be enhanced by using as evidence the regular occurrence of errors that could not be the result of imitation and therefore must demonstrate the development of rules or generalizations. Following this lead and applying it to second language learning, Corder (1976) suggested that the study of errors made by second language learners could in the same way provide evidence of their developing systematization of the language they were acquiring. In his now classic paper, precisely titled 'The significance of learners' errors', Corder suggested that errors of a systematic kind provided evidence of the nature of transitional competence, that is to say, the grammar or set of rules a learner used in producing sentences in the language he was learning. In a somewhat different model, but in general agreement, a paper by Nemser (1971) spoke of approximative systems—the term reflects the notion of successive approximations of target behaviour used at the time in work in programmed instruction.

Corder's proposal was particularly important, for it moved attention from the target language, or the target language and the native language, to the learner's own performance, and established this performance as a suitable object of research. The study of second language learning could thus move from the library to the classroom.

In thinking about the learner's performance as an object of study, Selinker picked up Corder's idea and tentatively tried out his own term: 'An "interlanguage" may be linguistically described using as data the observable output resulting from a speaker's attempt to produce a foreign norm, i.e. both his errors and his non-errors. It is assumed that such behaviour is highly structured' (Selinker 1969:71). The implication of this earliest formulation is that 'interlanguage' is a performance phenomenon, to be seen in the behaviour of second language learners attempting to emulate the target language speaker's norm or competence: the underlying structure is to be derived from the 'observable output'. In Selinker's next article (1971), the term 'interlanguage' lost its inverted commas and moved into the title, since when it has been the focus of many papers and the central concept holding together the 'SLA' school. There has been criticism of the work in the field; a review by Kohn (1982:173) maintains that: 'Today, however, much of the enthusiasm of the early days has died down, and it is no exaggeration to claim that the main achievement so far has been in accumulating new speculations instead of turning old ones into hard knowledge'.

A number of scholars have suggested explanations for this disappointment:

(1) the concentration on morpho-syntactic development and the failure to deal with semantic development (Ellis 1982)

(2) the failure to recognize the relevance of the learner's own standards of correctness and internalized linguistic knowledge (Kohn 1982)

(3) the misuse of concepts related to the target language (the comparative fallacy) (Bley-Vroman 1983)

(4) the failure to recognize clearly the specific features that distinguish interlanguages from other natural languages (Adjémian 1976)

(5) the failure to deal with variability (Dickerson 1974; Tarone 1979)[2]

(6) the failure to define the concept clearly (Bialystok and Sharwood Smith 1985).

The field nonetheless remains vigorous, and attempts to deal with criticism and incorporate new proposals. I see two connected problems with the notion of 'interlanguage': the tendency to confuse a process and a competence model, and the arbitrary use of the concept of language with minimal regard to questions of psychological or sociolinguistic reality.

In a competence model, our interest is in capturing the essence of the underlying system, without asking how it actually works. We attempt, in other words, to characterize in abstract or symbolic terms the system that best accounts for what we consider the facts of language. The form of the model is constrained by certain conditions; one vital criterion is the need to account for universalities that appear to be learned without adequate external evidence, a condition which explains the interest of psycholinguists after Chomsky in first language learning. But Chomsky's interest in language learning does not mean any commitment to psychological reality as a constraint on the model. Or, put another way: even if aspects of psychological and neurological reality will ultimately serve as important criteria for judging among competing competence models, the present state of knowledge of psychology and of the physiology of the brain precludes its use as a constraint. It is on the basis of these assumptions that most generative grammarians continue to claim independence of psychological criteria in their study of linguistic competence. But in spite of his use of competence terminology, Selinker seems to prefer a processing model.[3]

For Selinker (1971), interlanguage has a different 'psychological infrastructure' from normal language. But it is far from clear what the term interlanguage is meant to convey. Essentially, it would seem to make a claim that just as the structuralist explanation for the speech behaviour of people in their native tongue is an abstraction called language, the structuralist explanation for the speech behaviour of people in a second language is an abstraction called interlanguage. Thus, interlanguage is to be compared to language in the sense of 'langue' or grammar. The implication of this is clearest if we follow the Saussurean concept whereby language is an abstraction underlying the specific speech behaviour of members of a community, or the Chomskyan axiom that a grammar represents the knowledge of the idealized monolingual in a homogeneous speech community. In this sense, interlanguage would represent the knowledge of the idealized speaker in a homogeneous community of second language speakers. In other words, it is a claim that second language speakers share a system that is distinct from the system of native speakers.

While there are in fact situations where this can be true (for example, the development of a pidgin, a form of a language that is used only as a second language among communities isolated by geographical or social distance from the native speakers of the language), we are usually more interested in second language learners who consider themselves and are considered by others to be aiming at a variety represented in the language of native speakers. That there are deviations in their usage (performance), many of which are the result of deviations in their knowledge (competence) is true, just as it is interesting to seek out systematic similarities in these deviations that correspond to different first language backgrounds, different learning experiences, different goals and expectations, and even to the fact of this being a second language. In this sense, interlanguage might have been a useful name for the various Localized Forms of English (to use Peter Strevens's term) or Englishes (as Braj Kachru puts it) that make up the varieties of English as a World Language.[4] But there seems to be no more justification for postulating a different 'interlanguage' for individual second language learners than there is for postulating radically different languages for individual speakers of the same language who also deviate one from the other in systematic and unsystematic ways.[5] Just as there is variation among individual speakers of a language, sometimes socially recognized (for example, social and geographical dialects), and usually the target of educational tests and measurement, so second language learners are also likely to have marked deviations from the norm of the language they are learning. These deviations may be interesting to the extent that they have social significance, as when, for instance, evidence of non-native speech is used for positive or negative discrimination. To the extent that these deviations cast light on the nature of language learning, they are also interesting; the three related movements in applied linguistics calling themselves contrastive analysis, error analysis, and interlanguage have each provided frameworks for study that has had both practical and theoretical importance.[6] But in the typical case, the variety of language used by a second language learner is intended to be, and is usefully to be considered as, an approximation of that of a native speaker:

Condition 2
Native Speaker Target condition (typical, graded): Second language
learner language approximates native speaker language.

This is stated as a graded condition because the closeness of approximation will vary; it is a typical condition because there are cases where
the learner may not in fact aim at native speaker language.[7] This may be
because of the kind of speech to which the learner is exposed; the
teacher, for instance, may not be a native speaker, or may be distorting
the language he or she is using into the kind of foreigner talk that leads
to the development of pidgins.[8] Another reason may be connected to the
learner's lack of integrative motivation and consequent unwillingness to
adapt all the features of native speech, particularly a native speaker
accent.[9] At the same time, the condition does not deny the possibility of
finding evidence for systematic developments that do not follow native
speaker goals; a study such as Huebner (1985) shows the kind of
evidence that is revealing.

Selinker, Swain, and Dumas seem to say that to count as interlanguage all one has to find is evidence of similar strategies. But this
misses a point that has been central to linguistics at least since Saussure:
the social nature of a language. This was recognized by Corder earlier
when he called the approximative system an 'idiosyncratic dialect'; until
these strategies evolve into a socially recognized variety, they have no
more claim to the status of language than any other set of personal
characteristics of speech. From this point of view, there is no such thing
as an interlanguage. There are approximative systems, transitional
competences, evolving or almost static results of attempts by a second
language learner to understand the system of the target language.
Groups of learners with similar language backgrounds and similar
language learning experience have temporarily similar systems; similarly, learners isolated from native speakers of the language tend to
develop 'fossilized' systems or pidgins.[10] But there is some danger in
using a term for these idiosyncratic transitory systems that suggests the
kind of stability implied by calling them a language.

When the variety of a language used by people speaking it as a second
or foreign language achieves some kind of social status,[11] it seems
appropriate to give it its own label; but I see no a priori justification for
giving such a term to a cluster of varieties defined only on the basis of
their dissimilarity from a socially recognized variety. It would seem
clearer therefore to treat the word 'interlanguage' as an elegant variation
for second language. A more neutral term like 'learner variety' as used
by Klein (1986) or like 'language-learner language' used by Ellis (1985)
is probably to be preferred.

Davies points out:

> It is an interesting question, of course, whether native speakers also exhibit IL[interlanguage], but this is perhaps a question that should not be asked—not because it opens the Pandora's Box of the definition of the native speaker but because it trivializes and renders vacuous the whole concept. It needs to be restricted to second and foreign language learners and has value as a categorization of learning states in a second or foreign language. (Davies 1984:xii)

This misses a point. The value of Second Language Acquisition research that it derives from First Language Acquisition studies is the interest in learner varieties: in the transitional competence of a language learner as evidence of the learning process. The term 'interlanguage' appears to want to give a separate status to the objects of study in each case; this can be a misdirection. But there are other meanings, at least one other according to Davies and at least two others according to Ellis (1985:299). To the second, 'more rigorous' (Davies) use I now turn.

Variability

The line of research started by Corder has been particularly important in focusing on the systematic nature of the second language learner's knowledge of the language being learned. The underlying hypothesis is cogently worded by Klein:

> Every learner variety, no matter how elementary and inadequate it might be, constitutes a *system in itself* whereby the learner can meet at least some of his communicative needs. The efficiency of the system depends not only on the linguistic repertoire developed by the learner but also on the latter's proficiency in handling the system. (Klein 1986:57)

That there is a system is agreed, but, as Davies (1984) admits, 'What kind of system is so far unresolved', and as Widdowson (1984b) argues, it may be a mistake to assume that system means only rules. As Ellis puts it in his tenth hypothesis, dealing with linguistic output but clearly also referring to the linguistic knowledge of a learner: 'Language-learner language consists of (1) formulaic speech, and (2) utterances constructed creatively' (Ellis 1985:280).

In attempting to resolve this issue, one major problem that has faced students working in the tradition has been variability. Although to start with, interlanguage studies shared with the general Chomskyan tradition an unwillingness to deal with variation, which was pushed out into the periphery and treated as an issue for performance rather than competence models. The interest in variation in second language learning research starts with Dickerson (1974), who, in an article based on her dissertation, reported on a study of the phonology of Japanese speakers of English in which she proposed to treat the various stages of a learner's phonology not as static jumps (successive approximations) of a fixed grammar, nor as varying success in attempts to achieve the target language grammar handicapped by various degrees of first language interference, but rather as consisting of a series of variable rules, similar to the variable rules proposed by Labov as basic to any adequate grammar of a contextualized language.

The full implication of the issue of variability for interlanguage was first noticed by Tarone (1979). If interlanguage is governed by the rules of any other natural language, then it should turn out to have the same characteristics of variability as in other natural languages. Thus, the five axioms proposed by Labov (1969) will apply in general to studies of second language learning. There will be style-shifting, but in the case of a language learner, not all the socially appropriate shifts. These shifts will reflect the amount of attention paid to speech. As a result, there is special value in gathering evidence of the vernacular in informal usage. The observer's paradox here is that it is easiest to collect evidence in a situation where speech, because it is being observed, is not natural.

Littlewood (1981) has discussed the many kinds of variation that one might expect to find in a second language learner's speech. Variation within an individual learner is likely to result from changes in communicative function (redundant features will be omitted), changes in linguistic environment (as Dickerson shows, the learning of a phonetic rule involves slowly learning new environments to apply it), and changes in socio-situational factors (i.e. the changes between classroom and out of classroom performance). Littlewood speculates that the mechanisms involving first and second language acquisition are similar. He proposes, however, that second language learners have not only social norms, but also pedagogic norms, most evident in school situations. In separating the pedagogic norms from the social, he is drawing attention to the social artificiality of the normal classroom. He applies his theory to types of learners: the natural learner with low integrative motivation, the student with low integrative motivation to whom formal instruction is given, and the student aiming at social acceptance. The first of these will show the least, and the last the most, stylistic variation.

The variationists like Tarone are also clearly much concerned with discovery procedures. According to Tarone. who assumes that the goal of research is to describe the 'grammatical and phonological system which underlies learner performance' (1982:70), the best data to use are intuitional data supplemented by data gathered in actual meaningful communicative use: the former will give only a limited picture of the learner's system, for it will be a limited view of the target language. Tarone does not believe that these varying kinds of evidence show the existence of the same underlying linguistic norm, but rather that they show the existence of several linguistic norms, a continuum of styles ranging from a 'superordinate' style produced when the speaker pays the most attention to form, to a vernacular style produced when the least attention is paid. As far as one can see from available evidence, the vernacular style is the most impermeable to other influences:

> So, in these few studies where evidence is available on both the vernacular and the careful styles of second language learners, the evidence seems to show that the superordinate style is characterized by the presence of more target language variants, more socially marked native language variants, and (in some case) aberrant forms . . . .The evidence of style-shifting of this kind is quite sparse, but the evidence now available is consistent with the hypothesis that the IL[interlanguage] superordinate norm is more permeable to the target language and native language rule systems . . . (Tarone 1982:77)

Tarone points out the significant difference between her view of language knowledge and that implied by Krashen's Monitor Model. The Monitor Model assumes two distinct systems, one derived from learning and the other from acquisition; the variability model postulates a continuum, and so one system. The variability model, to the extent that it is concerned with competence rather than performance, is neutral as to conscious versus unconscious processes. And variability assumes influence from the native as well as the target system when the attention level is high.

Tarone has carried out a number of studies in support of her hypotheses. Tarone (1983) looks at some data on variability in the speech of second language learners, which show evidence of style shifting. Tarone (1985) tests the performance of Arabic and Japanese learners of English on oral and written tasks, and shows that style shifting occurs between narration and interview as well as between speaking and writing. Schmidt (1980) investigates foreign student production of sentences with second verb ellipsis such as in:

John is reading books and Bill comics.

The learners studied never produce such a sentence in free oral production (how common is it in native speech?); succeed with it 11 per cent of the time in elicited imitation, 25 per cent when asked to combine sentences in writing, and judge it grammatical 50 per cent of the time.

In a study of morphology of Japanese students learning English, Fairbanks (1982) describes a Japanese speaker of English who almost never uses the third person singular -s ending in casual speech, but nearly always uses it, for both singular and plural verbs, in careful speech. In the study by Dickerson and Dickerson (1977), Japanese students are reported to produce a correct variant of English /r/ before mid- and high vowels more often in word list reading than in dialogue reading, and least often in free speech. In a study of /θ/ variants produced by speakers of Arabic in their own language and in English, (Schmidt 1977), the high status Arabic variant turns up more in minimal pair and word list reading than in normal reading; the same pattern holds for it in English. Finally, Beebe (1980) reports variation in production of English /r/ among Thai learners between conversation and reading word lists. In final position, the correct form is more likely (72.5 per cent) in listing than in conversation (36.5 per cent); in initial position, the existence of a Thai status-marked pronunciation of initial /r/ reverses these results.

Data like these, Tarone argues, contradict what she calls the 'Homogeneous Competence Paradigm' described by Adjémian (1976:81) based on the Chomskyan model, which assumes that there is an idealized homogeneous competence of an idealized native speaker available to study through the speaker's intuition about his or her language, and to be studied in the case of second language learning, as of first, by seeking his or her judgements about the grammaticality of sentences. Variability between the grammar developed in this way and the learner's performance will be accounted for by the permeability of the system to other systems. In this view, interlanguage grammars (or, in my terms, the individual second language learners' grammars) are different from natural language grammars in that they may show permeability, fossilization, and backsliding. She prefers her own model, the 'Capability Continuum Paradigm'. 'Capability' is not linguistic competence, but a system underlying all regular language behaviour (Is it a limited communicative competence?). It is composed not so much of rules as of *regularities*. It is heterogeneous, made up of a continuum of styles. The critical controlling element is attention. It can be studied only by collecting natural speech material. Variability is more marked in careful styles, which are most permeable to first and second language interference. Learning is towards the vernacular. Learner interlanguages should meet all the constraints on natural languages; the system is not unique, but similar to first language acquisition, where there is evidence of dialect conflict.

To sum up what has been argued so far, variability sets a challenge to the structural model (as proposed by Chomsky), but rather than simply exiling its study to performance or accepting its centrality, Tarone proposes to deal with it, as Labov deals with a similar issue in first language, by postulating the addition of a socially-governed variable rule to the structural grammar itself. Thus, for Tarone as for others working in the Interlanguage model, knowledge of a language is essentially to be characterized in structural or competence terms. At the same time, as has been noted, others working in the model show, like

Selinker, a decided affinity for the use of neurolinguistic metaphors that are much more suitable for processing models.

Selinker's own attempt to deal with variability is set out in Selinker and Douglas (1985). After describing some sessions with a non-native speaker, they propose a number of hypotheses for further study in similar interviews. They accept Tarone's argument for stylistic variation, proposing that second language learners are not monostylistic. But to them, the most interesting source of variability appears to be what they label 'discourse domains'. Discourse domains, they say, are 'highly personal'; each learner creates his or her own, some used for specific purposes and others for more general purposes.[12] Specific purpose domains (for example, language used to talk about a specific technical purpose) may overlap with those of other second language speakers. This is an attempt to find in the speech of second language learners the same dimensions of variation that have been recognized in first language speakers, although Selinker's use of a novel framework for what he calls interlanguage may well slow down the work of recognizing similarities and differences.

From the point of view of specifying outcomes of second language learning, there are two important things to be learned from all this work. The first is the emphasis in interlanguage theory on the fact that a second language learner's knowledge forms a whole. This is summed up in the Language as System condition given earlier. At the same time, this condition needs to be modified to recognize that knowledge of a second language, like knowledge of a first language, is marked by variability:

Condition 3
Variability condition (necessary): Like first language knowledge, second language knowledge is marked by variability.

Several things follow from these two conditions. First, they raise important theoretical questions with discrete item approaches to language testing; this will be discussed later.[13] Second, they make clear the value of the work undertaken in interlanguage research in attempting to determine the nature of a second language learner's underlying grammar. Third, they make a distinction between 'knowing a second language' (even imperfectly) on the one hand, and on the other, 'language-like behaviour', such as reciting memorized but unintegrated chunks (words, phrases, or sentences) in the language.[14]

But the chunks do have their place; what has been said does not deny the validity of Widdowson's observation of the importance of learning unanalysed routines or 'schematic units' which do not conform to rules of the grammar (Widdowson, 1984b:328). One might reconcile the Language as System condition with Widdowson's point by suggesting that these 'schematic units', although not analysed or part of a productive grammar, can nevertheless form part of the systematic knowledge of the second language learner just as irregularities and exceptions can form part of the 'leaky' grammar of normal languages.

What we are dealing with here is the existence of a distinction in forms of language knowledge. Just as in first language acquisition there is a holophrastic stage in which unanalysed chunks make up the basis of the child's utterances, so too a second language learner starts off with unanalysed portions of the second language. As Bialystok (1981) remarks, the development of analysed knowledge, which permits recombination, is an important and independent stage of learning. The task is described by Klein (1986) as having two parts: breaking the stream of acoustic signals into their constituent parts, and learning the meaning of the parts.[15]

To capture the complementary nature of these observations, two contrasting conditions are proposed:

Condition 4
Unanalysed Knowledge condition (necessary, graded): Unanalysed knowledge (memorized chunks of the second language) may be used by second language learners, but unanalysed knowledge by itself provides for very restricted, language-like behaviour.

Condition 5
Analysed Knowledge condition (necessary, graded): As linguistic knowledge is analysed into its constituent parts, it becomes available for recombination; this creative language use may be enriched with unanalysed knowledge.

The two conditions are stated as necessary and graded; the second part of each, however, sets out typical graded effects of its application.

The second problem raised by interlanguage work is the intriguing (and controversial) issue of a model against which to judge a second language learner's ability. If we reject the implication of interlanguage theory that a second language learner's knowledge comes to form a consistent and reasonable goal in itself, we must ask what is the variety that is in fact the learner or teacher's goal; in other words, how do we specify the target language?

Variety of language

Variability as interlanguage research describes it is concerned essentially with variations that occur in the performance of the individual second language learner. This, following Tarone (1983), is assumed to be explained by the notion of attention, the same notion used for dealing with stylistic differences in the native speaker.[16] But how should we deal with the need to make a choice among socially recognized varieties of the target language? When teaching Arabic, should the target be the structures of the literary language or of one of the spoken varieties or of Modern Standard Arabic (Abdulaziz 1986)? With English, which of the many varieties is to be taught?[17] These decisions will have important effects not just on the content of courses and the selection of teachers, but, as later chapters will explore, on attitudes to language learning.

The ubiquity of the issue cannot be denied, and is particularly serious in a purely structural approach, which, in principle, excludes functional considerations. If one is looking for a description of the structures to be taught, one almost inevitably goes to the published sources, which, in the vast majority of accounts, provide normative accounts of the formal grammar of the written version of the language, usually in classic texts. Even in languages with as rich a grammatical tradition as Arabic and Hebrew, there are virtually no grammatical descriptions of the contemporary language, whether written or spoken. Thus, structural approaches will be severely limited if they wish to deal with the modern forms of the language. The power of normativism in the classroom is such as to impose new putative standards even where they do not exist.[18]

There is another issue concerned with variety. In the assessment of an individual's proficiency in a second (or for that matter a first) language, one central problem is distinguishing the degree of control from the kind of control. The structural model suggests generally that control is on a single gradient; the functional model generally recognizes that control is over a varied collection of styles, registers, etc. Of all the areas where this becomes important, the most serious is probably the implications of these approaches for understanding the proficiency of subjects who lack control of school-valued language abilities. The modern Western educational system, especially as it has developed since the attempt to make education universal, has placed its main values on a set of language abilities associated with a special kind of literacy.

This last idea can be most easily understood by looking at diglossia. Diglossia is a term proposed by Ferguson (1959) to designate cases where two markedly different forms of the same language are used for socially distinguishable functions. Thus, in German-speaking Switzerland, standard High German is the appropriate language for public formal higher functions, while Swiss German is appropriate for private and informal functions. The same two people, with similar educational background and social class, will switch from one variety to the other in different circumstances. Similarly, Classical Arabic is the language used throughout the Arabic-speaking world for H [high] functions (for example, writing, sermons, public speaking) while a local variety (or more precisely, a socially appropriate form of a local variety) is used for L [low] functions (for example, normal daily conversation). Now, while it is not inevitable, it is generally the case that this kind of diglossia is most marked in a strong distinction between the written and spoken languages. In the classical diglossic situation, medium and formality do not overlap: the formal written variety of language is the only one that can be written, and the informal spoken variety is the only one for natural speech. As a result, it becomes necessary to use a sort of 'read-aloud' version of the written language in formal situations calling for speaking. In some languages, this division is softened; thus, the insistence of the Royal Society (established in London in the mid-seventeenth century) on the Plain Style led to the development of an intermediate level in English, suitable for formal speaking and for all but the most formal writing.

But the existence of this intermediate style has in effect obscured rather than clarified one of the fundamental differences in styles of language, captured often (but not necessarily—see Spolsky 1986a) in the difference between a written and a spoken language, that of the continuum of autonomous verbalization. The continuum is marked at one end by an emphasis on working with the minimum non-verbal context, making points explicitly in words rather than relying on shared knowledge and environment. This distinction has been variously referred to: it underlies Bernstein's elaborated versus restricted code,[19] Ong's oral versus literate,[20] and Cummins's CALP versus BICS.[21] For our present interest, its most important consequence is the existence of a set of language-related abilities associated with the literate style and favoured in certain social groups and at particular times. These abilities are also the ones that are most easily tested, for a critical feature of those who control the style is their willingness to participate in socially determined formal language activities such as language tests. Indeed, Edelsky and her colleagues (1983) and Martin-Jones and Romaine (1986) argue convincingly that the CALP-BICS distinction proposed by Cummins is largely a result of a special kind of school testing. All of this emphasizes once again the critical importance of defining goals.

How might this be incorporated in our model of second language learning? The choice of goals does clearly impose important conditions on language learning. In the next chapters, where specifications for measurable language behaviour are proposed, this question will need to be answered more precisely. At the same time, this section has drawn attention to a number of potential areas that will be included in these specifications: first, some appropriate variety (or set of varieties) as a goal (Is a course in English as a second language intended to produce graduates with American or British accents? Is a localized form of English a satisfactory model?); and second, a decision on the weight to be given to control of academic language for school purposes. These might be stated as a necessary condition on goals of instruction:

Condition 6
Specific Variety condition (necessary): When one learns a second language, one learns one or more varieties of that language. As a

corollary, goals for a formal course of instruction need to specify the variety or varieties of language being taught.

The exact nature of the variety taught varies, but it is often the case that the fact that teaching takes place in an academic setting means that there is an emphasis on academic skills:

Condition 7
Academic Skills condition (typical, graded): Learning of a second language may be associated to varying degrees with the development of academic language skills.

It must be noted that these two conditions setting specific outcomes do not deny the existence of some common core, some general language proficiency which will be looked at in more detail in a later chapter. In the strict sense, when this is a defined variety (for example, the common core that some courses set out to teach), the condition applies to it too. In another sense, knowing any variety of a language involves knowing a large number of items, and as there is overlap in the items that make up varieties, learning one variety contributes to a greater or lesser extent to being able to use another.

In looking at variation, our emphasis has been on language knowledge, on what is known. But it has been a critical observation of modern language teaching that languages are not just known, but used. In understanding goals and outcomes, therefore, we need to ask not just about language knowledge but also about language use. This will be the task in the next chapter.

Notes

1   Usually abbreviated to SLA.
2   Selinker and Douglas (1985) is a report of one attempt to do this within the theory; they recognize the differences between special-ized and generalized knowledge of a language, and try to cross from a structuralist to a functionalist model. As can be seen from Ellis (1985), the variation models have now been incorporated in the general theory.
3   Davies (1984:xii) refers to the contrast between the 'product' orientation of interlanguage linguists and the 'process' orientation of interlanguage psychologists. But *product* is ambiguous: it might refer to surface performance or to underlying competence. Bialy-stok and Sharwood Smith (1985) try to define interlanguage as the underlying system, but are constrained to see it as performance.
4   Lowenberg (1986) shows the crucial distinction between these non-native varieties and interlanguage as a transitional variety: they have distinctive strategies in generalizing rules, and have developed norms of their own.

5 No more and perhaps no less, if we choose to accept the argument made by Householder and echoed by McCawley that there is no reason to assume that all members of even a homogeneous speech community have identical grammars. Coppieters (1987) shows that while native and non-native speakers seem to use French in the same way, they have very different intuitions about some sentences, suggesting to her differences in their competence or underlying grammars. The study is clearly an important contribution to questions on the nature of interlanguage.

6 See Spolsky (1979b).

7 Coppieters (1987) raises the interesting possibility that native-speaker-like performance may be based on different underlying competence.

8 See Chapter 11.

9 The classic cases are film actors or politicians who have maintained foreign accents in their otherwise impeccable English. The effect of integrative motivation is discussed in Chapter 10.

10 For discussion of fossilization, see Chapter 11. Huebner (1985) suggests that fossilization may well be less common than believed in cases where learners remain in contact with native speakers.

11 See Chapter 9 for discussion of how language varieties are socially defined by attitudes.

12 A parallel argument is presented by Dodson (1985) who proposes that bilinguals have a preferred language for 'every discrete area of experience (defined as domain, part-domain, concept-cluster or even single concept expressed by a single utterance)'.

13 See Chapter 4.

14 We often refer to this, quite appropriately, as parroting; the chunks of language produced by a parrot, even if they are associated with an appropriate clue, are not decomposable as in analysed language knowledge.

15 A separate task is learning to recombine the units. For a fuller discussion of Klein's proposals, see Chapter 11.

16 Bell (1984), as will be seen in Chapter 9, shows how individual variation is itself related to and derivable from social variation. Selinker and Douglas (1985), as described above, also accept the need to add the topical variation recognized by sociolinguists.

17 See for instance Prator (1978), Kachru (1986), Quirk and Widdowson (1985), Strevens (1987), Quirk (1987).

18 See for instance Sinclair (1985), Milroy and Milroy (1985).

19 See for instance Bernstein (1964) and, for an account of the controversy it led to, Atkinson (1985:102ff).

20 See Ong (1982).

21 See for example, Cummins (1979, 1984). For discussion, see Edelsky and others (1983), Rivera (1984), and Martin-Jones and Romaine (1986).

3　Knowing how to use a language

Duality of knowledge and skills

There is variation, as the last chapter established, not just in the items which make up linguistic knowledge, but also in the forms that this knowledge takes; the knowledge may be of unanalysed chunks or of recombinable constituents. A related but different distinction that is generally recognized is that between active and passive knowledge, better expressed perhaps as that between productive and receptive skills, for there is good reason to assume that the receptive skills of reading and understanding speech are just as active as the productive skills of writing and speaking.[1] At the most general level, this sets a special problem for any kind of language testing, for underlying knowledge can only be tapped as performance. Bearing this difficulty in mind, it is nonetheless important to note as a condition that individual learners vary in their productive and receptive ability:

Condition 8
Productive/Receptive Skills condition (necessary, graded): Individual language learners vary in their productive and receptive skills.

More specifically, it is typically the case that receptive skills develop before productive, and are in a non-trivial sense developed to a higher degree: more people can read works of literature than can write them.

Condition 9
Receptive Skills stronger than Productive condition (typical, graded): Receptive language skills (understanding speech or written text) usually develop before productive skills (speaking, writing) and usually develop to a higher level.

This last condition is often interpreted as setting an order for teaching the skills. It also becomes critical, as discussed in Chapter 7, in those cases where language learning anxiety sets major blocks to the development of productive skills.

But the difference between production and reception raises other interesting issues. One critical aspect surfaced in the debate over forms of second language knowledge. A feature of Krashen's Monitor Theory was the distinction he proposed between two systems of knowledge, one concerned with the unconscious implicit knowledge of rules underlying normal language use, and the second consisting of conscious explicit low-level rules available only under appropriate conditions for monitoring language use. While the proposal has not stood up to examination,[2] there is something important behind it.

The distinction it deals with is of course not a new one in second language learning. When the proponents of the Audio-Lingual Method put so much emphasis on the need for practice to establish automatic habits, their aim was to get away from the methods of the grammar-translation approach which, they complained, confused knowledge about the language with the ability to use it. The Audio-Lingual Method itself was challenged both because of its failure to show how one could go beyond the automatically drilled patterns that formed the basis for language-like behaviour to creative language use, and by the theoretical blows to psychological learning theory given by generative grammar. But the problem of distinguishing knowledge and use, and showing their connection, remained.

One suggestion of how to do this is provided by the work of Bialystok who, in a series of meticulous studies, has been exploring the effect of task on ability. Bialystok (1978) proposes a model to deal with differences in skill development. Her model is arranged on three levels, input (exposure to the language), knowledge (the way the information gained from exposure is stored), and output (the way the knowledge is used in production or comprehension). While allowing for variation in kinds of exposure, the input remains undifferentiated in the model. The main distinction occurs in the knowledge level, where Bialystok postulated three hypothetical constructs: Explicit Language Knowledge ('the conscious facts the learner has about the language'), Implicit Language Knowledge ('the intuitive information upon which the language learner operates in order to produce responses (comprehension or production) in the target language'), and Other Knowledge ('knowledge of the native language and of other languages, knowledge of the world, etc.')

The implications of this model have been worked out in a number of studies. Bialystok (1979) applies the model to judgements of grammaticality and shows that one can make a judgement about grammaticality either on the basis of knowledge of rules or on the basis of intuition; thus, the task of judging grammaticality is one that does not necessarily bias towards implicit or explicit knowledge. To express this, I propose two complementary conditions that make a distinction between the two forms of knowledge:

Condition 10
Implicit Knowledge condition (typical, graded): Language knowledge, analysed and so available for recombination, may be intuitive and so not be consciously available to the learner.

In this case, the speaker can produce correct forms and recognize incorrect ones, but has no easy way of talking abstractly about the reason why a form is correct or not.

Condition 11
Explicit Knowledge condition (typical, graded): Analysed language knowledge may be consciously available to the speaker who is able to state a rule or explain the reason for a decision to use a certain form.

Explicit knowledge is generally gained through formal teaching. It is sometimes referred to as 'knowledge about the language' rather than 'knowledge of the language', or as 'declarative knowledge', that is, knowledge that can be talked about.[3]

In a paper developing the theoretical model further, Bialystok (1981) reorganizes her earlier distinction between Explicit and Implicit into a distinction between analysed and unanalysed knowledge, and adds to this the distinction between automatic and non-automatic to give a four-way matrix of kinds of second language. The main claim of this model is that the extent to which knowledge is analysed and the extent to which it is automatic are independent.

In later papers (Bialystok 1982, 1984; Bialystok and Ryan 1985; Bialystok and Sharwood Smith 1985), Bialystok has made clearer the nature of her processing model of second language learning, a model that interestingly does not aim just to encompass (and explain) differences between adult and child second language learning but also to highlight differences between first and second language learning by including constructs and processes that are relevant to both. Knowing a language involves, Bialystok argues, two distinct components: '. . . the mental representation of systematic, organized information about the target language and the procedures for effectively and efficiently retrieving that knowledge in appropriate situations' (Bialystok and Sharwood Smith 1985:106). A second language learner may differ from a first language speaker in either of these components, or both. Similarly, because they are distinct, the learning of each may be independent, except that a structure must be represented mentally before it can be used.[4] Mental representations may be more or less deeply analysed (and so perhaps more abstract), but greater sophistication of analysis is not necessarily towards the target language norm, and reanalysis does not necessarily imply greater complexity. Nor does increasing competence (whether quantitative or qualitative) necessarily imply conscious awareness of the structure. There are likely also to be differences in quantity of knowledge between native speakers and language learners. Adults with extensive formal education learning a language in a classroom setting may have deeply analysed knowledge of a limited portion of the target language. Accordingly, a speaker's knowledge may be described quantitatively or qualitatively, and as conscious or not. While there are differences between first and second language learners in these dimensions, there are no a priori reasons to assume that the differences between the groups are greater than those within them.

Bialystok does not speculate on the form of representation; while her experiments do flesh out this abstract account, it is not certain that she could not accommodate any model of language structure; and to this extent her processing model is potentially consistent with current competence models.

The second component in her model is made up of the control procedures, referred to more precisely as 'retrieval' procedures. She states that there is no reason to assume that they differ in kind between first and second language use, but that there is a difference in 'efficiency', referred to as 'automaticity' in Bialystok (1982), and seen as the basis for fluency. Fluency is distinct from and independent of knowledge, so that a language learner may be accurate and hesitant, accurate and fluent, or inaccurate and fluent. This point is made by two conditions:

Condition 12
Automaticity condition (necessary, graded): Ability to use language knowledge varies in automaticity; this is shown by the fluency with which a person speaks.

Condition 13
Accuracy condition (necessary, graded): Ability to use language knowledge varies in accuracy.

Sharwood Smith (1986:13) points out the confusion in much research between competence models and processing models. He follows Bialystok in proposing a model that distinguishes between competence and control: 'Briefly, there are two fundamental types of change that can take place in language acquisition or language attrition—namely competence change or control change' Competence in his model is the same as it is in a generative grammar: abstract representations of knowledge, mainly in the form of analysed or unanalysed rules, stored in the long term memory. Control, in contradistinction, 'involves mechanisms which access knowledge in long-term memory and integrate the various bits of information that have been accessed in acts of utterance comprehension and utterance production' (Bialystok and Sharwood Smith 1985:14).

Much the same distinction, but with terminology borrowed from cognitive psychology, is expressed by Færch and Kasper (1986:51): 'Declarative[5] linguistic knowledge cannot be employed immediately but only through procedures activating relevant parts of declarative knowledge in speech reception and production.'

The distinction is at first glance appealing, but there are problems with it, for it is far from clear how to apply the definition. Assuming that the *integration* process, which looks very much like syntax, is part of performance (as Saussure perhaps considered syntax part of *parole* rather than *langue*), then it would work. But if competence involves syntactic rules, which are clearly needed to integrate 'bits of inform-ation' in comprehension and production, then how are control rules to be distinguished from competence rules? It appears they are not, but rather we need to distinguish 'knowing a rule' (declarative knowledge, competence,) and 'using a rule' (activated procedural knowledge or control).

Thus, Sharwood Smith distinguishes three kinds of control or process-related cross-linguistic influence. The first is using a previously estab-lished 'processing system' to control new developing competence; the second is 'falling back on well-automated processing mechanisms appropriate to the competence knowledge' of another language. The third kind of competence-related cross-linguistic influence is using for instance competence knowledge from the first language in the second. The first two are distinguished by frequency: the first is 'habitual' and the second 'stable'; the first is presumably distinguished from the third by 'tests designed to get around this "habit"', which will reveal that the learner knows but does not use the second language rule.

Somewhat less compromising are those approaches that do not attempt to retain a competence model as a part of the processing model. Jordens for instance holds that:

> There is, however, no direct link between an interlanguage rule system and interlanguage performance data. The learner's output is directly determined by rules of language *production* and only indirectly by the corresponding linguistic rule system ... One language production model that is both linguistically adequate and psychologically plausible is the procedural grammar for sentence formulation developed by Kempen and Hoenkamp (1982). (Jordens 1986:91)

The notion of dual knowledge is an interesting one; it is strong in its attempt to relate not just various kinds of second language learning but also first and second language learning. The empirical testing to which scholars like Bialystok and Sharwood Smith is submitting it gives us a clearer view of how it can be made precise, and helps us understand the inherent complexity of exploring the relation between a competence and a processing model, between knowledge and the ability to use it, between structure and function. Once again the complexity of language proficiency becomes apparent, and, even though the exact formulation might not be clear, it is valuable to propose a condition as follows:

Condition 14
Dual Knowledge condition (necessary): When one learns a second

language, one develops both knowledge and skills in using that knowledge. As a corollary, goals for a formal course of instruction or tests of proficiency need to distinguish between knowledge and use, as well as between various levels of automaticity and accuracy in use.

The dual knowledge approach is relevant not just to a view of the nature of underlying competence, but also relates directly to a central issue to do with learning. When learning a language is viewed as learning skills Johnson 1986, 1988, the process appears to be usefully broken into three (or two) phases. The first is the development of competence or declarative knowledge; in the case of adults, this might involve understanding the task to be performed. In the second or associative phase, the skill is performed, the declarative knowledge becomes procedural, errors are corrected, and parts of the task form an integrated whole. In the third phase, the skill is continually practised, and becomes automatic and faster. During this stage, the adult learner may lose the declarative knowledge and find it hard to explain the steps followed to perform the skill. [6] The conclusions to note here are, first, the distinction that has been made between (declarative) knowledge and use and, second, the fact that use can vary in automaticity.

Communicative competence

The view of a second language learner's knowledge implied in interlanguage work was challenged in two ways: work in variability called for fitting into the model the same kind of socially conditioned variation that Labov proposes for grammars of all languages, and the arguments of Bialystok show the implications of a processing model rather than a competence model for the question. Variability is more easily and more naturally handled within an approach which starts from the assumption that knowledge of a language must be described not in terms of underlying grammatical structures but in terms of general-izations about specific and varied language-related functions, a model that moves closer to a processing model in its insistence on starting with language use (performance). Such an approach may be seen in current interest in communicative competence. In his theoretical work, Chom-sky chose (perhaps unfortunately[7]) to use the term *linguistic competence* to refer to the underlying knowledge of an idealized native speaker of a language that enabled such a person to distinguish *grammatical* from *ungrammatical* sentences of the language. *Competence*, which is to be accounted for in the grammar, Chomsky distinguishes from *perfor-mance*, the latter including such factors as memory limitations (which, for instance, explained the constraint on the length of sentences that are grammatically infinite). Now this last illustration should help make clear that Chomsky was using the terms quite differently from their normal use; it is a mistake to confuse Chomskyan competence with normal ability. Be that as it may, his use of the term pre-empted others who wanted to talk about a language speaker's ability as linguistic competence; it further confined attention to the rules of the language considered appropriate to a Chomskyan generative grammar, with its basic limitation to sentence-length utterances and its exclusion of socially interesting variation.

The way was open then for Dell Hymes, building on Roman Jakobson's masterful analysis[8] of the functions of language, to propose the notion of *communicative competence*, defined by some as linguistic competence plus all other rule-governed aspects of language use, but by Hymes himself as something that contrasted with rather than supplemented linguistic competence: 'The heart of the argument is that extensions in the scope of linguistics to include pragmatics, discourse, text and the like, do not suffice, as long as the directions and foundations of linguistics itself remain unchanged' (Hymes 1985:10). The idea is particularly valuable in setting a wider goal for the second language learner, for it suggests that he or she be required to develop all the communicative skills of a native speaker and not just control of the basic grammar of the sentence.

In their excellent review of the issue, Canale and Swain (1980) recognize its relevance to both second language teaching and testing. Their approach to the question arose, they report, out of problems in measuring the achievement of students in French-as-a-second-language classes. They note some of the confusion between teaching approaches (grammatical versus communicative versus situational) and the theoretical uses of the terms. They point out (following Campbell and Wales 1970) that Chomsky uses the terms *competence* and *performance* in both a weak and strong sense. The weak sense is in the claim referred to earlier that there is a distinction between language knowledge and language use; the strong sense is a claim of a distinction between competence as the grammar and performance as the psychological factors involved in speech perception and production. As Campbell and Wales, and also Hymes (1972) point out, this approach overlooks the issue of appropriacy: the knowledge not that a sentence is well-formed but that it is appropriately used in a specific context. Hymes puts it like this:

> We have then to account for the fact that a normal child acquires knowledge of sentences not only as grammatical but also as appropriate. He or she acquires competence as to when to speak, when not, and as to what to talk about with whom, when, where, in what manner. In short, a child becomes able to accomplish a repertoire of speech acts, to take part in speech events, and to evaluate their accomplishment by others. . . (Hymes 1972:277–8)

Hymes goes on to distinguish communicative competence (knowing all the rules) from performance (actually using them).

Canale and Swain examine two controversial issues: whether communicative competence includes or is separate from linguistic, and whether one can usefully distinguish between communicative competence and performance. On the first, they are finally convinced that it is better to include linguistic within communicative competence so as to make clear their ultimate indivisibility; rules of grammar are meaningless (except presumably to the grammarian) without rules of use.

Jackendoff (1983) presents another strong argument for the primacy of linguistic competence and thus presumably for its recognition as the central component of any performance models. While competence models are not processing models and so do not usually make claims to represent the method of mental storage of the structures and rules they postulate, performance models are also process models, with consequent claims for the nature of the storage, which is itself a claim about the nature of competence. Put another way, Hymes, who argues that communicative competence is independent of linguistic competence, or Schlesinger and Carroll, who aim to develop performance grammars, still presuppose claims about the form of storage of knowledge, i.e. of a grammar, which is what a competence model is. Cognitive models that concentrate on 'procedural knowledge' also assume the necessity of defining 'declarative knowledge'. It does not seem possible, therefore, to ignore the question of the form of the grammar or to avoid the need to consider the relationship between competence and performance.[9]

Canale and Swain's own model of communicative competence involves recognizing three distinct but related competences, with definable boundaries. The three are:

> *Grammatical competence.* . . . knowledge of lexical items and of rules of morphology, syntax, sentence-grammar semantics, and phonology . . .
> *Sociolinguistic competence.* . . . sociocultural rules of use and rules of discourse . . .
> *Strategic competence.* . . . verbal and non-verbal communication strategies that may be called into action to compensate for breakdown in communication due to performance variables or to insufficient competence. (Canale and Swain 1980:29–30)

Within each of these components Canale and Swain recognize 'a subcomponent of probability rules of occurrence' to account for the '"redundancy aspect of language" (Spolsky 1968)'. The Canale and Swain taxonomy has led to a good deal of interesting work,[10] but major questions remain about establishing the boundaries and relations between the three proposed competences.

Kelly (1981), for example, prefers to deal with the issue as a performance problem: he analyses performance features such as noise in listening to speech. The work on communicative competence suggests, then, that the knowledge of a second language learner involves not just linguistic knowledge, but knowledge of a set of other rule-governed language systems, or a complex of such systems: learning a language involves not just learning the phonology, morphology, sentence syntax, and semantics, but also the pragmatics, discourse rules, rules of sociolinguistic appropriateness, and rules for verbal and non-verbal conversational strategies.

Hymes has proposed that this be dealt with by what he calls an ethnography of speaking, and a good deal of valuable research in this tradition makes clear the interesting complexity involved.[11] Another well-analysed area of communicative competence is speech act theory, developed particularly by philosophers of language like Searle and Grice following Austin. Austin's contribution was to point out that utterances are acts: that they can be classified not just as to what they say but as to what they do; and Searle showed the complexity behind the listener's ability to discern that a seeming statement like 'The salt is at your end of the table' is in fact regularly and systematically interpretable as a request. Grice identified the 'general principles of co-operative behaviour' that make it possible for listeners to work out the likely illocutionary value of utterances. As these features of language were identified, it was not long before people asked how they were learned, and since 1975 a number of researchers have been looking at how children acquire these rules in their first language. And from there, it is clearly a short step to ask the same questions about second language learners.

This was done by Schmidt and Richards (1980), who, after a useful summary of the speech act literature, pose a number of useful questions for research in second language learning. They point out the obvious relevance of speech act theory to communicative language teaching; an approach that stresses communication must certainly benefit from a theory that will provide at least a taxonomy. Speech act theory, they suggest, should help in defining the situations in which second language learners receive meaningful input. Speech acts should provide a suitable area for studying inferencing (How do non-native speakers understand the inference of speech acts? Does foreigner talk involve making inferences more explicit?), transfer (How universal are the pragmatic rules and what kinds of misunderstanding occur across languages?), appropriateness (How does it vary cross-culturally?), and generalization.

There are by now a good number of cross-linguistic studies of speech acts. An early study by Blum-Kulka (1982) compares the speech act rules of learners of Hebrew with those of native speakers. She aimed to cast light on three hypotheses: the existence of some universal principles in speech acts, such as the ability to infer communicative intention; the existence of culture and language specific conventions of social appropriateness; and the development of a kind of interlanguage of pragmatics on the part of learners. The second language learners in her study generally knew what was required of them; their responses were contextually appropriate; but their answers were significantly different from those of the native speakers. Some of the differences could be explained by the limitations on linguistic devices available to the learners, but there was a general tendency for the English learners of Hebrew to choose much less direct strategies than native speakers. Thus, for example, most English speakers (in English or in Hebrew) opened requests for directions in the street with an attention-getter ('Excuse me. . .Can you tell me. . .') while all but one Hebrew speaker completed this item with a direct question ('Where is. . .'). In work in a similar vein, Thomas (1983) describes some cases of what she labels 'cross-cultural pragmatic failure'; calling it cross-cultural allows her to deal with social class variation (note that all of Blum-Kulka's subjects were university students).

Another study of the learning of pragmatics of a second language is the project carried out by Edmondson and his colleagues (1984). In a model similar to Blum-Kulka's (they form part of an international group that meets regularly to discuss their work), they set out to gather empirical evidence of the pragmatic behaviour of native speakers of English (the target), native speakers of German in German, and Germans learning English. The resulting data have lent themselves to elaborate and fruitful analysis of each language's preferred patterns and of the learners' subsequent performance, and are an important step in developing a rich account of the pragmatic knowledge involved in learning a second language.

Looking at expressions of gratitude, Eisenstein and Bodman (1986) were surprised to discover that even advanced learners of English, including some who had lived in the United States for some years, had major difficulties. Such descriptions as these both permit study of the process of second language learning, and provide additional sources for specifying the kind of knowledge that must underlie various kinds of communicative proficiency.

This by no means exhausts the complexity of attempting to describe communicative competence; indeed, it may be considered a tentative step into a vast area. When one sees the richness of analysis possible in studies such as those by Ferguson (1976) or by Brown and Levinson (1978) of politeness,[12] it is clear how much more detail is possible. This work in contrastive pragmatics is further evidence of the complexity of the knowledge that the second language learner must acquire.

The view from theory

How have the existing theories of second language learning dealt with these issues? If we look, for instance, in Dulay, Burt, and Krashen (1982), the answer would seem to be, not at all. Communicative competence, discourse, pragmatics, speech acts; these terms are completely absent from their book, as they are from the theory. There is mention of *communicative proficiency* but it turns out to be the ratio of local to global errors, the latter being defined as 'errors that affect *overall sentence organization*' and as a result 'significantly hinder communication'. (op. cit.:191) Thus, it is clear that the Monitor Model is by choice a microlevel theory of the learning of sentences and not a general theory; while it will be seen to claim that such learning depends on active communication, it has no concern for the nature of the communicative process itself or for the macrolevel of developing larger proficiencies.

In this and the last chapter, I proposed some conditions that call for considering language knowledge as a whole, and that call for distinction between knowledge of a language and ability to use it. As there are second language learners who may wish to learn the grammar of a language but not to speak it, I propose this as a typical condition expanding on the Dual Knowledge condition, as follows:

Condition 15
Communicative Goal condition (typical, graded): Language learners may aim to achieve various degrees of control of a language for communicative purposes.

Second language learning theorists have taken a number of different paths in their characterization of language knowledge. The followers of interlanguage theory tend to describe a second language learner's knowledge as characterized by a set of rules similar to those of the target language, forming a complete whole but differing in significant ways from the rules of the target language. With the influence of the variationists, they now seem to accept that many of these rules will be variable, perhaps expressed as Labovian variable rules. In actual practice, the rules they have considered are limited to a number of interesting morphological and phonological features. There is also the added complexity involved in recognizing the specific variety of a language that is being taught.

Work in the dual knowledge tradition has made clear that it is not enough to talk about knowledge, but that it is necessary also to account for use. One approach is to be found in the psycholinguistic studies of scholars like Bialystok, whose work connects second language learning to other studies of learning, and provides the basis for understanding differences between fluency and accuracy and in degrees of each. A quite separate tradition, following on work in linguistics, philosophy, sociolinguistics, and ethnography, looks at the nature of rules for language use and the ways in which second language learners acquire them. The effect is to enlarge our view of language knowledge. To see an attempt at more precise specification of second language knowledge and ability, and more importantly, to consider actual methods of measuring it, there is benefit in looking at a more practically oriented field, that of language testing. This will be the task of the next two chapters.

Notes

1   See for instance Titone (1985).
2   For arguments against this particular proposal, see Gregg (1984), Long (1983a), Spolsky (1985c), McLaughlin (1987).
3   For a study of the practical implications of the distinction, see Levin (1972).
4   While Bialystok sees these two components as being logically ordered in this way, it is not clear that the ordering has practical significance: the mental representation on which a procedure is based at a given point in time might be wrong and later replaced.
5   Declarative knowledge is underlying knowledge, more or less competence in the Chomskyan sense. Procedural knowledge is knowledge involved in acquiring and performing skilled operations, more or less what is sought by those who call for performance grammars.
6   Neurophysiological studies show organic changes at the synapse as automatization occurs.
7   Hymes (1985) discusses the uses of other terms like 'proficiency', 'abilities' and 'communicative habits', and notes: 'That "competence" became a term of reference, of course, is due to Chomsky.'
8   Jakobson presented this model in the 'Closing Statement: Linguistics and Poetics' at the 1958 Conference on Style; see Sebeok (1960: 350–77). Hymes was present at the conference (Hymes 1985:13) and acknowledges the influence in his development of the notion of 'ethnography of speaking' and later use of the term 'communicative competence'.
9   I suspect that the requirements of models based on Parallel Distributed Processing (Rumelhart and others 1986) might well, as Sampson (1987) argues, produce a revolution in their call for much more atomic specification of linguistic units than do current processing models.

10 An interesting study of strategic competence is reported by Paribakht (1985).
11 For a bibliography of research in the ethnography of speaking, see Philipsen and Carbaugh (1986).
12 Davies (1987), for instance, compares politeness formulas in English and Moroccan Arabic as the basis for teaching them to second language learners. The volume edited by Wolfson and Judd (1983) contains a number of studies showing aspects of the learning of greetings, partings, invitations, and other socially relevant skills.

4 Structures and functions

The approach from language testing

For a general theory of second language learning to be testable, it must include a precise method of specifying the goals and outcomes of learning. In the last two chapters some of the theoretical problems involved in such a specification were discussed, and a few general principles proposed that could be derived from theories that have dealt with second language knowledge. To arrive at greater specificity, it will now be advantageous to look at the issue from the point of view of the field that is most directly concerned with the precise description and measurement of second language knowledge, namely second language testing: this approach follows from the belief that something cannot be measured until it has been defined and identified.

The question of what it means to know a second language turns out, like all good questions, to have many possible answers. When someone asks you 'Do you know such and such a language?', your answer may take one of several forms, three of which are typical:

(1) 'I only know a few words.'
(2) 'I can read professional material in it.'
(3) 'Not as well as my wife does.'

There are other kinds of answers possible, but they will generally be analysable as referring to one (or a combination) of three kinds of claim:[1]

As in (1), a claim that one knows certain parts of the language—which I shall call the *Structural claim*
As in (2), a claim that one can use it for certain purposes—I shall call this the *Functional claim*
As in (3), a claim that one has a certain level of general knowledge of the language—I shall call this the *General Proficiency claim*.

Behind each of these claims is a different notion of what is involved in knowing a language, and while they overlap in certain ways and are clearly hierarchical in ordering,[2] the difficulty (or impossibility) of specifying that overlap is a central issue not just of applied but also of theoretical linguistics.

Each claim derives, in fact, from a different theoretical concept of the nature of knowledge of a language, and each has different empirical consequences. The first approach assumes that knowledge of the language is best described, as is the language itself, by describing its structures. It takes the form therefore of a grammar and lexicon, setting out to list the various items and rules on each of the levels that are thought to be required to account for the language. The structural description of the language then provides a basis both for describing an individual's knowledge of it ('X has not yet mastered the past tense', 'B has trouble with the passive transformation', 'Y is a basilang speaker'[3]) and for preparing tests and curricula.

Testing structural knowledge

In a structural approach to language testing,[4] we set out to discover the atoms, as it were, of language proficiency: to list the individual linguistic items that make up knowing a language and then test each one, or, more practically, test a selected or random sample of them. We seek evidence in other words that the learner knows the constituent elements of the language. The approach lends itself to the requirements of psychometric theory; the universe we wish to test is assumed to consist of a large number of equally relevant and equally valued items; sample theory determines how to select representative items from this universe; classic or Rasch[5] statistical techniques establish the reliability of the sample.

To carry the approach into practice requires access to a theory of linguistic analysis and description. The important work in this field was Lado's (1961) classic book on language testing, which started to build the critical and necessary bridge between language testing and language description. In his book, Lado considered virtually all kinds of language tests, but he was particularly strong and influential when he showed the way that linguistic skills could be broken down in accordance with contemporary structural linguistic theory into their smallest components, permitting the tester to focus on precise areas of difficulty.

A structuralist model is most likely to be a competence model, that is, a claim dealing with underlying knowledge rather than a process model, one which attempts to show how the organization of the knowledge has direct results in performance. As a consequence, a structuralist model of language knowledge makes no claims about how to observe or measure that knowledge, happily leaving that task to the psychometrist. This appears in the alliance between structural linguists and psychometrists that marks what I have called the modern or scientific approach to language testing (Spolsky 1977).

Language tests based on this approach are what Carroll (1961) has called discrete point tests, because they test knowledge of individual or discrete items selected from the structural description of the language. The criticism of them as tests is that the theory does not give any clear grounds for justifying the selection of one item rather than any other. There are at least four reasons why it is difficult to generalize from a discrete point test beyond the items included in it: the principle that second language knowledge forms a systematic whole; the existence of variation in second as well as first language knowledge; the absence of reasoned valuation for any item but the probability of the existence of differences in such values; and the general uncertainty of the correctness of any specific list of items however it may be selected. Because of this, a discrete point test gives a theoretically limited view of the knowledge of the person tested. It is of course useful in diagnostic and achievement testing, where the decision on the relevance of the item to the curriculum has been made on another level, but a test of individual discrete items does not provide a satisfactory picture of linguistic knowledge.

In spite of this limitation, there is obviously a good deal of truth (if not all the truth) to be revealed by discrete point testing of the items that an individual knows, and it is important to remember that learning a language involves learning individual items.

Condition 16
Discrete Item condition (necessary): Knowing a language involves knowing a number of the discrete structural items (sounds, words, structures, etc.) that make it up.

This condition is important both for testing and in setting a definition for *K*, the linguistic outcome set up in Chapter 1. It is particularly important for what I am calling the microlevel. This is in essence the working level of language learning, for items are added one at a time. Research in the Second Language Acquisition (SLA) tradition has so far managed to deal only with a small subset of the structural items that make up this aspect of language knowledge. In the first years there was a concentrated focusing on a few morphemic items in English, and more recently this has been expanded by adding a number of syntactic features of interest to studies of universals. But a vast range of other aspects of language knowledge is still untouched. At the same time, it is important to remember that the Language as System condition described in the Chapter 2 means that any new item added may lead to a reorganization of the existing system, and that items learned contribute in crucial, but difficult to define, ways to the development of functional and general proficiency. Even if we had more coverage of structural items in the research literature, there would be good reason to look at functional analyses.

Testing integrated functions

In the same year that Lado's book on language testing appeared, a major article by John Carroll (1961) drew attention to another kind of approach. Tests of individual linguistic items are all very well, Carroll said, but there is also an important place for what he called integrative tests: tests that integrate a large number of different discrete items by calling on the subject to perform some function or task using the target language.[6] Knowing a language involves these integrated skills as well.

Condition 17
Integrated Function condition (necessary): Knowledge of a language involves control of one or more integrated functional skills.

The functional approach is based on the assumption that the internal nature of language knowledge is best captured by detailing the many uses to which the language can be put. At the first and simplest level, it starts with a four-way division into active and passive (or better, productive and receptive) control of the spoken and written languages; this four-skills approach was standard in the development of the Audio-Lingual Method, but ultimately was shown to be inadequate.[7] More recent forms of the approach aim, therefore, to list exhaustively the various possible functions of language, including all the notions that can be expressed in it. This approach is embodied variously in the communicative competence model, the notional-functional curriculum,[8] and the interest in teaching and testing pragmatics discussed in Chapter 2.

While it can be presented more or less as a competence model (as Canale and Swain (1980) suggest), a functional model is more easily conceived of in a process framework, for its greatest interest is in the performance side of the phenomenon. While competence models do not include processing claims, process models generally include a view of the form of knowledge; and there are models (for example, Krashen 1982, Bialystok 1978, 1982) that assume that the knowledge base includes details of history—knowledge gained in different ways is marked differently—as well as details of usability. Functional goals are stated usually in performance terms, as 'X can do the following'. They may also include a criterion statement such as 'with ease', 'fluently', 'without serious mistakes'.

The simplest functional test assumes the possibility of describing language proficiency as the ability to perform some defined tasks that use language. The idea is both practical and theoretically satisfying, but there are important problems involved and these must be faced if we are to understand the limitations of such a test. The fundamental limitation is the ultimate impossibility of a direct translation from functional to structural terms.[9] Just as physics had to learn to live with its principle of uncertainty, so linguists must learn to accept models that do not expect direct and precise relations between form and function. Speech act theory has made quite clear how many different structures can be used for the same act: the felicity conditions for a request can be met by an imperative sentence (Please shut the window), a statement (The window is still open), a question (Could you shut the window?), or an exclamation (How cold the wind is today!); it can also be met by a variety of non-verbal gestures, by grunts, by significant looks, etc. Of course one can study the pragmatic value and sociolinguistic probability of choosing each of these structures in different environments. This is the goal of an ethnography of communication, which starts its analysis with functions, but the complexity of this task is so immense that we cannot expect ever to come up with anything like a complete list from which sampling is possible.

The second limitation, and the one I will be concerned with in this chapter, is the problem of determining which of the many functions which language fulfils should be included in a test of language proficiency. In a less test-oriented approach, it might be assumed that all items will be taught and tested; the question then is one of ordering rather than selection. If it were possible to arrive at a complete list, sampling theory might help select from it; but as the list remains theoretically open, so we must find some criterion other than chance to validate the statistical probability of our selection.

If we cannot select items on a chance basis, we need to have some appropriate criteria. One is frequency, but while this is useful when selecting vocabulary items, it is likely to be less feasible in the case of functions. A more typical criterion is a common-sense model of usefulness, and it is this that underlies the approach to language testing that seems to be the most functional in its underlying principles. The use of scales in language testing may be earlier than the work of the Foreign Service Institute testers, but their work was probably the most thorough, and once the long secrecy had been broken in Wilds (1975), the best discussed and most generally emulated approach to language proficiency scales. Work on the Foreign Service Institute scale started in 1956 (Sollenberger 1978); the first step was the development of a six-point scale (from 0 to 5) for abilities in the skills of speaking, reading, and writing.

The changes in the scale over the next twenty years are interesting to note. The levels were renamed, and descriptions were expanded. The wording of the scale in the two earlier versions and in the latest version adopted by the Inter-agency Language Roundtable (ILR) makes clear how contextualized it is: it is written for the purposes of a US government office in rating the language skills of its employees. While the scale is sometimes referred to as an absolute one, it is clearly relative to the context for which it is intended.

The assessment of skills, the actual rating, is carried out in the classic Foreign Service Institute oral interview by two trained examiners who probe the subject's level of performance. Use by the Foreign Service Institute over a period of thirty years has led to considerable refinement; the spread of the technique first to other US government agencies,[10] then to more public domains, has led to an increased understanding of the process and its potential. John Carroll (1967) used the technique in his important study of the ability of college foreign language majors; John Clark (1978) more recently developed a version suitable for high school students; and others, including, for instance, Elana Shohamy (1983) and Shohamy and Reves (1985), have explored its practicality for foreign language testing.

It was in some measure the success of these last developments that encouraged American university teachers of foreign languages to use the notion of scales to establish proficiency goals for foreign language teaching.[11] As is readily apparent, the ACTFL[12] Guidelines derive directly from the Foreign Service Institute scale, with some general modifications and a somewhat different set of details. First and most obvious is that the overall range of the scale is modified so that it offers more divisions at the lower end: what is 0—0+ in the Foreign Service Institute scale occupies two renamed levels in the ACTFL Guidelines. Level names in the ACTFL Guidelines are chosen to be more suitable for school and university use. The other major modification is that, besides the four original scales for the four basic language skills of speaking, listening, reading, and writing, the ACTFL Guidelines include a scale labelled Culture for such skills as knowledge of greeting behaviour and knowledge of literary commonplaces of the foreign language. The generic scales are worded much as the Foreign Service Institute scale, but the specific language scales add structural details.

The descriptions are vivid and useful, showing the steady progression that might be hoped for in a student in a modern fluency- and communicative-oriented foreign language classroom, preparing to visit the country whose language he or she is learning and in the meantime engaging in appropriate simulation activities. The descriptions of the other skills are similarly communicatively oriented, so that reading starts with 'simple elementary needs such as names, addresses, dates, street signs . . .' and moves through 'menus, schedules, timetables' and 'popular advertising' to (at the high intermediate level) 'social notes, letters . . ., summary paragraphs . . . from familiar news'. Edited prose fiction comes in at the advanced level, short stories and novels at the superior level. The reading skills are in fact an excellent account of functional literacy in a native language; had we had them at the time, we would have been spared a good deal of the work we did to develop a functional literacy test used by the Israel Defense Forces. [13]

One of the great advantages of the scale and guidelines approach is that it lends itself to several important uses. The guidelines provide a method of communication with lay people, for the descriptive statement has more meaning (or rather, clearer meaning) than a numerical score, where a single number has to bear several different interpretations.[14] It answers the most direct questions about the face validity of a test. It lends itself to direct (or ingenious indirect) translation into an authentic[15] and reliable[16] test and into valuable curricula.[17]

Necessary or imposed order

The Foreign Service Institute scales appear at first glance to be logically ordered: they seem to chart the steady progress of a foreign service officer from a stumbling semi-tourist to a skilled and successful diplomat. But other orders are in fact possible: one needs only to mention the not uncommon pattern of the academically trained scholar who proceeds through grammar and reading of literary texts to polished written skills, and then adds spoken skills only when given an opportunity and a need to do so. The various arguments for the primacy of speech were more rhetorically effective than empirically based: the order of teaching and learning a foreign language is much more a matter of choice and circumstances than dogmatic theorists would like. But even if this were not so, there would still be many learners whose goals and learning opportunity do not permit the pursuit of other goals through communication.

One obvious example of this is the teaching of Hebrew to Jews outside Israel, a paradigm for many other cases where the need for access to a liturgical language or to classical religious texts sets a quite different ordering of skills from that involved in a communicative model. Thus, just as a Hebrew school outside Israel might want (or need) to spend its first years preparing its pupils to take an appropriate part in their bar mitzvah ceremony, so a Koranic school might give first place to rote reading.[18] A similar case would surely also be made by those interested in specific purpose reading skills, among which the pursuit of access to other language literatures has a very respected place.

Let me summarize the argument this way. A functional set of goals, especially one based on a communicative approach, exists in a social context, and involves a precise definition of the social roles to be performed by the learner. Where this is consistent and common, as in the US Foreign Service, or in the Council of Europe notion of the Threshold Level for tourists and occasional visitors,[19] it is not unreasonable to develop a scale that proceeds through the skills. Similar but competing scales can be developed for other social roles. Thus, the US Defense Language Institute might reasonably adapt the Foreign Service Institute scale to a number of specific military purposes, or for Hebrew, we might want to have a communicative track, a liturgical track, a religious textual track, a secular textual track, to mention the most obvious. If it cannot be based on a single social goal, a single set of guidelines and a single scale could only be justified if there were evidence of an empirically provable necessary learning order, and we have clearly had difficulty in showing this to be so even for structural items.

One way around this problem might be to attempt to set up a kind of multiple branching approach. Rather than forming a single continuous scale, the various skills might be visualized as being laid out on a complex grid of alternate tracks, so that designing a programme (or a test, which is after all its mirror image) is something like selecting a Chinese meal: one from A, two from B, one from C, etc. I must admit I like the image, but find it hard to work through the reality. Nor am I attracted by the alternative view of an infinite number of distinct tracks, for items will clearly be repeated in various paths. We need, it seems, a model capable of deriving indeterminate results from determinate rules. The most obvious candidate for this is a preference model.

How might the preference model provide a solution to our present problem? It is by accepting that the outcomes of language learning form a complete set of such preferences. For any given learning goal, weightings determine which features should be included. Thus, in the training of a telephone operator for a multilingual business, the probability of languages, topics, requests, and responses will all contribute to a final description. Language learning theory may provide some notion of suitable ordering of the items,[20] and so a language tester might choose to start with this as the basis for his or her work, as a first set of specifications for the test. Beyond this minimum, a needs assessment survey is one way to set up a scale: a description of the specific tasks we expect the learner to be able to perform, and the importance we attach to each.[21] Thus, we should normally expect functional goals to be an intrinsically unordered set; the social context in which the instruction is to take place will determine a weighting of importance, and various other relevant conditions [22] will combine with these to determine ordering. We see then the potential danger of accepting any single set of ordered goals for all instruction, which is the essential proposal of the ACTFL Guidelines. Except when we are dealing with a homogeneous population and social context, profiles are better reports of functional ability than anything based on absolute ranked scales.

Goals for learning Hebrew—an example

The issue of the ordering of goals may be illustrated with the example of the problems of teaching the Hebrew language outside Israel. There are a large number of detailed functional goals that might reasonably be considered to make up knowledge of Hebrew; one might be willing to say that a person has learned Hebrew (knows Hebrew) if any (or any combination or all) of them has been mastered. While these outcomes are more or less distinct, many of them can be further broken down into other discrete skills. Ideally, together they add up to a description of the ability of the educated native speaker, but any one or any combination is a possible outcome of language instruction for a second language learner, and any one or combination may in fact have been chosen as the first or major goal of instruction of a specific programme.

There are many programmes teaching Hebrew whose goals would be met if they attained a minimal mechanical reading level; others would want to follow a communicative route through the functions; others might want to start with translating Biblical Hebrew. There are programmes whose designers would agree that some form of communicative language use is a first goal; others would reject this completely, or place it only after more important goals had been met. There is likely to be controversy about the place (not just the desirability) of other goals as well. A secular Jewish teacher, for instance, would consider that reading and understanding the Bible in Hebrew is a reasonable and achievable goal, while a religious school, which would place a much more demanding interpretation on the notion of 'understanding' the Bible, would consider that it would not normally be achieved in a school programme. There are a number of ultra-orthodox schools which oppose the use of Hebrew for any secular or general communicative functions, although learners who have achieved high levels of proficiency in biblical and religious Hebrew will often be capable of speaking Hebrew, albeit with a marked accent.

This analysis shows that the ordering of a scale such as that of the Foreign Service Institute or of ACTFL is natural only within an agreed or imposed set of goals, and that the ideology of the programme or the specific goals of its students or teachers play a major part in determining which set of goals is appropriate and how they must be ordered. Consider how this applies to the proposed goals for Hebrew instruction. Rather than attempting to map them onto some absolute scale or guideline, we might rather consider how each is valued according to one of a number of major rationales[23] that might be given for teaching and learning Hebrew in the Diaspora. Rationales too are a fairly open set, but if people are asked why they teach Hebrew, or why they are learning it or sending their children to a school where it is taught, there are nine answers that are likely to occur with reasonable frequency:

(1) It is valuable for maintaining Jewish values and heritage.
(2) It is needed for Jewish religion and religious life.
(3) It is a symbol of Jewish ethnic and national identity.
(4) It is associated with Zionism and going to live in Israel (aliyah).
(5) It is useful for visiting Israel.
(6) It is required for some useful examinations.
(7) Knowing any second language is valuable.
(8) You need Hebrew to take part in a bar mitzvah or a bat mitzvah ceremony.

(9) You need Hebrew to prepare for a professional career as a rabbi or Jewish teacher.

Now, it is clear that each of these rationales would put various degrees of weight on each of the possible goals of instruction: for instance, the skills associated with reading prayers receive weight from the rationale of Jewish religion and religious life, while the rationale involving Zionism and living in Israel puts weight on the communicative goals. The full picture is set out in Table 4.1.

Goals	Rationales
1 follow a service in Hebrew in a prayer book	R
2 lead a service from a prayer book in Hebrew	RVT
3 understand the meaning of the prayers in Hebrew	VT
4 carry on a simple conversation in Hebrew	NZB
5 join in a discussion with speakers of Hebrew	TNZB
6 read bar/bat-mitzvah portion in Hebrew	M
7 follow radio news in easy Hebrew	ZB
8 follow the television news in Hebrew	ZB
9 understand a lecture in Hebrew	ZV
10 understand a play in a Hebrew theatre	V
11 understand signs written in Hebrew	ZB
12 read a newspaper in easy Hebrew	NZB
13 read a normal Hebrew newspaper	NZB
14 read modern Hebrew Poetry	VX
15 read a short story in simplified Hebrew	VX
16 read an Israeli novel	V
17 write a personal letter in Hebrew	NZB
18 write a business letter in Hebrew	BZ
19 write creatively in Hebrew	VNX
20 read and understand the Bible in Hebrew	RT
21 read the Bible in Hebrew and translate it	RT
22 fill out forms in Hebrew	ZB
23 study all school subjects in Hebrew	NZ
24 study Jewish subjects in Hebrew	NZL
25 study Jewish religious subjects in Hebrew	Z
26 talk on the telephone in Hebrew	ZB

Key to rationales
V   Jewish values and heritage
R   Jewish religion and religious life
N   Jewish ethnic and national identity
Z   Zionism and aliyah
B   Visiting Israel
X   Examinations
L   Linguistic sophistication
M   Bar mitzvah or bat mitzvah
T   Becoming a rabbi or teacher

Table 4.1   Goals and rationales for learning Hebrew

From a study of Table 4.1, we can see that the most suitable ordering of goals for a specific programme will probably be determined by these ideological weightings plus a number of other relevant conditions. Thus, one would expect to find quite different orderings of importance being proposed in the various kinds of Jewish day schools, such as Zionist religious schools, Zionist secular schools, ultra-orthodox non-Zionist schools, establishment academic schools, or minimalist schools. The final ordering of the goals, then, would involve at least two different criteria: any natural ordering (some skills are by definition easier than others; others include sub-skills that might therefore reasonably be expected to precede them), plus the ideological weightings, the socially and individually determined values that set priorities in goals for learning. In a later chapter we will see an empirical test of the relation between goals and skills; the important point at this stage is to note that any ranking of functional goals into a single scale, such as that proposed by the proponents of the ACTFL Guidelines, is necessarily limited to a specific ideology of language teaching. This general principle is summarized in a condition as follows:

Condition 18
Integrated Skills Weighting/Ordering condition (typical, graded): The weighting (relative importance) and ordering of integrated skills are dependent on individually or socially determined goals for learning the language.

In this chapter the study of language testing has so far shown us that knowing a language and how to use it involve knowledge and control both of a number of structural items and of a number of pragmatic, integrated functions. I will in the next chapter want to consider how these might be summed or related: in the meantime, we have again seen the complexity of language proficiency, and so the necessary complexity of any model that attempts to describe how it is acquired.

Notes

1 For a somewhat richer and much less parsimonious taxonomy, see Stern (1983: 341ff).
2 General proficiency is made up of one or more functional abilities, and both depend on control of an appropriate number and mix of structural items.
3 I read Schumann (1978a and elsewhere) as using this term to claim that the speaker so described uses a grammar containing certain structures that are similar to those in a pidginized form of the language he or she is speaking.
4 Identified by Carroll as the 'discrete point test'.

5   For discussion, see the articles by Anthony Woods and Rosemary Baker, and by Grant Hennings and his colleagues in Volume 2, Number 2 of *Language Testing*.

6   In a way, both functional and overall tests might be considered integrative. I will look at overall tests, that is, tests that assume some kind of general language proficiency, in the next chapter.

7   See for instance Titone (1985).

8   See for example Munby (1978).

9   Kennedy (1987) provides an excellent illustration of this problem when he identifies nearly three hundred linguistic devices for expressing the notion of temporal frequency in academic English and considers some ways of deciding which of them to teach.

10   In its latest version, it is called the ILR test, signifying some agreement on its use by the other US agencies which together with the Foreign Service Institute of the Department of State make up the Inter-agency Language Roundtable.

11   See *ACTFL Provisional Proficiency Guidelines* (1982); also Liskin-Gasparro (1984).

12   American Council for the Teaching of Foreign Languages.

13   The work was carried out by Robert Cooper, Raphael Nir, and Bernard Spolsky.

14   The polysemy of grades and scores is a cause for major concern to all responsible testers and test users. A single score may mean (or may be interpreted as) an assessment of the student's proficiency level, or achievement relative to others, or level of effort, or as a warning or reward, or as a prediction of future success.

15   For cautions on the use of the word 'authentic' see Widdowson (1979:163–172), Stevenson (1985), and Spolsky (1985a).

16   Provided the evaluators all undergo common training.

17   See *Foreign Language Annals*, 17, 5, (1984), 485–489.

18   See Wagner and Lotfi (1983).

19   See van Ek (1975).

20   But ordering is almost certainly a matter of preference. It is because of the complexity of applying the many different criteria involved that there is no agreement in the order that various textbooks present their topics.

21   Cf. Munby (1978).

22   See for instance Spolsky (1985d).

23   Compare the discussion of rationales for bilingual education in Lewis (1980).

5 Measuring knowledge of a second language

The idea of general proficiency

The tests of functional skills discussed in the last chapter are integrative rather than discrete point tests; they measure not knowledge of specific structural items but the integration of those items into defined language functions (Carroll 1961). A test of overall or general proficiency is also integrative, but it starts from somewhat different principles.

The attempt to test overall language proficiency is justified by the belief that there is some fundamentally indivisible (even if technically analysable) body of knowledge varying in size from individual to individual such that individuals can be ranked according to the extent that they have the knowledge. While it admits of some gross and not necessarily rankable variations (X can speak but not write, Y functions better in formal situations while Z has better control over informal language), it aims to express the subject's control of the language by a measure on a single scale or gradient, an assumption it shares with those who believe in the value of a single IQ score, or that a percentage grade in an examination is a unidimensional statement of ability. It turns up in practice in claims for general proficiency scores derivable either as a general factor underlying batteries of tests of various kinds or as the special trait measured by some privileged test methods like the cloze and dictation. The term proficiency and the emphasis on discovering it through test performance mean that this model, while talking about knowledge, is also more likely to be oriented towards modelling the process of language use than towards understanding underlying competence.

Having shown how knowledge of a language is to be broken down into structural and functional components, it might seem surprising that I am still willing to treat of language ability as general proficiency. But to say that linguistic and communicative competence are divisible does not necessarily rule out the claim that there is a core of common knowledge of a language underlying the specific abilities of a speaker. I would agree then with a statement by John Oller in which he recognizes the undue constraint of binary logic:

> the holistic, global aspects of language use, or other cognitive performances, do not exclude particulate, analytic and discrete

elements. Indeed, it seems that in an adequate theory the holistic elements must depend on the interaction of the relatively analytic components. Hence, the idea that global and particulate models were incompatible must have been quite wrong. . . It would seem that both views are needed and that they can complement each other rather than contradict one another. (Oller 1983:36)

The argument for the claim of general language proficiency goes something like this. While we cannot specify a minimum of structural knowledge or communicative competences, we can make some general claim about the ranking of one individual relative to him or herself at other times or relative to other people, so that we can say 'X knows more of this language now than last month' or 'X knows more than Y'. We can specify this difference in one of three ways: by a test of structural knowledge (the more items known, the greater total proficiency), by a test of functional knowledge (the more functions controlled, the greater total knowledge), or by an overall test which is a special kind of functional test that taps the generalized ability more directly. The claim for this may be expressed in the following condition:

Condition 19
Overall Proficiency condition (necessary): As a result of its system-aticity, the existence of redundancy, and the overlap in the usefulness of structural items, knowledge of a language may be characterized as a general proficiency and measured.

Let us look at the evidence on this question from work in second language testing. We saw earlier that many of the arguments in second language learning turn on questions of discovery procedures; the arguments between Tarone and Selinker discussed in Chapter 2 over variability, for instance, turned in part on how to elicit data and what to consider as data. Tarone introduced into the field of interlanguage study the notion that linguistic variation can (in part) be accounted for by differences in the attention paid to language according to the task set the speaker. The functional approach is also fundamentally behaviourist in that it aims to describe a phenomenon (language knowledge) in terms of observable performance. It takes, therefore, considerable interest in questions of discovery procedures.

In linguistics, there have been three main methods of obtaining data:

(1) observation (recording, analysis, judgement) of natural language performance or written records of it
(2) introspection or self-report
(3) formal elicitation of performance so that it can be recorded, analysed, or judged.

Linguists in the philological tradition who worked with written texts, and structural linguists who put similar emphasis on the need to work with a natural corpus of spoken material, both used the first method, setting a high value on authenticity. In practice, however, structuralists were willing to elicit spoken forms (method (3) above) and to ask native speakers for their judgements about forms (a version of method (2)). Transformational grammarians in general obtain evidence by the process of introspection, making up their own examples if they are native speakers; sociolinguistic surveys also often rely on self-report. Labov (1969 and elsewhere) has been the main critic of these various methods, showing both the systematic problems of self-report and the paradox of trying to observe natural (and so unselfconscious, unobserved) behaviour.[1] He has been concerned specifically with capturing the underlying explanation for variation between the results obtained by the various procedures which tap different levels of style.

Second language tests necessarily presuppose theories of the nature of second language knowledge; the problem, as I once expressed it (Spolsky 1973), is to find a way of having someone perform his or her competence. Language tests fall naturally into three main groups: tests of specific structural knowledge, tests of specific functional abilities, and tests that claim to measure general proficiency. The arguments for the former two are fairly clear, but the third has been a matter of quite fierce controversy.

Cziko (1984) looks at some of the problems with empirical models of communicative competence, distinguishing descriptive and theoretical models like Canale and Swain's from working models such as those used in testing. If these models of the components of communicative competence represent distinct abilities, he argues, it should be possible to show them distinctly in tests of proficiency; they should occur as factors in tests. To investigate this question, we would typically give two tests of the specific abilities we wish to study (Cziko's example is a reading skills test and a speaking skills test) to a group of subjects, and we would interpret a high Pearson product-moment correlation as evidence of relationship and a low one as evidence of independence of the two skills being tested. But there are problems: a low correlation could result from one test having failed to spread the subjects out sufficiently, or a high one might not recognize that while the rank order is the same, the students are in fact very strong at one and very weak at the other skill. Cziko shows the various patterns of language background that might produce equivalent results, and the various ways that patterns of proficiency vary when the tests used are norm-referenced (based on the performance of a specific group of learners). He argues, therefore, that the use of absolute or criterion-referenced tests, not influenced by any specific population, is essential before one can start to make useful and meaningful correlations between tests of various skills. His conclusion is that only with 'the use of criterion-referenced language measures designed to reveal the true skill patterns of language learners, together with appropriate statistical analyses and extensive language background information' (Cziko 1984:37) will we be in a position to study the working of the various factors or components making up communicative competence.

Work in language testing research has been concerned with clarifying as much as possible the relations between the various kinds of testing tasks and the specific abilities that they measure. The multiple-trait, multiple-method studies of language testing encouraged by Stevenson's (1981) pioneering work on the relevance of construct validity to language testing is essentially concerned with attempting to separate the various strands built into language tests. In practice, it has turned out to be simpler to think up new tests and testing techniques than to explain precisely what it is that they are measuring. Certain conclusions are however safe. First, there is a strong correlation between various kinds of language tests. Part of this comes from the fact that they are all formal tests: thus, subjects who for various reasons do not test well (who become over-anxious, or who are unwilling to play the special game of testing, i.e. answering a question the answer to which is known better by the asker than the answerer) will not be accurately measured by any kind of formal test: there will be a large gap between their test and their real-life performance.[2] A second part of this correlation might well be explained by some theory of overall language proficiency.

The idea of overall language proficiency was originally derived from Carroll's (1961) notion of integrative language tests. The argument was presented first as follows: 'The high correlation obtained between the various sections of TOEFL [Test of English as a Foreign Language] and other general tests of English suggests that in fact we might be dealing with a single factor, English proficiency . . .' (Spolsky 1967:38). In a subsequent paper, the acknowledgement to Carroll is spelled out:

> Fundamental to the preparation of valid tests of language proficiency is a theoretical question: What does it mean to know a language? There are two ways in which this question might be answered. One is to follow what Carroll (1961) has referred to as the integrative approach and to say that there is such a thing as overall proficiency. (Spolsky *et al.* 1968:79)

There are empirical and theoretical arguments presented for this claim. The empirical argument follows from the work of a number of language testing scholars, including Holtzman (1967), who were at the time reporting very high correlations between various language proficiency measures. It was further supported by a series of studies by Oller and some of his colleagues who, using factor analysis, were struck by the power and importance of a common first factor that Oller labelled 'unitary language competence'.

There is considerable doubt over the validity of this statistical argument.[3] The use of one kind of factor analysis, exploratory principal components analysis, tends to exaggerate the size of the first factor. This statistical technique, because it does not start with a hypothetical model of the underlying factors and their relationships, sets up a general component that includes in it much of the unexplained scatter. The statistical argument over language proficiency parallels similar debates over the notion of a single measurable factor of intelligence. The key argument between Thurstone, who claimed that there were seven underlying mental abilities, and Spearman, who argued for one, depended on the statistical techniques they used. Thurstone showed that Spearman's analysis of results of tests to produce a one-vector solution that he labelled g (a general intelligence factor) is theory bound and not mathematically necessary. By using a different technique, Thurstone produced his own three- vector solution, and then proceeded to reify the three vectors as primary mental abilities. But there is no reason to believe that Thurstone's own primary abilities are not themselves dependent on the tests used; with more tests added, one could use the same statistical technique to show more kinds of primary ability. Gould (1981) argues convincingly that the statistical tests that have been used in this debate do not in fact make it possible to distinguish between single and multi-factor causes. He is particularly critical of the reification of the results of factor analyses. Oller (1984) has acknowledged the criticism of the statistical basis for his claim and is now much more hesitant.

Oller's arguments are not only statistical, but relate in part to the notion of an expectancy grammar. The theoretical argument presented in Spolsky (1968) is not statistical either, but focuses attention on the link between the creative aspect of language, the fact that speakers of a language can understand and create sentences they have not heard before, and the work of Miller and Isard, working within information theory, on the importance of the ability to understand language with reduced redundancy. The information theory model was particularly important because it treated language in an independent way; as Chomsky's earliest work demonstrated, the probability analysis it used was quite different from a structural linguistic analysis. Tests that mask the message randomly (dictation with or without noise[4], or the cloze test[5]) might then be considered independent, non-linguistically determined measures of language proficiency. If they are tapping specific abilities, they are doing it in a more or less random way, and so are testing a random conglomerate of specific items. Indeed, the weakness that Klein-Braley (1981) spotted in the cloze test was its use of the word, a more or less linguistic unit, as the unit to be deleted, and as she showed, this very fact meant that a specific cloze test was biased towards measuring specific structural features.

The C-test that Raatz and Klein-Braley (1982) have proposed tries to overcome this problem by deleting not words but parts of words;[6] it is thus further from being a measure of structural ability, and so closer to a general measure. According to this argument, the best (because most general) measure of this kind would be a written equivalent of the dictation with noise; the visual noise too would need to be added randomly, and as equivalent to the white or pink noise of the aural test, one would use some form of visual blurring for the written passage. One might want to argue that a test like this is functional if not structural, but the very absence of content validity and obvious task authenticity in the cloze and the noise test is what makes these tests so abstract and non-specific. It is of course possible to find ways to make the tasks seem authentic,[7] but the very fact that an effort is needed makes my point. All these studies continue to provide support for the notion of general language proficiency as stated in the condition, however difficult it might be to measure it with accuracy. One of the important results of this condition is the possibility of developing a common core of items to be included in a general introductory course;[8] as a general rule, specific purpose teaching of a foreign language follows the teaching of this common core.

Essentially, then, we have seen that there are both in general theory and in language testing theory and practice three interrelated but not overlapping approaches to describing and measuring knowledge of a second language: the one structural, the second functional, and the third general. Anybody who knows a second language may be assumed to have all three kinds of knowledge, and they are related but not in any direct way, so that any description on one dimension alone is just as likely to be distorted as a description on the basis of one aspect of one dimension (for example, vocabulary knowledge only for structural knowledge, or greeting behaviour only for functional).

Relating the models

The discussions so far have led to certain important distinctions. First has been the basic distinction between competence, seen as an abstract set of rules accounting for underlying knowledge, and performance, defined as observable behaviour. Note that there is no claim in the notion of competence that the system of rules is identical with the form of mental storage of those rules, although such claims are usually made in performance or processing models.

A second set of distinctions has involved some form of the theoretical division of competence into various components, such as linguistic, pragmatic, and sociolinguistic. The first component, Chomskyan linguistic competence, accounted for by the grammar of the language, is itself sub-divided into at least the following sub-components: phonetic representation, phonology, syntactic structures and rules, semantic structures and rules, correspondence rules between syntax and semantics, and lexicon.[9] While the division into these sub-components is generally accepted, the boundaries between them are not clear, nor is there agreement about the boundaries between the grammar and the second major component, also clearly a kind of competence, the pragmatics, or the general rules of language use. There may be a third component, sociolinguistic competence, defined informally as socially specific rules of language use. It is also possible to treat pragmatics and sociolinguistics together, the former dealing with universal and the latter with local society-specific rules.

The third distinction is that between separate components of language knowledge, whether structural or functional, and the notion of general language proficiency, defined operationally within information theory as the ability to work with reduced redundancy.

Now an obvious question that follows after making these distinctions is to ask how the parts are related. I have already mentioned the question of the relation between competence and performance and accepted arguments that favour building the latter on the former.[10] At the same time, we must note that there are strong arguments presented against any such connection: those who wish to develop performance grammars see no link between the rules of an interlanguage (competence) and the observed data; Jordens (1986) postulates instead rules of language, such as the procedural grammar proposed by Kempen and Hoenkamp (1982).

An equally difficult challenge is set if we wish to consider the relation between structural and functional descriptions. This issue is faced on a practical level by those who take on the complex task of intertwining productively a notional-functional syllabus and a structural one. Why this should be difficult is clear if we look at the same task tackled on a theoretical level by those who have attempted to trace the connection between speech acts and the many different formal structures that realize them.

The most elaborated analysis of functional language competence is the work in the speech act theory that we have described earlier. Bach and Harnish (1979) attempt to relate linguistic structures and speech acts. Their answer, however, does not satisfy. The key problem faced by those working to relate the functional and formal characteristics is the very absence of the possibility of one-to-one mappings. Not only are there many different forms of words that I can use in making a request:

Please shut the window.
Close the window, please.
Close it, please,
Do it, please.

but also there are many different syntactic structures that may be used:

Will you close the window?
I want you to close the window.
I am cold.
When will you close the window?
I haven't been feeling well lately.
The window is open.

Given the difficulty and perhaps theoretical impossibility of specifying precisely the relation between structure and function,[11] it is necessary to include both approaches in the model, and to be willing to describe language proficiency in both functional and structural terms.

Testing practice and theory are important because they reinforce our understanding of the complexity of the knowledge of a second language that may be achieved by, and measured in, a learner. Only a highly detailed battery of tests and observations will lead to the kind of precise profile of knowledge and skills that accurately portrays the results of learning. In practice, we will often be constrained by pragmatic considerations to limit our attention to a simple slice of this complex reality, but when we do so, we need to keep in mind the practical and theoretical limitations of what we have done.

Linguistic outcomes in a general theory

To summarize what I have been saying in these last two chapters, a second language learner's proficiency in a specific language or variety (*K*, the outcome of language learning) may be described in one of three ways:

(1) In terms of mastery of specific elements of the (autonomous) linguistic system. Such comments may be absolute ('X has complete control over the verb system of L_x'), comparative ('X knows the vocabulary of computers in L_x as well as a native speaker'), or evaluative ('X has good control of the phonology of L_y'). Instructional goals may be formulated in structural terms, such as lists of grammatical structures or of lexicon to be taught.

(2) In terms of ability to function in the language. The statement can be general (for example, control of the written rather than the spoken language), specific as to functions ('X knows enough L_x to reserve a hotel room') or notions ('X can express anger in L_y'), related to specific situations (formal or informal), or topics, or registers. These specific abilities may be grouped to form arbitrarily defined clusters, as in the Foreign Service Institute scale, but are better organized as a list of possible goals from which appropriate sets can be chosen

according to the ideology or rationales underlying the learning (or testing) situation.

(3) In terms of a hypothesized general proficiency. In practical terms, because measurement of this will depend on a specific functional instrument, it is probably best to treat it as a special kind of functional ability.

It is clear that there is a hierarchical relation between these three approaches. The more structural items you control, the more functional ability you have; and the more functional abilities, the greater the level of your general proficiency. But there is no one-to-one mapping possible between the levels, nor can one specify uniquely or exhaustively which items on the lower level are reflected in a chosen higher level ability. [12] While there is a theoretical relation between these three approaches, then, the impossibility of making it specific and explicit means that we need to state clearly which model we are using and present our own precise definition of language proficiency.

There is no point in setting out here a taxonomy of possible goals; every language teaching curriculum is based on such a taxonomy, whether explicitly or implicitly. As Mackey (1965) showed, the specification of these goals is a minimum first step in language teaching analysis. I am arguing here that its recognition is also a necessary first step in a general theory of second language learning; there is no way to make sense of seemingly contradictory data and opinions without returning regularly to the issue of specifying the outcome of the learning process. In the introduction to a volume on research in cross-linguistic interference, Kellerman and Sharwood Smith (1986:7) make a 'plea for modularity', calling for 'a differentiated approach to the various areas of language, given the apparent and hitherto underestimated degree of complexity of crosslinguistic influence.' Given this variation at the microlevel of individual second language proficiency, it is not surprising that, as we explore the various factors that account for learning of more generalized proficiencies, we will need to note the various ways in which the factors interact with the multitude of possible outcomes whose surface we have been exploring.

How then should the learner's knowledge of a second language (the linguistic outcome) appear in a model of second language learning? How should K_f (and for that matter K_p) be defined in the formula proposed at the end of Chapter 1? First, it needs to be stated as a set of preference rather than necessary conditions. Second, it needs to be stated as an open condition, definable within determined characteristics for any specific situation.

The linguistic outcomes have been discussed in a number of separate conditions: these may all be summarized in the following general condition:

Condition 20
Linguistic Outcome condition (typical, graded): Prefer to say that someone knows a second language if one or more criteria (to be specified) are met. The criteria are specifiable:

(a)   as underlying knowledge or skills *(Dual Knowledge condition)*
(b)   analysed or unanalysed *(Analysed Knowledge condition; Unanalysed Knowledge condition)*
(c)   implicit or explicit *(Implicit Knowledge condition; Explicit Knowledge condition)*
(d)   of individual structural items (sounds, lexical items, grammatical structures) *(Discrete Item condition)*
(e)   which integrate into larger units *(Language as System condition)*
(f)   such as functional skills *(Integrated Function condition)*
(g)   for specified purposes (see, for instance, *Academic Skills condition, Communicative Goal condition*)
(h)   or as overall proficiency *(Overall Proficiency condition)*
(i)   productive or receptive *(Productive/Receptive skills condition)*
(j)   with a specified degree of accuracy *(Variability condition; Accuracy condition)*
(k)   with a specified degree of fluency *(Automaticity condition)*
(l)   and with a specified approximation to native speaker usage *(Native Speaker Target condition)*
(m)   of one or more specified varieties of language *(Specific Variety condition)*.

Given the amount of redundancy in language (the justification for assuming the existence of overall proficiency), lack of specificity will not necessarily be fatal—a second language learner will often be able to perform untaught or unspecified tasks, but the accuracy of any model will depend on the precision of the description of K.

Allowing for this fuzziness or contamination effect, we should expect that any statement of a condition in the model of second language learning will have as its result clause a specific outcome; the overall form of a condition would then be like this:

If (specified condition), then (specific linguistic outcome).

For example, when we are considering the effect of age on second language learning, we will find statements of the following kind useful:

If the learner is young, then pronunciation is better.
If the learner is older, then learning of grammar is faster.

Similarly, in looking at the learning of Hebrew by Jews in the Diaspora, the specific list of statements might include:

If the learner is religiously observant, he or she is more likely to be able to read a Hebrew prayer book.

As we will see, statements of this kind, with some degree of precision as to probability for each part (the degree of certainty of our knowledge of the accuracy that the condition has been met, and the degree of probability of the outcome), form the basic rules of the model, which will further aim to show the weight of each rule in a specific situation.

The distinction between structural items and functional abilities will also turn out to be a critical one, setting as it does the challenge of integrating microlevel theories of the learning of individual items (such as the morphological or syntactic items that are the focus in Second Language Acquisition studies) with macrolevel theories of the development of the more extensive kinds of language proficiency studied by those who work in the Social Psychological tradition. It is to these issues that we now turn.

Notes

1 For a discussion of the relevance of this to second language learning research, see Wolfson (1986).
2 See Spolsky (1984, 1985a).
3 See for instance the first seven papers in Hughes and Porter (1983).
4 In a noise test, subjects are given dictation from a tape to which randomly generated ('white') noise has been added.
5 In a classic cloze test, the person taking the test is required to fill in missing words in a passage of continuous prose; the words are deleted on a non-linguistic basis (for example, every seventh word). The term is also used for tests where the decision to delete is made on a linguistic or pedagogical basis (i.e. certain parts of speech, or key words) but these rationalized cloze tests do not fit the point made here.
6 In the C-test, the second half of every second word is deleted.
7 Stevenson (1985) has shown how students may be convinced that the tasks are authentic and reflect real-life events, but the artificiality remains.
8 Carter (1987) discusses some of the problems in devising tests to establish a core vocabulary.
9 For discussion, see, for instance, Jackendoff (1983:9).
10 A criticism of Chomsky's formulation was that he seemed on the one hand to treat performance as a wastebasket for anything that would not fit into competence and on the other hand to set up his own statement of what kinds of regularities would be admitted to linguistic competence.

11   This task is undertaken for literary interpretation by Schauber and
     E. Spolsky (1986) using a preference model.
12   In practical terms, one does of course try to do this: a language
     course is an attempt to specify the functions and items that make up
     some generalized level of proficiency chosen for a particular set of
     students, and the Language for Specific Purposes approach involves
     trying to determine the items most useful for the functions
     associated with a specific domain.

6   The psycholinguistic basis

The human learner

The parts of a multi-faceted model of the kind being explored in this book have no set or necessary order. The model presented at the end of Chapter 1 suggested a cyclical arrangement, with outcomes coming to influence the social context, which itself influences the learner (through motivation), the learning situation, and the expected outcomes (goals). It also allowed for interaction between the various constituent parts, so that there is no single starting point. Further, the relative importance of the factors that make up the model can vary according to complex combinations of circumstances. In a competence model, the order of application of rules may be relevant in the case of necessary conditions; the application of typicality conditions, which may, as we have seen, be contradictory, depends on their relative weight or importance rather than on their order.

In a processing model, order may often be important, but this is not necessarily the case: one of the most interesting recent discoveries about the brain is its ability to process a multiplicity of information simultaneously, a property emulated in the newest generation of computers and underlying the Parallel Distributed Processing model discussed at the end of the final chapter of this book. Such a model is also implied by the assumption that learning of a language proceeds on multiple levels: one does not learn sounds first, then words, then grammar, but adds items of various kinds in no fixed order. Nonetheless, having begun, as it were, at the end, with our consideration of the complexity of language proficiency—the outcome of language learning —it will be convenient to try to set some order for the consideration in this chapter and those to follow of the conditions that help account for the nature of this outcome.

Because of the relevance of a second language learning model to those concerned with language teaching, I have chosen to arrange the chapters with reference not to process but to the criterion of the ease with which the factors concerned are susceptible of external modification. I start, then, with those conditions that are least under the control of an individual language teacher and move progressively to those where the teacher's intervention seems easiest. This order will have certain echoes in the application of the theoretical model, for it will move us from generally necessary conditions in this chapter to mainly typicality conditions at the end. But it must be stressed that this order of arrangement is purely for convenience of writer and reader; the latter should not be surprised if the former seems occasionally to jump about following other principles of association. The order I have adopted is similar to that of Stern (1983): he uses the term conditions in a different way to me.

The absolute and necessary condition for second language learning is a human learner. While this may at first glance seem trivial and obvious, it is in fact interpretable as an empirically verifiable claim of some critical theoretical importance.

Condition 21
Human Learner condition (necessary, postulate): A general theory of second language learning deals with the learning of a second or later language by a human being who has already learned a first language.

Two alternative possibilities are worth considering. One might want to set as a requirement for a general theory of second language learning that it account for the learning by an animal of anything other than its natural communicative system, i.e. the training of animals and birds to respond to human signals and to produce signals interpretable by human beings. Alternatively or in addition, one might choose to require that a general theory of second language learning account for the possibility of programming a computer to produce or accept a natural language. Jackendoff (1983:12) rejects the possibility of computer modelling as a constraint on a semantic theory because of the difference between present day computers whose processing is serial and the brain, the processing of which is interactive and parallel. But it would seem that Expert Systems (in Artificial Intelligence) are in fact an attempt to develop models with properties very similar if not identical to the preference model, and of course Parallel Distributed Processing itself (Rumelhart and others) applies the brain metaphor to computer design. While I would not like to disregard the value to be achieved by studying animal communication systems or the possibilities of computer processing for the light that both can throw on human capacities, accepting either of these requirements would greatly complicate our task. A decision to require them must depend on some good evidence of their more than generalizable similarity to human second language learning. This evidence would come from an understanding of the physiological processes underlying human language use. For this reason, we will start this section with a consideration of the nature of the central physiological organ underlying language, the brain.

A great deal is known about the brain, but, as Hatch (1983:198) says, although we have learned to name all the parts, we still do not truly understand what happens to language input or how language output is formed. Obler (1983:159) characterizes our knowledge of the requisite neurophysiology as being 'quite rudimentary at this time'; while there has been important work with creatures such as the snail, 'neuro-scientists are as yet unable to describe the physiological process(es) related to the processing of language'. The covering of the black box remains opaque, but there are a number of more or less informed and more or less plausible guesses about how it might work, and some more or less imaginative guesses about the implication of these guesses for second language learning.

Some things are accepted. There appear to be differences in the function of the two hemispheres of the brain, with the right hemisphere specialized for music and the recognition of complex visual patterns, and the left specialized for analytical ability and some aspects of language. It also seems that sensory input goes to special parts of the brain. Certain areas have been shown to be especially related to language functioning. Broca's area, in the cortex, is important; when it is damaged, there are problems in speech production (and not just articulation). Trauma to this area can produce Broca's aphasia, one of the signs of which is telegraphic or agrammatic speech. Wernicke's area also is involved in speech, but a trauma here does not seem to affect grammar so much as meanings; in addition, comprehension is affected. Other areas seem also to be involved.[1]

There is no consensus among experts, Hatch tells us, on the match between brain structures and language functions: they range from the 'strong localists' to the hemispherists, the latter claiming that any specialization of the hemispheres is a matter of inhibition of a special kind. Drawing generalized conclusions from research is still very difficult, a result, as Obler (1983) remarks, of the limited techniques and methodologies used in neurolinguistic studies of bilingualism and second language learning and the special populations which have been studied.[2] It is, then, hard to generalize from these to the behaviour of normal people.

Underlying work in neurolinguistics there are, Obler says, a number of assumptions that are generally taken for granted. It is assumed that the only difference between the organization of the language of the brain-damaged patient and that of the normal person is that when there is damage, something is missing; that all groups of people have the same brain organization for language, with minor differences for special groups; that brain organization is fixed at birth and changed only by damage; and that some areas of the brain are specifically committed to language. In addition, it is assumed that language is organized in the brain non-redundantly; that a theory that accounts for 80 per cent of the data is solid; that there is and there will be found a one-to-one correlation between psycholinguistic processes and brain structures; and that laterality studies are worthwhile (Obler 1983:162ff). It will be obvious that there are good reasons to question many if not all of these assumptions; if, for instance, we found it difficult to conceive of one-to-one mapping of language structures to functions, why should we expect to be able to go from either to brain structures? In point of fact, as Fromkin (1987) points out, the exact location of breakdowns is of no interest to the linguist. Rather, just as linguistic theory suggests to the student of neurolinguistics the kind of components involved in language processing, so neurolinguistics can provide another kind of evidence for the existence of these suggested modules.

But there is always the temptation to try to build detailed models. One of the most optimistic of scholars in the field is Lamendella, who asserts that:

> The nervous system may be viewed as being composed of a set of *neurophysiological functional systems* definable by their anatomical constituency, their synaptic connections with other structures, and their internal organization. Each such neurofunctional system and the subsystems which make it up are responsible for a given *domain of functional activity* identifiable by the input/output relations of that system, as well as by its internal processing activity. (Lamendella 1977:160)

Primary language acquisition, Lamendella says, takes advantage of innate systems, which are available up to the critical period, a hypothetical age at which the language acquisition device no longer operates,[3] after which second language acquisition is still possible, but only using somewhat different systems. It is different from foreign language learning.

At first reading, one might be forgiven for failing to notice the crucial move from the leap of imagination in the first sentence—'may be viewed as'—to the absolute assertions that follow. It is important to keep reminding oneself that there is no neurophysiological evidence what-soever for any of the 'systems' being proposed, nor for their loss.

What does this all give us? Galloway (1981) summarizes research evidence on the neuropsychology of bilingualism and second language performance. There are a number of hypotheses that have been tested, considering stage, manner, modality, environment and age of acqui-sition, cognitive style, language specific, and socio-ethnic factors. Using either dichotic listening or tachistoscopic viewing tasks, right ear (left hemisphere) and right visual field (left hemisphere) advantage has been studied. Advanced second language learners and bilinguals appear to be equally lateralized in each of their languages. Numerous attempts have been made to disentangle the complex results, and there is a modified stage hypothesis current that claims that there should be greater right hemisphere involvement when adults are in early stages of learning in an informal environment. There is also a possibility of greater left hemisphere involvement in second language learning when subjects are monitoring, or when they have learned the language through reading. There are a number of studies that suggest that language in some bilinguals is more evenly divided between the hemispheres than in monolinguals. There are reported differences (in contradictory directions) according to age of learning. There are hypotheses, but no hard evidence of language-specific differences (Hebrew versus English) and ethnic differences (Navajo versus other groups). Galloway concludes with a number of very cautious generalizations, then points out methodological weaknesses of the data (for example, very few tasks, word rather than sentence based).

A series of papers at the 1981 TESOL Convention summarized the state of the art in the field of neurolinguistics and second language acquisition (Cohen 1982). Seliger (1982) considered the possible relevance of the right hemisphere after language had become lateralized in the left hemisphere, and thinks it could be useful. Genesee (1982:316) reviewed the literature of bilinguals, and concluded that: 'The best clinical evidence available suggests that the two languages of the bilingual are not subserved by different neurophysiological substrates.' The studies of lateralization are all constrained by available techniques; they have conflicting results, but it is possible to argue that '. . . use of right and left hemisphere-based processes may be deployed differently by those who acquire the SL [Second Language] late relative to the first language, and that these strategy differences may characterize processing of both the first and second languages' (op.cit.: 318).

While the stage hypothesis has been extensively studied, the results are so contradictory that Genesee assumes either that stage is masked by another unidentified factor or else the techniques used are insensitive to stage differences. There are some indications that there may be greater right hemisphere involvement in informal second language learning than in formal. Genesee also concludes with the need for caution in accepting even these results. Scovel (1982) warns against any notion that these results will be directly applicable to any teaching method.

To sum up, the body of hard data on the neurolinguistics of second language learning comes nowhere near matching the enormous amount of speculation or the large number of studies. As Obler concludes:

> Practitioners [of neurolinguistics] are painfully aware that our reach exceeds our grasp. While we are able to define with relative ease the questions we will eventually want to answer, the methodologies we currently have available to study them approach the topics at too gross a level, or cannot be controlled, or are relatively distant from giving us information about the actual neural basis of the language behaviours we observe. (Obler 1983:185)

Even if there is not hard evidence of what linguistic functions are controlled by specific parts of the brain, there is a good deal that has been inferred from behavioural changes. One important question is the effect of brain damage on the ability to learn a second language. This is not a topic on which we have a great deal of evidence, but it has been looked at in connection with the careful monitoring of the various immersion[4] programmes for teaching French in Quebec.

In one study, Trites (1981) looked at a group of children who had serious problems in early immersion programmes. These were children who had been diagnosed through a test of tactual performance as having difficulties associated with a maturational lag in the development of temporal lobe regions of the brain. Genesee (1983) questioned Trites' findings and argued that the diagnosis was not clear, for the children did poorly on a whole range of other tests. Moreover, there is no evidence of how these children would have done in a monolingual programme. Contrary evidence has been presented by Bruck (1978, 1982), who studied a group of children who were judged to have learning or language disabilities on the basis of reports by their teachers and results of a short diagnostic screening test but were otherwise of normal levels of intelligence. A group of such children in a bilingual early immersion programme were compared with a matching group in a non-immersion programme; the two groups developed linguistic, cognitive, and academic skills at similar rates, both groups being slower than non-disabled children. The disabled students in the immersion programme developed proficiency in French to the level that they could cope with classroom instruction in the language 'within the limits imposed by their disability'. Genesee (1983) concluded that the extra language learning did not impose an educational disadvantage on low-IQ or learning-disabled children. In any case, it is clear that learning disability as defined in these studies is not a block to learning a second language and functioning in it.

The difficulty of making hard claims on the basis of evidence like this results from the fact that when we are studying a person with some kind of brain damage, our evidence may just as well be of the working of a reorganized brain as of a brain with one section omitted. This point will become clearer if we consider other kinds of physiological defects and their effects on second language learning. Let us start with a trivial but instructive example. Someone with a broken arm speaking a language that encourages the use of frequent large non-verbal gestures clearly suffers from a speech impediment, but will usually be able to overcome that difficulty by modification in intonation and stress. Or consider a person temporarily prevented from speaking as a result of oral surgery; a combination of gestures and the use of written messages will be a possible substitution technique. Subjects with speech impediments develop compensatory mechanisms. Someone who is partially deaf develops lip-reading skills. Children who are blind from birth use fewer words containing the bilabial consonants normally learned by visual clues. In all of these cases, there has clearly been reorganization and ways of replacing the missing part, but the modified performance does not give definite evidence of the organic change.

These arguments, then, work against setting neurophysiological necessary conditions on second language learning that are any different from those we would set on other learning activities. Our first necessary condition, that we are concerned with a 'human being', does not need further precise categorization; we assume that 'human being' is defined by the normal set of rules, with the normal necessary conditions (alive, conscious of the outside world, in control of some non-reflex responses) and the normal typicality conditions (intact body, functioning sense organs). Just as the absence of a typicality condition (the loss of a limb or the impairment of a sense organ) does not lead us to consider someone as not human, neither does it rule out the possibility of second language learning. This principle is captured in the following condition:

Condition 22
Physiological Normality condition (necessary): Any physiological or biological limitations that block the learning of a first language will similarly block the learning of a second language.

This condition also deals with cases of other handicaps such as deafness or visual impairment; whatever difficulties these handicaps set for first language learning will also be present for second language learning. Thus, one would expect students with impaired hearing to have special problems with learning the sounds of a second language, and blind students to have difficulties with observable sounds (especially bilabials) and semantic areas such as locatives.[5]

The argument from linguistic theory

There is an argument for a biological basis for language learning in current linguistic theory. The current view of first language learning, as Cook (1985) points out, has as a central feature Chomsky's observation that children show evidence of knowing things about language that appear not to have been gained from their outside experience. From this, Chomsky postulates that there are certain language properties inherent in the human mind, which form a Universal Grammar. The Universal Grammar is not a set of particular rules but a set of general principles about the possible form of grammatical rules: a metagrammar, to be precise. These Universal Grammar rules include 'parameters' which are specifically applied by the grammars of individual languages: 'The grammar of a language can be regarded as a particular set of values for these parameters, while the overall system of rules, principles, and parameters is UG . . .' (Chomsky 1982:7). This UG or Universal Grammar, Chomsky suggests, is present in the brain and develops as the child grows, given certain environmental 'triggers': '. . . a central part of what we call 'learning' is actually better understood as the growth of cognitive structures along an internally directed course under the triggering and potentially shaping effect of the environment' (Chomsky 1980:33). To learn a language, a child must receive positive or negative evidence of the form of a specific language in order to fix the parameters for that language. The Universal Grammar may all be present from the beginning and applied only as needed, or it may itself develop over time.

Cook (1985) emphasizes three important restrictions in the argument. First, the theory deals with linguistic or grammatical competence or knowledge of a language and not with what Chomsky calls pragmatic competence and defines as the ability to place 'language in the institutional setting of its use, relating intentions and purposes to the linguistic means at hand' (Chomsky 1980:225).[6] Second, Chomsky (1982) makes clear that the principles of the Universal Grammar are more important than the rules: a grammar is the specification of the way in which parameters are set. Third, there is a distinction between the 'core' grammar set by the Universal Grammar and 'peripheral' marked constructions that might have other sources (Chomsky 1980:8). In practice then, the child sets parameters according to the basic principles of the Universal Grammar in accordance with its experience; while it 'prefers' to apply these Universal Grammar principles, for a periphery of marked features it may use other processes. There is, however, no reason to assume that the core develops first; unmarked structures may emerge late; frequency may have an effect (Chomsky 1981:9). Hypothesis-testing may be an explanation, but it is to be seen as choosing from a limited number of possibilities set by the Universal Grammar.

When this theoretical position is applied to second language learning, Cook argues that the same argument should apply: a second language learner comes to show evidence of knowing facts that he or she has not been taught. But there is a vital difference: the second language learner already has available a grammar that itself has involved applying the principles of the Universal Grammar. The question then arises as to whether the learning of a second language can still involve fixing parameters in the Universal Grammar.

This question is answered in the negative by the Critical Period Hypothesis proposed originally by Lenneberg (1967), which claims that after a certain age the principles and parameters of the Universal Grammar are no longer accessible to the learner. Building in part on studies of imprinting in young animals (at a certain stage ducks adopt any moving object as their mother), it has been argued that unless a child learns a certain part of language by a critical period, then this aspect will not be learned. This is held to account both for the failure of adults to regain full language proficiency after traumatic aphasia (in contrast to the way that young children go through the language learning process again) and for the similar difficulty that post-adolescent learners have in acquiring full control of a second language, especially of its phonology. There is general agreement with Cook's claim that the Critical Period Hypothesis has not been established, especially because of the evidence that second language learning is possible.

Of greatest importance to our present interest is the postulation of a biologically inherent process, a Language Acquisition Device, if we want to use the metaphor, related in complex ways to general cognition and expressible in terms of a Universal Grammar which consists of a set of principles and a set of parameters to be set for a specific language.

In Chapter 8, where we return to the issue of the Universal Grammar in considering the extent of its relevance to second language and its interaction with other previous language knowledge, we shall need to reconsider some of these issues. At this stage we are concerned with the issue of biological constraints. If the theory is correct, the Universal Grammar is as much a part of a human being as is any other physiological organ; its absence leads to a serious disability. It is important to note that the Universal Grammar arguments do not lead to a graded or typicality condition: there is no evidence to suggest, nor theories that argue, that some people are endowed with better Universal Grammars than others. The variation in individual capacities will need to be sought elsewhere.

The relevance of age

I have discussed the claim that all or crucial parts of second language learning are dependent on some innate preprogrammed mechanism, identical or similar to the Language Acquisition Device proposed for first language learning. A second claim is that this mechanism is differentially available, according to age (the Critical Period Hypothesis) or according to the nature of affect or input conditions (Krashen's hypotheses concerning the learning-acquisition distinction, the affective filter, and comprehensible input).

Like other questions we are dealing with, the age issue is also a result of blurring of boundaries: in a model looking only at informal second language learning and bilingualism, we naturally tend to assume that children learn languages better than adults; when we are studying what happens in our own foreign language classroom, we often believe that the best age for learning was the year before the students came to us; and the measure we choose of language proficiency usually determines who will be shown to have learned best in a comparative study. Educational systems usually arrive first at a decision of optimal learning age on political or economic grounds and then seek educational justification for their decision.[7] For all these reasons, the research evidence on the question is far from clear or conclusive.

But the theoretical importance of the issue is considerable. If differences between first and second language learning can be accounted for by age differences (as in the Critical Period Hypothesis), then we appear to have a biological basis for learning (a developmentally related biological innate programme).

On the other hand, if Krashen is right about the differential availability of an acquisition processor at all ages, we have a ready explanation both for the comparative failure of most foreign language teaching methods (they deal only with the monitor, and so with low-level minimally useful rules) and for the limited success of large numbers of adult second language learners who are restricted either developmentally or affectively to monitor learning.

In a study of the age of learning, Fathman (1975) looked not just at overall performance but at the order of learning specific structures. She had two interesting conclusions: first, that age of learning did not seem to make any difference in the sequence of learning of these items, and second, that age of learning made a difference in performance on phonology (where younger learners did better) and morphology (where there was an advantage for older learners).

The issue of the order of learning turns out to be important. Let me set out the basic problem. There are three possible determinants for the order in which someone learns language items:

(1) The order of presentation
(2) Something in the structure of the material learned
(3) Something in the nature of the language learning process.

The first of these in its pure form assumes that the order of learning follows the order of presentation. Just as I learned French before German because it was taught in my high school in the first year while German was taught only in the third, and just as I learned Hebrew vocabulary related to the prayer book and the Bible before I learned vocabulary concerned with daily life, because I first learned Hebrew in a religious school, so this approach assumes that the learning of morphological and syntactic rules and forms follows the order of the school syllabus. Perhaps a more realistic view of this input theory would allow for the fact that I might have been absent from school or worrying about a football game when some item was taught, but the implication is clearly that changes in order of learning follow changes in order of teaching. But if it could be shown that people learning a second language in informal situations through natural exposure all show a similar order of learning items, this approach would fail.

The second possibility is to assume that languages are in fact structured in such a way that logically one must learn certain things before others. Just as, in mathematics, learning to add comes before learning to multiply, so one might expect language learners to learn to control simple sentences before compound ones. This could be supported by evidence of the earlier learning of linguistically less complex items. It must be pointed out, however, that attempts to define complexity have not in general been successful. Also, the assumption is questioned by Chomsky's distinction between a core grammar explainable by universal and language specific rules and a peripheral grammar consisting of unanalysed chunks, the order of learning of which, Chomsky argues, is not to be explained by the nature of the rules but by exposure.

The third possibility is to assume some effect of the learning process itself: either some internal preprogramming (a concept to be explored in more detail later), or through creative construction in accordance with some universal set of strategies, or through transfer from the native language (but this would not explain cross-linguistic similarities).

It is the third of these explanations that would be most sensitive to changes with age (although studies of input are showing the variation in input addressed to children and adults). If the process is biological, it should show changes with age: either one should be unable to learn certain things before a certain age (as in Piagetian models) or one should lose the plasticity of childhood as an adult. Indeed, one of the major arguments for a biological basis for all language learning is that after puberty second language learning is not as completely successful as before it. Let us look at some of the evidence that can bear on this issue.

Felix (1981) studied the first eight months spent by 34 ten- and eleven-year-old German children learning English in a 'liberal audio-lingual' classroom, where most of the classroom activity was repetition exercises, pattern drill, and strictly controlled question-answer dialogues (there was instant correction of all errors, and no spontaneous novel utterances were allowed). Clearly, the classroom gave virtually no opportunity for natural exposure, nor did these children have any exposure to English (except to that used in pop music) outside the classroom. As Felix points out, this setting gave the researchers an admirable opportunity to consider three important issues: the similarity between the utterances of these students and those of learners in naturalistic situations; similarities in sequence of learning between this classroom situation and natural situations; and evidence of student independence of the didactic policy of the teacher.

Felix makes the point of his comparison very clearly:

> Is second language learning in the classroom a creative construction process in the sense defined by Dulay and Burt (1974a, 1974b) or do classroom learners basically rely on behaviouristic habit formation processes? This question centers on an even more fundamental issue,

namely whether or not man is equipped with two or more distinct mechanisms to acquire language depending on the situation in which learning takes place. (Felix 1981:91)

In his paper, Felix looks at four structural areas: negation, interrogation, sentence types, and pronouns. His conclusions are important enough to be quoted in his words:

> Judging from the data presented in the preceding sections the number of structural parallels between the utterances of tutored and naturalistic [L2 and] L1 learners is in fact striking ... This observation suggests that at least some of the principles that govern naturalistic language acquisition also determine the processes by which students learn a foreign language under classroom conditions. (op.cit.:108)

While there was clear evidence of effects of the environment, there were stronger tendencies controlling learning, nor did interference have any explanatory power.

We will need to look at the likelihood of an innate order again; for the moment, let us assume it and ask how we can account for commonly observed differences between child and adult learning. The notion is often presented as the Critical Period Hypothesis referred to earlier. This is held to account both for the failure of adults to regain full language proficiency after traumatic aphasia (in contrast to the way that young children go through the language learning process again) and for the similar difficulty that post-adolescent learners have in acquiring full control of a second language, especially of its phonology. If the observations are correct, there are two possible explanations: time (i.e. younger learners have more time to learn) or timing (i.e. the stage at which learning begins).

One very interesting study that bears on this question is Swain (1981), who looks at the relative advantages of early and late starts to immersion programmes in Canada. At least since Ervin-Tripp (1974) showed some of the ways in which older children learn certain aspects of language more efficiently than younger children, a good deal of evidence has been accumulated that being young is no more an advantage in language learning than in many other aspects of life. In spite of this, Swain was surprised to find that late immersion learners had many better results than early immersion learners.

> One group of students tested, who were in grade 8 at the time of testing, had 100% of their instruction in French in kindergarten and grade 1; 80% in French in grades 2 to 5; and 50% in French in grades 6 to 8 totaling over 4000 accumulated hours of French. The other group of students, who were in grade 10 at the time of testing, had 30 minutes a day of FSL [French as a Second Language] instruction in

grade 7 followed by 70% of instruction in French in grade 8, and 40% in grades 9 and 10 totaling approximately 1400 hours of French. The performance of the early immersion students was superior to that of the late immersion students on a test of French listening comprehension . . . However, the performance of the late immersion students was superior to that of the early immersion students on a French reading comprehension test . . . and was similar to that of the early immersion students on a French cloze test . . . (Swain 1981:3–4)

For school-related learning, at least, and in the circumstances of French immersion programmes in Canada (Swain emphasizes the sociological context and the fact that it is the majority child learning a minority language), an earlier start has much less effect than one might have expected. One must look also at the data on production to see if this holds up. Swain's study does not contradict the general agreement that there are certain aspects of second language learning, especially the more school-related tasks (and the areas that Krashen ascribes to the monitor), that older learners have more success with; nor does it contradict the general finding that the earlier one starts to learn a language, the more success one has in developing native-like pronunciation.

Let me sum up the evidence on the issue of age of learning. There is a good deal of evidence, summarized in Dulay, Burt, and Krashen (1982), about the effects of starting to learn a second language while young. Studies by Oyama (1982a) of a group of Italian-born male immigrants who had been living in the US for periods of five to eighteen years showed that the age of arrival had a major influence in the presence or absence of a noticeable accent, but length of stay (five to eleven years versus twelve to eighteen) made no evident difference. In a study of Cuban immigrants reported by Asher and Garcia (1969), age of arrival was also the main factor in accounting for accent, but when the time in the country was less than five years, length of stay became significant. Seliger, Krashen, and Ladefoged (1975), in a study based on self-report, again find age of arrival to be significant. It should be noted that all these studies assume a minimum initial period (say five years) for someone who is young enough (under 9 to be fairly sure of success, under 15 to have a good chance of it) to acquire a native like accent. And all these studies report the existence of a noticeable minority who are exceptions: in Oyama, the results are averaged, but the score for the youngest group is 1.27 (1 is accentless) and for the oldest is 3.72 (5 is a heavy accent); in Asher and Garcia, 7 per cent of the oldest arrivals have near native accents, and 32 per cent of the youngest have a slight accent (none have a definite accent, but 16 per cent of the middle group do); and in Seliger, Krashen and Ladefoged there are small groups of the youngest with and the oldest without accents. This lack of perfect correlation surely argues against any absolute biological basis, and leads me to propose a preference rule:

Condition 23
Native Pronunciation condition (graded, typical): The younger one starts to learn a second language, the better chance one has to develop a native-like pronunciation.

It should be noted that the statement of this rule does not attempt to explain the observation; whether it is a question of time, or plasticity of muscular co-ordination, or openness to new language ego. What is important at this stage is to see that we have found no support for a necessary condition even in the area of pronunciation.[8]

There is less evidence on differences in grammar than in phonology. Oyama (1982b) reports some grammatical tests favouring younger arrivals, and Patkowski (1980) found that written transcriptions of oral interviews with sixty-seven immigrants who had come to the US before the age of fifteen and been there at least five years were more likely to be rated as native-like grammatically the younger the immigrant had been on arrival. In the school-learning of testable items of morphology and syntax, on the other hand, there is evidence that older learners learn faster than younger.[9]

A study by Harley (1986) of the learning of various aspects of the French verb system by younger and older anglophone children in immersion programmes makes clear the complexity of the issue. She studied selected samples of children in grade 1 and grades 9 and 10 after each had received about 1,000 hours of French immersion instruction. Detailed analysis of verb use in interviews, story repetition tasks, and translation tasks, showed some advantages for the older children, particularly in lexical control and control of semantic time differences, but on a good number of measures there were no significant differences between the groups. General similarities emerged in the order of accuracy in the various items studied, suggesting more or less similar acquisition processes. A comparison of the late immersion group with a group of the same age who had had 3,500 hours of instruction showed advantages for the latter, but once again there were many features on which there was no advantage. Finally, there was evidence that IQ scores correlated better with total scores on the verb measures in the case of the late immersion group than in the others.

Up to what age these and other effects work has not been looked at very much, but Seright (1985) reports a study in which younger adult French-speakers aged 17 to 24 developed aural comprehension faster in a short-term programme than did matched pairs of older adults aged 25 to 41. The study did not reveal any specific cause for the results.

Assuming that these complex age differences are established, what are the possible explanations? There are essentially four to be considered: the biological, the cognitive developmental, the affective, and the environmental. We have already touched on the biological; here, I will simply say that there does not seem to be convincing evidence for the suggestion that there is a critical period, associated with lateralization, such that language learning after lateralization is different, and thus there is no reason to set this as a necessary condition.

When we turn to look at a cognitive developmental explanation, we can certainly assume that the kind of formal abstract tasks called for in much classroom teaching of foreign languages is likely to be more within the competence of the older child or adolescent. Swain in fact argues convincingly that much of the school training given in the native language is likely to be useful to the second language learner in developing related skills. This clearly is connected to the task-related abilities studied by Bialystok (see Chapter 3), and supported by Harley (1986) in her finding that the score in IQ tests is related to the learning of French verbs in late immersion students. I propose a preference condition to capture this point:

Condition 24
Abstract Skills condition (typical, graded): Formal classroom learning of a second language is favoured by the development of skills of abstraction and analysis.

The affective hypothesis is summarized by Schumann (1975). Having reviewed the various studies concerning the importance of attitudes, motivation, and personality in second language learning that lead him to develop the acculturation model which we will discuss in a later chapter, and having noted the weakness in the neuropsychological arguments for a critical period, he proposes an affective explanation for children's greater success in certain aspects of language learning. Essentially, he follows Macnamara (1973), who argues that children learn better than adults because they try harder at communicating with their peers. He goes on to suggest that the reason adults often do not get involved in this 'real communication' essential to learning may be socialization:

> That is, because of the way society functions, adults may not usually be provided with extensive enough opportunity to develop their second language skills through genuine communication with speakers of the target language. Although this position must be considered, the position most consonant with the affective argument is that problems with the adult's attitudes, motivation, and/or empathic capacity which are brought about either by general social-psychological development or language and culture shock prevent him from getting involved in communication which will lead to successful language acquisition. (Schumann 1975:232)

This may be summed up in a further typicality condition:

Condition 25
Child's Openness condition (typical, graded): The greater openness to external influence of a child favours the learning of a second language in informal situations.

The final argument, that children learn languages in different environments from adults, is clearly true. In Chapters 11 and 12 I will mention studies that can show ways in which learners of various ages might in fact receive quite different levels and kinds of assistance from their interlocutors. It is to be noted that Schumann recognizes the differences in communicative needs that might come from these differing sociological conditions, although he prefers to relate them to the learner's attitudes. To capture this influence of the child's social situation, I propose the following condition:

Condition 26
Child's dependence condition (typical, graded): The social situation faced by a child in a second language environment favours second language learning.

In this analysis of the question of age, it is striking that once again something that is sometimes thought to be simple turns out on closer examination to be much more complex. The notion that young children pick up second languages more easily than older learners is clearly challenged by evidence of areas in which the latter do better. The question that needs to be asked is thus not whether older or younger learners do better, but rather what goals are suitable at various ages and what conditions lead to greater success in learning specific parts of a second language at various ages. Starting with the general and universal, we have been forced to look more closely at the individual. The next chapter, then, will carry further this investigation of individual differences.

Notes

1   See Geschwind (1979) for a full proposal.
2   The methods include the study of aphasia (language breakdown) and of laterality (tachistoscopic or dichotic presentation of stimuli), the use of split-brain patients, the anaesthetization of each hemisphere, the electric stimulation of cortical sites, blood flow studies and evoked potential studies of the brain, and psycho-linguistic experimental techniques like stroop testing, onset time studies, and lexical decision tasks. The research is carried out on special populations such as: '. . . aphasics, split-brain patients, dyslexic children and children with other developmental learning

disorders, hemi-decorticate patients . . . . left-handers, deaf signers, illiterates, exceptionally talented individuals (for example, idiots savants, musical prodigies), bilinguals and women' (Obler 1983:160). Studies have focused on aphasia, aphasic syndromes and recovery patterns, and attrition patterns in patients with dementing diseases. There have also been studies of the attrition of a non-used language in a healthy subject. It is very difficult, Obler (1983) concludes, to untangle the interplay of the three dimensions of method, population, and topic.

3 See later in this chapter, page 90ff. for discussion of the Critical Period Hypothesis.

4 In immersion programmes, classes of students who speak one language learn a second by receiving all or most of their instruction for a year or more in the second language. The classic cases are the French immersion programmes for English speakers in Canada. Early immersion is usually in the first two years of elementary school; late immersion may be in the seventh or eleventh grades. See Genesee (1987).

5 For a review of the case of teaching a foreign language to blind children, see Nikolic (1986). Danesi (1988) considers the implications of what he calls 'neurological bimodality', the differences in hemispheric preferences, for second language learning in a classroom situation.

6 Cook points out that Chomsky (1980:230) finds the term communicative competence wrong, for there are many purposes of language beyond communication.

7 Clyne presents arguments for teaching second languages in primary schools in Australia and includes a number of studies which conclude that 'a second language can be successfully acquired by children who start at any of the grades considered in this study' (1986:131).

8 Flege (1987) similarly concludes that there is no evidence for the Critical Period Hypothesis as it effects pronunciation; Patkowski (MS) argues with Flege, and takes the position that the evidence is 'consistent with the notion' of the hypothesis even if it does not prove it. As Patkowski points out, the lack of long-term studies looking not at short-term effects but at the ultimate level of attainment means that the question remains open.

9 See for instance Ervin-Tripp (1974) and Morris and Gerstman (1986).

7 Ability and personality

Individual differences

To say that older or younger learners are better or worse is not normally considered a breach of egalitarian principles, for most of us have our turn at being young and old. Proposing some other explanations for difference is more questionable, for labelling one learner as inherently less qualified than another runs the risk of establishing or justifying permanent divisions among people. Consider explanations based on intelligence, for example. There is certainly a good deal of evidence that human beings vary considerably in whatever ability or abilities may underlie the construct that is labelled intelligence. To what extent is intelligence, however defined, not just a necessary condition, a mark of humanness, but also a graded condition relevant to learning, including second language learning? Part of the answer to this question is tied up with the question of the relation between general cognitive ability and specific language ability, which may be summed up in two claims:

(1) There is a language-specific ability or faculty, distinct from other cognitive abilities.

The work of modern generative grammarians is based on this claim, and sets out to justify it by showing the existence of language-specific principles such as those proposed for Universal Grammar. The second claim is that:

(2) This language-specific ability must be consistent with other aspects of the cognitive system, because it interacts with and makes use of them.

Jackendoff presents this claim as the 'Cognitive Constraint':

There must be levels of mental representation at which information conveyed by language is compatible with information from other peripheral systems such as vision, nonverbal audition, smell, kines- thesia, and so forth. If there were no such levels, it would be impossible to use language to report sensory input. (Jackendoff 1983:16)

He suggests that one can in fact go further than pointing out the need for interfaces between the various sensory modalities and propose, as a strong form of Piagetian developmental theory, a hypothesis of the existence of conceptual structures universal and innate but specifically developed by experience:

The Conceptual Structure Hypothesis
There is a *single* level of mental representation, *conceptual structure*, at which linguistic, sensory, and motor information are compatible. (op.cit.:17)

Cook (1985) argues that there is no reason to suppose that the 'mental faculty of language' depends, as Piaget would claim, on certain cognitive operations; he is, however, missing Jackendoff's point when he says that there is no necessary connection between language and other faculties. But, as Cook points out, there are other ways in which the language faculty and the other cognitive faculties are related. Just as language development is tied to physical development in specific ways, such as the influence of the development of the nervous system on phonology, so the use of certain language abilities depends on the availability and development of certain general cognitive abilities. Cook mentions the example of the constraint of short-term memory on sentence length. Jackendoff says that the richness of semantic structure is dependent on conceptual richness, which of course relates language to cognition.

There is a clue here to an important set of distinctions. In some of the conditions discussed so far, there is a basic necessary condition that must be met, a sort of core minimum. At the same time, there is clearly the possibility of stating a graded condition. It is, for example, generally accepted now that both innate and environmental conditions must be met for language to be acquired: the grammarians have given us reason to believe in the necessity of the innate Universal Grammar, and they fully agree with others that there is need for exposure to the language.[1] Now it is clear that there is variation in the amount of exposure. Might not there also be variation in the quality of the innate component?

The argument is at first sight an appealing one. If human beings are not created equal, we can more easily avoid any share of responsibility for the various inequalities they suffer. It is also potentially a socially irresponsible theory, one that can lead to racism and other forms of discrimination against persons considered innately inferior. There is therefore good moral reason to set a particularly strong requirement for proof on biological explanations of differences between human beings.

If we apply this principle to the possibility of language learning, we should first stress the universality of the language faculty (and so by definition of the language learning ability) in non-pathological human beings. As there are no significant biological differences between first and second language learning (rejecting the Critical Period Hypothesis), there is no reason to expect to find that differences in the *fact* of second language learning are biologically explainable. There is still the possibility of biological influence on the *quality* or *quantity* of second language learning. While it may well turn out that a good many of the differences in individual second language learning achievement can be accounted for by environmental factors, it will still be necessary to look at two potential explanations for differences that could have an inherited or biological basis, namely intelligence or general cognitive ability, and language aptitude or specific language ability.

Intelligence

There has been a controversy between Oller and others over Oller's (1981 and elsewhere) claims that general intelligence and language proficiency are more or less the same thing. This argument follows from his claim for the existence of a general factor in language proficiency[2] and the high correlation of IQ scores with the results of language tests. The issue is also related to the various attempts of Cummins (1980, 1983, and elsewhere) and some of his colleagues to chart the difficult seas of the relations between school abilities and non-school social communicative abilities, an issue tied up with problems of assessing intelligence and comparing social class differences. The explanation for their observations lies, it was proposed in earlier chapters, in the special problem of gathering evidence of both language ability and general intelligence; both make use of various kinds of tests, and there is good reason to suspect that we are dealing then with their shared components tapped by the very process of testing. Moreover, both do depend (accepting Jackendoff's hypothesis) on the richness of conceptual structure. At the same time, both are at the mercy of the particular cultural bias of the testing instrument. The most that can safely be said is that there is a strong relationship between the scores in intelligence tests and the scores in formal tests of school-related language abilities.

This point is very well illustrated by a study by Genesee (1976) in which he looked at the relevance of intelligence as measured by standardized IQ tests, to the success of English-speaking pupils in immersion and non-immersion French programmes in Montreal. Genesee's study was aimed at investigating the value of an immersion programme for other than the middle-class children of average or above average intelligence whose parents had been its instigators. Students in each of three levels of immersion programmes (early immersion students in grade 4, grade 7 immersion students at the end of their first year, and late immersion students in grade 11), together with a control group in French as a second language programme, were classified for intelligence according to scores on the Canadian Lorge-Thorndike Test of Intelligence and then given a battery of French tests. At all grade levels and in all tests, intelligence predicted test performance. A sub-sample was selected, including students of above average, average, and below average intelligence, and interviewed in French. The interview, which was taped, involved the description of a cartoon story in French and a short conversation on the cartoon or other matters. The tapes were rated by two native speakers independently on five dimensions: listening comprehension, pronunciation, grammar, vocabulary, and 'communicativeness' or fluency. On these measures, while there were differences for level, there were no differences within level according to intelligence; in face-to-face interviews, judges could not distinguish the performance of the below average students from the others. However, the IQ scores were good predictors of performance on the more academic, literacy-based measures. Among the late immersion learners, who started at grade 11, Genesee (1976) and, in another study, Tucker, Hamayan, and Genesee (1976), evidence was found of statistically significant correlation of IQ with communication skills as well. Genesee (1987) speculates that this might be a result of the more academic approach of the late immersion programme or of the greater tendency of older learners to use 'conscious, intellectual strategies'. As these studies did not specifically check out these hypotheses, and as they did not include other relevant factors such as attitude or anxiety, the question must remain open. Harley (1986) also found that IQ scores correlated better with scores in a French verb test in the case of older pupils that in the case of those who began younger: the cognitive abilities involved help make up for later and lower exposure.

To sum up, while intelligence is a predictor of the learning of school-related academic language skills, it does not generally seem to predict the learning of communication skills, even as shown in school-administered interview situations. This may stated as a graded typicality condition:

Condition 27
Intelligence condition (typical, graded): The ability to perform well in standard intelligence tests correlates highly with school-related second language learning (i.e. in functional terms, such tasks as reading and writing of academic material in formal language and as performing abstract tests of structural knowledge) but is unrelated to the learning of a second language for informal and social functions, except perhaps in the case of older learners.

This condition might be stated somewhat more precisely, as follows:

(a) If the learner receives a high score in a standard intelligence test, he or she is likely to score equally well in tests of formally taught language skills. We should expect, therefore, to find a significant correlation between intelligence test scores and formal school language test results.
(b) Whether a learner receives a high or low score in a standard intelligence test is irrelevant to his or her acquiring social and

communicative functions in a second language in untutored situations. We should expect to find therefore no correlation between intelligence test scores and casually observed social control of the second language.

(c) In the case of older learners, however, the nature of the learning situation (for example, an appeal to intellectual learning) or the established use of intellectual learning strategies might lead to an effect.

Genesee's conclusions are important. Just as all children, with exceptions in pathological cases, are able to develop functional control of their first language, so it is reasonable to assume that all can acquire a second language. In 'natural' learning situations, such as the second language environment or an immersion programme, IQ differences are limited in their effect to the kinds of skills that IQ tests measure—academic and literacy-based. In formal classroom learning, where these skills are emphasized, the effects are stronger. If this is true of general cognitive ability, does it also apply to specific language aptitudes? This will be the topic of the next section.

Aptitude

Intelligence was one of the factors considered as a candidate for predicting language aptitude. The question faced by those who tried to develop language aptitude tests was what other measures would predict language learning in a school situation. The original model proposed by John B. Carroll remains a viable one.

While the earliest language aptitude tests date from the 1930s,[3] the important work was done by Carroll and Sapon (1957) developing the *Modern Language Aptitude Test* and a decade later, the *Elementary Modern Language Aptitude Test* (Carroll and Sapon 1967) and by Paul Pimsleur with his *Language Aptitude Battery* (1966). As Stern (1983) remarks, these tests are interesting not just for their practical usefulness but also for their theoretical claims, the most obvious of which is that language aptitude is not a single factor, but a cluster of specific abilities. By analysing the components of each of the tests, as Stern does (1983:371), several main components are seen to be postulated:

(1) A number of specific skills related to auditory ability: the ability to discriminate among sounds, interpret them, associate them with written symbols, remember them. Note that this component is itself further analysable into skills that will be differentially important according to the outcomes proposed for the course. While the component is primarily concerned with an approach to teaching the spoken language, it has components that assume that such teaching will be accompanied by writing.

(2) A number of tasks showing grammatical sensitivity: with or without the aid of a translation, the subject is asked to make some judgements about the grammatical relations of some sentences in a foreign language. No knowledge of grammatical terminology is needed. The test is written.

(3) Test of memory, involving memorizing and recalling words in a new language.

The Pimsleur battery does not use this last item, but does include a test of word knowledge in the first language and measures of general academic achievement and motivation.

The measures of aptitude were validated in a number of studies by Carroll (1963) and Pimsleur (1963, 1966); in all these studies, language aptitude was consistently found to predict second language achievement. Similar results were reported by Gardner, Clément, Smythe, and Smythe (1979).

There have been criticisms of the concept of language aptitude. Oller (1979) in his proposal for a general factor of language intelligence suggests that language aptitude tests are measuring it too, but, as Gardner (1985:23) points out, this is directly contradicted by studies showing its independent existence. Neufeld (1974) argues against it on the basis of the fact that all individuals can learn a second language, but is missing the point that aptitude is intended to explain differences in achievement rather than the fact of learning.

Since Carroll's original work, interest in language universals and in natural language learning has tended to draw attention away from individual differences in aptitude. The issue has been raised again in studies by Skehan (1986b) in an attempt to deal with the underlying complexity of language aptitude and its relation to first language acquisition and second language learning. Skehan's work has been a follow-up to an earlier study of the first language development of two cohorts of children born in England in the Bristol area in 1969–70 and 1971–72 (Wells 1985). The Wells study showed a great deal of variation in individual first language development, so that, on the measures used, some children were years ahead of others. Skehan has been studying the same children when they started to learn a foreign language at secondary school, trying to find the relationships between their development of first language proficiency, their foreign language aptitude (in particular grammatical sensitivity and inductive language learning ability) measured later, and their actual achievement in learning a foreign language.

Skehan's studies have shown two strong predictors of the language aptitude that he measured when the children were aged 13. First was 'a general language processing capability': the children who had developed faster in their first language (as shown by measures of sentence structure complexity and Mean Morpheme Length of Utterance) were those who later tended to have higher scores on foreign language aptitude tests. Even more predictive of later aptitude was another cluster of factors, independent of syntactic development, which was made up of the results of earlier tests of first language vocabulary, the students' family class background, and the educational level and literacy standard of their parents. Skehan suggests that this second cluster is to be interpreted as evidence of the development of 'ability to use language in a decontextualized way'.

It would seem that the aptitude tests are especially concerned, as of course they should be, with the learning of a language for school-related purposes and in a school situation. The assumption remains that they measure, in a school-related way, aspects of aptitude that are likely to be important in accounting for part of the individual differences in informal learning. Each, in other words, taps a graded component of necessary human abilities: the ability to discriminate the sounds of the new language, the ability to break the stream of speech into constituents and to generalize about its structure, and the ability to remember its words. Without some core minimum ability, no second language learning is possible; from this point of view, everyone has basic aptitude. The more each capacity is developed in a learner, the faster control will be attained and the higher the potential level of success achieved. This may be summarized in three specific aptitude conditions:

Condition 28
Sound Discrimination condition (necessary, graded): The better a learner can discriminate between the sounds of the language and recognize the constituent parts, the more successful his or her learning of speaking and understanding a second language will be.

While this condition has obvious common-sense support, it is much harder to demonstrate in practice. Blickenstaff (1963) showed that pitch discrimination correlated with foreign language attainment at beginning levels in high school, but became less significant at the more advanced levels. Brutten and others (1985) found no evidence of the effect of auditory abilities on proficiency with more advanced English as a second language students, but will continue to look at more elementary levels.

Condition 29
Memory condition (necessary, graded): In learning a new language, the better the learner's memory, the faster he or she will learn new items and the larger his or her vocabulary will be. This ability may vary for learning words aurally and visually.

Condition 30
Grammatical Sensitivity condition (necessary, graded): Beyond the necessary minimum ability to 'derive a grammar' implicitly, the better a learner's ability to recognize constituents and develop or understand

generalizations about recombination and meaning (whether from explicit or implicit generalizations, in whatever forms), the faster he or she will develop control of the grammatical (and pragmatic) structure of a second language.

Skehan argues that second language learning aptitude is in important ways not just a 'residue' (Carroll 1973) of first language development but the 'second or foreign language equivalent of a first language learning capacity', and that it is therefore a major component of second language learning. Aptitude, he believes, must account for the differences ignored by Universal Grammar explanations. There is good reason, he argues, to consider it relevant to informal second language learning too. Though second language learning capacity is tapped by tests that appeal to conscious skills and explicit formulations, it is, he believes, implicit and can occur unconsciously in informal learning. Auditory coding capacity is as important in informal learning as in formal; without it, there cannot be the basic perception of the units of speech. Memory is of obvious importance in informal learning; at later stages, the load of lexicon to be stored and retrieved efficiently is very great. Skehan concludes, then, that 'each of the components of foreign language aptitude are not relevant exclusively to formal instruction'. He argues further that the skills involved in 'decontextualization' are likely to be of great value in informal situations where the language learner is left to him or herself.

Further support for these views is provided by two empirical studies, the first by Wesche (1981). Students in a Canadian Public Service Commission language instruction programme were divided into three streams on the basis of an aptitude battery and interviews: a group with high analytic abilities, one with high memory skills, and one with matched skills. The methodologies offered each group varied: the first group was encouraged to analyse: the second was given situationally based material and a great deal of material to memorize, and the third received more traditional, audio-visual material. There was a significant interaction between learner types and methods: students did especially well when matched with the appropriate methodology.

In the second study, Skehan (1986a), using techniques developed earlier (Skehan 1980), studied a group of learners in intensive foreign language courses in the British Armed Forces, and found by cluster analysis a natural grouping into three: two successful groups of learners, one with high analytical ability and average memories, and a second with average analytical ability and good memories, and a third, with 'fairly flat' aptitude profiles, some of whom were successful learners.

Both these studies show the importance of aptitude, not as a single factor but as something with definable components, that interacts in logical ways with kinds of exposure and methodology.

There remains the serious question of the relevance of these special abilities for learning in non-formal situations. In the case study to be reported in Chapter 13, we will see evidence that suggests that aptitude is relevant in formal situations where there is little variation in attitude or kind and amount of exposure. The aptitude measures turn out to be excellent predictors of achievement in French, where attitude is homogeneous, teaching is academic, and most students have had similar amounts of exposure. It does not predict Hebrew proficiency, which in the study is better accounted for by attitudinal factors and learning opportunities. Rather than saying that aptitude is irrelevant in natural learning, I would propose that its effects are most to be noted in early stages of learning.

A second issue, on which no evidence can be adduced but speculation seems reasonable, is the existence of special aptitude for the more advanced social communicative skills (ability to persuade and influence in a second language) seldom directly measured in language tests. To separate out these skills could well correct the imbalance that results from the concentration of attention on academic skills.

Learning styles and strategies

We have seen a distinction between learners who can use their grammatical sensitivity and those that can use memory. There are other individual differences that interact as strongly with kinds of teaching, and these are called learning styles or strategies. Here I am concerned not so much with conscious learning strategies[4] as with (usually) unconscious sequences of operations that accompany, and presumably influence, the learning of a language. As Bialystok (1985) argues, this aspect is most usefully studied by looking at first and second language acquisition together. It was pointed out by Macnamara (1973) that language learning involves children in a number of different and developing strategies or approaches. Clark (1973) showed the value at one stage of learning that there is in using context: children learning spatial terms interpreted the terms according to physical context (the activities of the experimenter) rather than verbal instruction. Another strategy documented by Clark is overgeneralization, the extending of a term to cover a wider range of objects. An important strategy described by Bowerman (1982) is chunking, the learning of large unanalysed chunks of language and inserted as thought appropriate into contexts. Each of these strategies has been shown to be relevant to both first and second language learning.

Now, it must again be stressed when we are dealing with cognitive matters that in certain kinds of second language learning situations, especially in those concerned with the classroom learning of school-related abilities, there will be special aptitude for certain aspects of those abilities. I will start with a couple of trivial examples. If a language teacher takes into account the neatness of writing or of typing, a student who has a good hand or can type well will do well. If the emphasis is on the learning of abstract grammatical generalizations about a language, a student who excels in abstract verbal learning will do well. Similarly, if the learning situation emphasizes the learning of complex rules of politeness (for example, in learning to speak Thai or Japanese), the student with sensitivity to social relations and their expression will do well.[5]

Learning strategy or style are terms used to describe identifiable individual approaches to learning situations: specifically, Keefe (1979:4) defines them as 'cognitive, affective and physiological traits that are relatively stable indicators of how learners perceive, interact with, and respond to the learning environment'. Reid (1987) identifies six major style preferences generally studied: the first four are preferences for visual, auditory, kinaesthetic, and tactile styles of learning, and the last two are preferences for individual or group differences. She asked a number of university students, the majority foreign students studying in the US, for their preferences, and found considerable variation in the results. The foreign students' preferences were markedly different from those of native American students. Some of the differences that showed up were that the foreign students as a whole preferred kinaesthetic and tactile learning styles, and most groups did not like group learning. Students at the graduate level were more likely to prefer visual and tactile learning; undergraduate students more likely than graduate students to favour auditory learning. There was some interaction of chosen field of study and learning style preferred; for example, engineering and computer science students were more likely to prefer tactile learning than humanities students. The higher the students' English test scores, the more similar they were to American students' preferences; similarly, the longer they had been in the US, the more their preferences were like those of American students. There were also clear effects for language or national origin: Korean students were the most visual, Arabic and Chinese the most auditory (and Japanese the least). Within all the groups, however, there remained major individual differences.

As Reid (1987) points out, there remain a large number of important questions to ask about learning preferences. The research is largely based on self-report; it would be interesting to have studies to show that students do actually use these strategies, and more important perhaps, that they benefit from the opportunity to use them. That they are not fixed is clear; experience leads to modification, but the likelihood is high that group and individual preferences will affect the performance of students in appropriate and inappropriate learning situations. To summarize this factor, I propose a general condition:

Condition 31
Learning Style Preference condition (typical, graded): Learners vary (both individually and according to such characteristics as age, level, and cultural origin) in their preference for learning style (visual, auditory, kinaesthetic, and tactile) and mode (group or individual); as a result, learning is best when the learning opportunity matches the learner's preference.

Personality

The example of learning styles or strategies makes the transition from aptitude to attitude, from a matter of intellectual to affective preparation, from the learner's abilities to his or her personality.

Attitudes and motivation are more a part of the individual learner than of the society, but as they are so very greatly influenced by the social context, I will leave their treatment to Chapters 9 and 10. In this section, I want to deal with personality factors that at the outset might be assumed to be independent of social context, although they may predict an individual's social behaviour and they may be differentially interpreted and valued (and so reinforced) in various social groups.

The main studies concerning personality are those of Guiora and the University of Michigan Personality and Language Behavior Research Group. The theoretical framework is summarized in Guiora and Acton (1979). The original proposal for 'collaborative research between the discipline of clinical psychology and the language sciences' was made by Guiora, Lane, and Bosworth (1968) and their initial interest was sparked by clinical questions. By transposing the focus of study from other aspects of behaviour to language, it was hoped to achieve greater empirical validity. Their basic question was: 'How will language affect personality development and how will personality development in turn affect language behaviour?' (op.cit.:195). One series of studies has considered the impact of gender marking in a language on gender identity, and they have shown that Hebrew-speaking children are more successful earlier than Finnish- and English-speaking children on the Michigan Gender Identity test. In a related study, this was shown to have no effect on ascribing sexual connotations to words in a comparison between Hebrew- and English-speaking college students. Whatever conflict gender versus sex sets up, it seems to be resolved by the age of five. One area they have been particularly interested in is the ease with which young children develop native pronunciation. Their explanation involves three basic constructs, summarized in Guiora:

> The choice of authenticity of pronunciation as the realm of behaviour for testing hypotheses about empathic capacity was based on the notion that both pronunciation ability and empathy are profoundly influenced by the same underlying processes, namely permeability of

ego boundaries. In order to sharpen the conceptual focus, a mediating construct, *language ego,* was introduced. Like the concept of body ego, language ego is a maturational concept and likewise refers to self-representation with physical outlines and firm boundaries. (Guiora, in Guiora and Acton 1979:198–9)

During developmental stages, boundaries are permeable; once ego development is finished, the flexibility or plasticity of ego boundaries varies from individual to individual. Pronunciation, Guiora believes, is 'the most important contribution of language ego to self-representation'. Permeable boundaries are not weak or unhealthy; a healthy ego is well-defined, but there are people who can move back and forth between languages and the 'personalities' that go with them.

Guiora's central explanation for the importance of personality factors in second language learning is that language is not just a means of communication but a basic method of self-representation, incorporating 'in a unique blend intra and interpersonal parameters, cognitive and affective aspects of information processing, allowing a view of the total person . . .' (Guiora 1982:171). Learning a second language involves confronting a different organization of perception and conceptualization. Fundamental is the Whorfian view that language is to be treated as

a manifestation and as an engine of that intricate and many-colored fabric we call personality. In short, I treat language as a psychological process that interweaves and interacts with other psychological processes, transitory or stable, in an ever-evolving fashion, to influence, change, determine the ultimate matrix described as behaviour . . . Language, native language has an effect, accelerating or retarding, on the development of certain cognitive structures . . . The differential schemata [of a second language] may serve to stress the difference, to seal in the uniqueness of one's own world, or it may present an opportunity to experiment with the alternative hypothesis. (Guiora 1983:9–10)

Because our native language carries our personal self-representation as well as our 'national-cultural epistemology', we naturally cling to it.

There have been a number of attempts to validate this paradigm. A first approach using the Micromentary Expression test (a measure of empathy based on ability to recognize changes in a woman's expression on a film) did not hold up. A more successful experiment suggested that students became less inhibited and pronounced an unknown foreign language (Thai) better after consuming a small amount of alcohol. In another study, the quality of foreign language pronunciation is more improved by hypnotism in the case of hypnotizable students than in the case of less hypnotizable students.

This latter is a study by Schumann, Holroyd, Campbell, and Ward (1978). In it, twenty student volunteers (no details on background) were given a modified version of the Harvard Group Scale of Hypnotizability, tested on their ability to pronounce Thai words under three conditions (baseline, hypnosis, and post-hypnosis), and then given the Stanford Scale of Hypnotic Susceptibility. While hypnosis did not significantly improve pronunciation, and while the highly-hypnotizable subjects improved non-significantly and the low-hypnotizable not all, when groups were defined not by the Stanford Scale but by self-rating of how deeply they were hypnotized, the group believing themselves to be deeper improved both during and after hypnosis; the other group actually deteriorated. But as the authors point out, there are also other problems with the study which can be considered no more than suggestive. Guiora's report of this experiment is perhaps over-positive. There are, he says, other studies under way. I mention finally an essay by Clarke (1976), which carries some of these notions even further. Impressed by the studies of Guiora, Gardner, and Schumann, he speculates about second language learning, first by comparing it to schizophrenia, and then by comparing it to the culture shock suffered by members of a traditional society when brought into a modernized society. He talks in particular about the problems of foreign students coming to the United States.

In spite of the attractiveness of many of these arguments, the research evidence, as Gardner (1985:37) puts it, offers little reason for optimism but should encourage further study. While these studies have not reached the stage that I feel it possible to attempt to describe personality conditions for second language learning, there is clearly something of importance here. One might speculate, for instance, about the differential preferences of the introverted and extroverted learner, the former benefiting from conditions of learning that permit quiet introspection and the latter from approaches that encourage immediate public performance.[6]

This kind of personality difference will draw attention to the probable weakness of making simple generalizations such as the claims for the silent period in the work of Krashen, Terrell, and Asher. For some learners, a silent period is clearly essential; for others, it is likely to be of little value, and may even lead to lowered motivation. We might also like to consider that approaches like those of Gattegno, Lozanov, and Curran represent attempts to modify conditions in such a way as to overcome the effect of personality matters.

Running through this latter issue is a general distinction among learners in terms of their expectations about the language learning task.[7] A second language learner brings to the language learning situation a set of notions about what is involved in the task; these expectations interact with personality factors and the actual learning situation to determine the strategies that the learner will adopt. Let me make this clearer with some typical examples. The early second language learner (the bilingual who is virtually learning two languages as a first language) quickly comes to learn that the two languages serve in the same way as two styles or registers in a single language: some people expect you to use one language or register, and others expect you to use the other. The later second language learner is more likely to consider second language learning like the aspect of first language learning that is most salient, usually the learning of vocabulary. The learner who has had a solid dose of formal grammar either in a first or second language will ask similar questions in a new language learning situation. The person to whom a language serves specific social or instrumental functions will ask how to say the appropriate things. The person who sets very high demands on his or her control of language will similarly expect to achieve a high level of control of the new language, and will often be inhibited from trying to learn if there is some danger of being misunderstood or considered less than highly skilled. Expectations may also be socially widespread; Strevens (1978) cites the 'national myth' that the English cannot learn foreign languages. Methods for relaxation of anxiety, such as those of Gattegno, Lozanov, and Curran, or approaches that call on adults to act like uninhibited children, are aimed at dealing with this last situation. In each case, though, the learner's assumptions of what to expect are likely to determine the strategies that will be tried and the kinds of results that will lead to reinforcement.

Condition 32
Expectations condition (typical, graded): A learner's expectations of the outcome of language learning interact with the learner's personality factors to control the selection of preferred learning strategies.

The working of this condition will be one that has a major influence on the learner's willingness to persevere with the complex and difficult task of language learning.

Anxiety in second language learning

There are a number of reasons for assuming that an anxious learner will not be a good one. Anxiety will distract from the task of attending to and remembering new items; it will discourage from the practice that will establish items. A number of earlier studies (Gardner and Lambert 1959; Tarampi, Lambert, and Tucker 1968; Chastain 1975) failed to find evidence of the effect of general anxiety on second language learning. One problem has no doubt been in finding a good way of measuring anxiety. Scovel (1978) also suggested that clearcut results are made more difficult because anxiety can have two effects that cancel each other out, leading to facilitation in some cases and interference in others. Up to a point, an anxious learner tries harder; beyond this level, anxiety prevents performance.

Gardner (1985:33) has a simpler explanation; he proposes that there is what he calls situational anxiety, specific to language learning, overlapping with general classroom anxiety but not identical with it. In a number of studies, he found support for this notion. Gardner and Smythe (1975) showed that there were correlations between general classroom anxiety and French classroom anxiety; the latter, however, was the one that loaded on the same factor as measures of French proficiency. Gardner, Smythe, Clément, and Gliksman (1976) found high negative correlation of French classroom anxiety with achievement in eleven of fifteen cases in a Canada-wide study; the only better predictors were aptitude and motivation. Clément, Gardner, and Smythe (1977), in a factor analysis of French-speaking students learning English, found an 'English self-confidence'[8] factor that included English classroom anxiety, English use anxiety, self-ratings of English competence, experience with more than one language, attitudes to the English course, motivation to learn English, and English achievement. Their explanation of this is as follows: '. . . self-confidence (with a concomitant absence of situationally relevant anxiety) develops as a result of positive experiences in the context of the second language and serves to motivate individuals to learn the second language' (Gardner 1985:54). In his LISREL-interpreted studies, Gardner (1985: 161) also reports evidence for the existence of a latent variable—anxiety—established by measuring French classroom anxiety and French use anxiety. However, the study shows anxiety as an effect of low initial proficiency and motivation, but not as a cause of low final achievement.

The general recognition by teachers of the existence of anxiety specific to language learning has been supported by clinical observations reported by Horwitz, Horwitz, and Cope (1986). Anxiety is most often focused on listening and speaking, with difficulty in speaking in class being the most common complaint of anxious students. Anxiety also shows up in other stressful situations such as tests. Horwitz and her colleagues argue for the existence of an anxiety specific to foreign language learning, conceptually related to three other specific varieties. These three are communication apprehension (a kind of shyness that interferes with talking to other people), test anxiety, and a generalized fear of negative evaluation. Foreign language learning anxiety contains elements of all three, but is more than just a combination of them; it is also largely influenced by the threat to a person's self-concept in being forced to communicate with less proficiency in the second language than he or she has in the first. From discussions with a number of students in beginner foreign language classes who identified themselves as anxious, Horwitz developed a Foreign Language Classroom Anxiety Scale, a thirty-three item scale scored on a five-point Likert Scale ranging from 'strongly agree' to 'strongly disagree'. Some illustrative items are 'I start to panic when I have to speak without preparation in my language class' and 'I am afraid that my language teacher is ready to correct every mistake I make'. In continuing studies (Horwitz 1986), the scale has been shown to be reliable and its construct validity supported by evidence that it can be discriminated from tests of other kinds of anxiety. Two studies have shown significant correlations between foreign language classroom anxiety as measured by the scale and final grades in language classes; this effect was independent of the effect of test anxiety on the final grade. The correlations reported are about −0.5.

In order to focus more specifically on situated personality factors, Ely (1986a) has studied a class of first and second year Spanish learners. He finds support for a construct of Language Class Discomfort,[9] which seemed to lead to a reduction in willingness to take risks in class,[10] and indirectly to a decrease in class participation.[11] This in turn had a deleterious effect on oral but not written accuracy.

There is good evidence, then, to consider that there is a specific kind of anxiety that in the case of many learners[12] interferes with second language learning. The condition may be stated as follows:

Condition 33
Second Language Learning Anxiety condition (typical, graded): Some learners, typically those with low initial proficiency, low motivation, and high general anxiety, develop levels of anxiety in learning and using a second language that interfere with the learning.

To sum up, this chapter has looked at evidence from linguistic theory and psycholinguistics on some of the conditions for second language learning that are present in the learner. The emphasis has been on those factors included in the model at the end of Chapter 1 as ability and aptitude although we have also touched on attitude as it shows up in the individual personality. The factors share a relative lack of access to external influence: they are not easily changed. As a result, their direct relevance to language teaching is either in selecting students for special kinds of training or in providing explanations of the likelihood of success or failure of various kinds of learning situations.

Notes

1 As Cook (1985) points out, Chomsky argues that even 'pure' learning theories of behaviourism assume an innate ability to make associations between stimulus and response.
2 See the discussion in Chapter 5.
3 For example, the Foreign Language Prognosis Test (Symonds 1930).

4   Oxford (1986) presents a taxonomy of second language learning strategies and sketches the implication for learning and teaching practice.

5   Brian Parkinson and Jennifer Higham (1987) are working to distinguish 'good' from 'bad' learners, speculating on the influence of laziness and 'some sort of block against formal learning'.

6   This also relates to the learning style preferences discussed earlier in this chapter.

7   Strevens (1978) cites low expectations as a cause of failure to learn languages. Expectations are also involved in what Gardner (1985) refers to as self-confidence (see page 114).

8   But note Yule, Yanz, and Tsuda (1985) who point to evidence of a more complex relation between self-confidence and accuracy than is here implied; second language learners can be confident and wrong.

9   For example, 'At times, I feel somewhat embarrassed in class when I'm trying to speak.'

10 For example, students who disagree with the statement 'In class, I prefer to say a sentence to myself before I speak it.'

11 Based on observation.

12 An interesting question not yet answered by research is how many learners are to be classified as anxious; in the case study reported in Chapter 13, it is about 10–15 per cent of the population. The rate is probably higher among adult learners.

8   The linguistic basis

Contrastive analysis

The language learner does not start with a *tabula rasa*. As studies over the past thirty years have shown, even the acquisition of the first language presupposes some degree of preprogramming or innate language-specific capacity, representable as a hypothesized Universal Grammar. In the case of second language learning, there is in addition to this the knowledge that the learner has already acquired of the first language.

During the heyday of the Audio-Lingual Method, contrastive analysis occupied a central place in the field of applied linguistics as the principal contribution that linguistics could make to language teaching. As originally formulated by Charles Fries (1945) and developed and popularized by Robert Lado (1957), the task of contrastive analysis was seen as the comparison of the structures of two languages and the mapping of points of difference; these differences are 'the chief source of difficulty' for the language learner, and they can 'form the basis for the preparation of language texts and tests, and for the correction of students learning a language' (Lado 1957).

Essentially, contrastive analysis worked in a structural model; it assumed (before Chomsky) a kind of competence model in which one set of knowledge (the learner's first language) came into contact through the learning process with a second set of knowledge (the target language). Where the two structures matched, learning was easy; where they differed (in form or use), a difficulty arose that needed to be overcome. The principle may be stated in a general (and under-specified) Language Distance condition.

Condition 34
Language Distance condition (necessary, graded): The closer two languages are to each other genetically and typologically, the quicker a speaker of one will learn the other.

This general condition assumes two specific conditions, as follows:

Condition 35
Shared Feature condition (necessary, graded): When two languages share a feature, learning is facilitated.

Condition 36
Contrastive Feature condition (necessary, graded): Differences between
two languages interfere when speakers of one set out to learn the other.

The working of these two conditions was assumed to be the major factor
in second language learning, and the main contribution to be made by
linguistics, which could provide a listing of shared and contrastive
features.

Contrastive analysis developed in the US at a time when the dominant
school in linguistics was pre-Chomskyan structuralism, one of whose
principal tenets was the notion that languages must be described in their
own terms and neither in terms of another language (grammars based on
Latin or other traditional models were a frequent target) nor on the basis
of theoretical universals. Contrastive analysis thus provided a framework for the development of useful pedagogical grammars. It provided
justification also for selective practical and eclectic descriptions of those
aspects of a language which were most needed by language teachers
through the days that followed the development of transformational
generative grammar and in the continuing uncertainties produced by the
absence of an accepted single paradigm for language description. At
their worst, contrastive grammars seemed to assume that all learners
needed was to be taught some new way of analysing the differences
between their language and the one being learned; at their best, they
recognized that a pedagogical grammar is only a first step in the process
of developing teaching materials.

Sridhar (1976) has a very good summary of the contemporary
controversies, the major emphasis on phonology and syntax, and the
large gaps left; it is only recently that there have been attempts to deal
with the contrastive semantics and pragmatics clearly implied in the
initial Fries-Lado formulation. The theoretical basis for contrastive
analysis remained weak. The problem is simply posed: ideally, a
contrastive analysis is a simple mechanistic drawing together of the
details of two complete grammars that have been written in similar
terms. For structural linguists, such grammars were theoretically
impossible, for each grammatical concept had to be defined in terms of
the language for which it was developed and of that language alone. On
the other hand, transformational generative grammars assume the
existence of universals, so that (theoretically) a complete transformational grammar would already be a potential contrastive analysis with
all other languages. In practice, then, contrastive analyses that tried to
cover 'approximately the same ground that the language teacher is
called on to deal with explicitly in the classroom' (Langacker 1968) were
of considerable practical value during the structural period, but lost
their theoretical support once generative grammars started to be written.

It is important, as Fisiak (1983 and elsewhere) has shown, to
distinguish this American version of contrastive analysis, which was

motivated by applied linguistics, from the earlier and continuing European tradition for the synchronic comparison, for theoretical reasons, of languages. This latter activity parallels (but somewhat surprisingly does not seem to have close intellectual ties with) similar work, especially in the US but also in Europe, in the search for linguistic universals. Thus what Fisiak calls theoretical contrastive analysis has continued to flourish, as witness his statement in the preface to *An Introductory English-Polish Contrastive Grammar* of which he is co-editor:

> The present *Grammar* is not a PEDAGOGICAL (i.e. applied) CONTRASTIVE GRAMMAR. It is not interested in setting up hierarchies of difficulty or explicitly defining areas of potential interference. It does not interpret linguistic facts in pedagogical terms. It is entirely neutral towards any form of application. (Fisiak *et al.* 1978:7)

Fisiak (1983:20) defines a 'theoretical contrastive study' as a contrastive analysis of similarities and differences between two languages: it may aim simply at an 'exhaustive' comparative description which will be an end in its itself and 'which in turn may help to verify claims postulating universality of given rules or items of grammar . . .' (Fisiak 1983:20). He points out that the central problem of this work continues to be the problem of comparability, the finding of a way to overcome the established difficulties of both formal and semantic equivalences. The development of a theoretical basis for pedagogical contrastive grammars also remains to be done.

In the last few years, for a number of reasons,[1] the contrastive analysis hypothesis has lost a good deal of its earlier popularity and respectability; error analysis and interlanguage studies have moved it to the fringes of practical and theoretical interest. One of the reasons for this has perhaps been that applied contrastive analysis was too clear on its distinction between competence and process: the grammar of a contrastive analysis is a description of language competence or knowledge, and the only process postulated is interference or transfer. Error analysis was much more process oriented, and interlanguage, while nominally a theory of linguistic competence, often involves complex blends with a process model.

This issue underlies the attempt by Lehtonen and Sajavaara (1983) to proclaim communicative contrastive linguistics. They suggest that the recent increasing emphasis on communicative approaches to language teaching has 'brought about simultaneous shift from declarative knowledge over to procedural knowledge, which means, in the present context, dynamic linguistic and communicative processes being seen as a central area subjected to analysis instead of static structures of grammar' (Lehtonen and Sajavaara 1983: 81). They regret the continuing absence of 'true performance grammars, which are based on natural language use and which rely on the processes of speech production and reception' (op.cit.:83).

In this statement, we are once again forced to confront the differing claims of a competence and a processing model. I therefore make again the point that a competence model makes no claim about processing; it aims to present a description of a set of facts about language that will account for observable utterances without postulating a method of storage, or production, or comprehension of those utterances. There are, it must be pointed out further, only practical reasons why a competence grammar is limited to sentences or syntax; Chomsky assumes the possibility of a competence model of language use (pragmatics); and it is a fundamental argument of this book that the model proposed by Jackendoff for semantics shows how this can be done. On the other hand, a processing (or performance) model like that sought by Lehtonen and Sajavaara, or Schlesinger, or Hatch, or Bialystok, dealing as each of them does with how storage, or production, or reception takes place, necessarily presupposes a theory of what it is that is stored, or produced, or received; in other words, it is forced ultimately to face the same challenge as a competence model.

It is not clear that in looking at the topic of this chapter we can avoid this difficulty, however much we may want to, for the issue before us is the essential one of what influence a second language learner's knowledge of the first language (to be accounted for in a competence model) has on the learning of the second (a processing matter). That is to say, we cannot afford the luxurious indifference to application that Fisiak pretends; in fact he too turns out to be responsible in his practice if not in his preaching. We are forced, then, to confront the very issues that Fries and Lado raised, the potential significance for a language learner of the differences and similarities between his or her first language and the language he or she is trying to learn.

The original weakness of the contrastive analysis hypothesis was its failure to go beyond a statement of difference to a supportable theory of difficulty. As Brière (1968) showed, and many others have demonstrated since then, difference by itself does not predict difficulty; often there is more difficulty in practice with structures that are similar than with structures that are different. Secondly, as work in the error analysis and interlanguage traditions has made clear, interference or transfer from the native language is only part of the problem, for a good number of the errors made by language learners seem to be unrelated to the learners' native language, showing signs rather of the same kind of overgeneralization or hypothesis testing that has been proposed for native language learning. Thus, Dulay and Burt (1974) were able to claim that most of the errors they found in a study of children learning English as a second language were 'developmental', like those made by native speakers in learning their own first language, and only a few could be considered genuine cases of interference. Later more sophisticated studies make similar though more cautious claims.

At the same time, it is hard to see how we can avoid a general claim for the influence of distance between first and second language on the learning process and for the effect of the Language Distance condition. Thus, it has been suggested that distance between languages might be roughly measured as the time required for a speaker of one to learn to use the other. Now obviously there are all sorts of qualifications necessary—the issue of criterion level is certainly important, as is the attitudinal effect of sociolinguistic situation,[2] but all other things being equal, we should expect it to be quicker to learn a closely related language than a more distant one. The original observation that formed the basis of contrastive analysis was true; it has simply proved difficult to state it explicitly or to note all the necessary qualifications that are prerequisite to empirical testing.

Universals and contrastive analysis

The importance of the principle and the difficulty of applying it specifically mean that we need a better framework to account for the fact that a second language learner's knowledge of his or her first language has some effect on his or her performance in the new language. For this reason, the attempt by Eckman (1977) to restore a refined contrastive analysis hypothesis to the centre of attention deserves careful study.

Eckman (1977) set out to revise the hypothesis by incorporating in it some principles of Universal Grammar; he argued that as a result of this modification, one should be able to make statements that do not merely describe differences but also predict difficulty. As he points out, the original form of the contrastive analysis hypothesis involved a strong claim for prediction of ease or difficulty. Lado (1957) suggested that items in a foreign language that were similar to those in the native language would be easy; those that were different would be difficult. The claim did not hold up in practice, as Brière (1968) and others showed, and a weak form of the hypothesis was proposed and formulated as follows:

> In contrast to the demands made by the strong version, the weak version requires of the linguist only that he use the linguistic knowledge available to him in order to account for observed difficulties in second language learning. It does not require what the strong version requires, the prediction of those difficulties and conversely of those learning points which do not create any difficulties at all. (Wardhaugh 1974: 181)

This weak version, Eckman argues, is nothing more than an unfalsifiable heuristic for analysing student errors and thus is quite uninteresting as a claim about second language learning. He prefers, therefore, to consider the stronger version and its potential modification in application to a specific case, that of voiced and voiceless obstruents in English and German. A taxonomic contrastive analysis of the phonology of the two languages shows that one area of difference is that in word-final positions, German (in contrast to English) does not have both voiced and voiceless forms, but only voiceless. But the analysis makes no prediction of direction of difficulty; it offers no suggested explanation for the observable fact that in practice, the difference is a bigger problem for the speaker of German learning English than it is for the speaker of English learning German.

One explanation might be to propose as an additional principle that it is harder to learn a new contrast (as the speaker of German must in learning English) than to learn to drop a contrast. But there is no support for this principle, and indeed contradictory evidence in the comparative ease with which English speakers learn the new contrast required in producing the initial /ʒ/ of French *je* (I). Nor does a generative analysis seem to help much, for the German facts are captured best by a terminal devoicing rule: looked at in this way, we would expect that the English learner would have the greatest difficulty, for he or she would have to learn an additional rule.

Eckman's solution to this key problem is to propose a notion of typological markedness, defined as follows: 'A phenomenon A in some language is more marked than B if the presence of A in a language implies the presence of B; but the presence of B does *not* imply the presence of A' (Eckman 1977:320). Applying this to the case under consideration, there are languages with only voiceless obstruents, and others with both, but no language with just voiced obstruents. Thus voiced obstruents are more marked and more difficult to learn. Eckman's view may be interpreted as a proposal to add to the Shared Feature condition and the Contrastive Feature condition a modification that applies to contrastive features:

Condition 37
Markedness Differential condition (necessary, graded): Marked features are more difficult to learn than unmarked.

Eckman's markedness differential hypothesis calls for a systematic comparison of the target and native languages and of the universal markedness relations; it then predicts that areas of the target language that are more marked than the native language will be more difficult, depending on the relative degree of marking, while difference in form without difference in marking will not cause difficulty. Eckman goes on to quote a study of markedness relations of obstruents that produces a typology and thus a hierarchy of the directionality observed in the German-English case, and offers a similar explanation for the French-English case cited above. He then analyses an area of syntax, the English relative clause, and shows that the predicted orders of difficulty derived from the hypothesis for Chinese, Japanese, and Arabic speakers do hold in a study of actual errors. He concludes by speculating on the underlying validity both of contrastive analysis and of typological markedness as predictors of difficulty.

Eckman (1981a) applies these principles to the analysis of the rules required to account for the English speech produced by two native speakers of Spanish and two native speakers of Mandarin. Some of the rules required to account for their production are, though independent of the rules of both the native and target languages, in fact rules that occur in other natural languages; one, however, does not appear to exist in any natural language. Eckman (1981b) restates these general principles and describes an empirical study of the difficulties of Cantonese and Japanese learners of English with word-final obstruents. The speech of two students from each language was recorded under a number of conditions; transcription and analysis revealed that while the Cantonese students tended to devoice a final obstruent, the Japanese students tended to add a schwa. Neither of these rules comes from either the target or the native languages, but both are strategies (rather than natural language rules) to deal with the difficulties produced by the variation in markedness, involving both maintaining the underlying representation of the target language and producing a form consistent with the phonetic constraints of the native language.

There have been some developments of Eckman's proposal. Rutherford (1982) considers markedness as a useful concept to explain a number of phenomena in second language learning, as elsewhere in language. The fundamental discussions of markedness follow Clark and Clark (1978: 230), who held that 'complexity in thought tends to be reflected in complexity of expression', with complexity of expression being stated in terms of markedness (Greenberg 1966). As a corollary to this notion is the principle of contextual neutralization; the unmarked form is the one that appears when the contrast is not made.[3] Rutherford reviews various uses of this concept in second language learning studies, and finds the earliest in a suggestion by George (1972) that unmarked forms are more easily learned. He shares with Kellerman (1979) a concern that Eckman's model seems to fit only a relatively small part of syntax, and approves of the proposal by Odmark (1979) that markedness is part of the learner's assumptions about the target language, and is thus useful in error analysis. Rutherford reviews a number of studies where markedness seems valuable in explaining otherwise random-seeming variations. He concludes that markedness should be a valuable explanatory concept not just at the levels of phonology, morphology, and syntax, but also in discourse.

In a related but independent study, Gass (1979) set out to study language transfer, looking for evidence of the effect of universal grammatical relations independent of native language interference (and presumably other language learning strategies). Looking at the learning of English relative clauses by adults from a number of different native languages, she showed that their difficulties were predicted partly by a universal 'accessibility hierarchy', proposed by Keenan and Comrie, and partly by intralingual transfer.

The same area is studied by Tarallo and Myhill (1983). Their aim is similarly to distinguish effects of first language transfer from effects of universals. Their methodology is particularly novel, in that rather than, as Gass, looking at a number of speakers of different languages learning English, they look at a number of speakers of English learning other languages. The students, some in their first and some in their second year, were asked to mark sentences as being grammatical or ungrammatical. Their analysis agrees with Gass in showing the existence of non-target language influences, but they differ with her on the nature of these influences and some of her generalizations.

A paper by Zobl (1983) proposes that the markedness hypothesis be tested against the projection principle (Peters) as an explanation for the ability of the second language learner to project views of the target language on the basis of comparatively little data. He attempts to show how some anomalies in Gass's results can be explained this way, and some of the data presented by Rutherford also lends itself to this analysis.

Universals and second language learning

Eckman's hypothesis and the Markedness Differential condition introduce Universal Grammar into second language learning theory, by claiming that universal markedness constraints act independently on language differences to account for interference and facilitation in learning. There are stronger claims to be made, such as the suggestion that it is Universal Grammar itself that provides the third factor. White (1985) has given an interesting account of claims for establishing a relation between universals and language-specific influences in second language learning. She reports an attempt to exploit current theories of Universal Grammar, and in particular the notion that some principles in a Universal Grammar are subject to 'parametric variation'. As discussed, this means that while a specific principle is universal, languages will differ in the scope they give to the working of the principle. White hopes in this way to be able to predict not just intralanguage problems but also interlanguage transfer, a worthy if difficult goal.

These ideas are also considered by Cook (1985), who describes first a 'consensus' view of Chomsky's current theory of Universal Grammar and language acquisition. In this, a grammar of a specific language is seen as a selection from possible forms allowed by Universal Grammar, which is itself a set of general principles that leave certain parameters open: 'The grammar of a language can be regarded as a particular set of values for these parameters, while the overall set of rules, principles, and parameters is UG . . .' (Chomsky 1982:7). The 'language faculty' or Universal Grammar develops in the brain, triggered by appropriate external stimuli: 'a central part of what we call "learning" is actually better understood as the growth of cognitive structures along an internally directed course under the triggering and potentially shaping effect of the environment' (Chomsky 1980, cited by Cook).

Cook points out three critical facts: the theory concerns grammatical and not pragmatic competence; rules are of less importance than they were in earlier forms of the theory; and core grammar is to be distinguished from peripheral grammar, the former the result of the growth of a grammar as so far described, and the latter 'a periphery of marked elements and constructions' (Chomsky 1980:8) that are unaffected by Universal Grammar. As Kean defines it:

> The core is the highly restricted set of grammatical principles and parameters specified in the theory of Universal Grammar (UG); the principles are invariant, absolute universals, and the parameters are those properties of grammar which are necessary but which have varying realizations in particular core grammars (e.g. basic word order). The periphery consists of language-particular phenomena outside the domain of the core; while all languages have a periphery, the properties of the periphery are not defining properties of the grammars of natural human languages (e.g. they may turn on properties of weak generation). (Kean 1986: 80)

This principle has important consequences for the theory of learning. Core solutions are to be preferred, depending only on triggering; peripheral knowledge is marked, and learning it is more demanding. There can be independent structures in the peripheral grammar or there can be systems related to the core grammar by relaxing certain of their conditions; thus, there can be a continuum. But Chomsky goes on, this does not necessarily affect order of learning:

> We would expect the order of acquisition of structures in language acquisition to reflect the structure of markedness in some respects, but there are complicating factors; e.g. processes of maturation may be such as to permit certain unmarked constructions to be manifested only relatively late in language acquisition, frequency effects may intervene, etc. (Chomsky 1981:9, cited by Cook).

The summary presented by Cook is as follows:

> To sum up, the hypothetical picture of L2 [second language] learning that emerges is that the learner contributes a set of language principles and unfixed parameters; the evidence he encounters enables him to fix the parameters into a new grammar. While his first language affects his acquisition, it cannot help him acquire those parts of grammar that vary from one language to another. He also encounters evidence that does not fit Universal Grammar, for which he has to adopt more marked solutions. . . Because of his greater maturity he does not have the same restrictions as the native child . . .
> (Cook 1985:14)

We might try to express Cook's views in a condition expressing the effect of Universal Grammar on second language learning:

Condition 38
Shared Parameter condition (necessary): When both native and target language have the same setting for some parameter of Universal Grammar (= have the same rule), minimal experience will be needed to trigger the correct form of the grammar.

When there is a difference between the parameters in the two languages, however, we require preference conditions; the third follows from Chomsky's recognition of the relevance of frequency to acquisition:

Condition 39
Unmarked Parameter condition (typical): Prefer to use the unmarked (core, Universal Grammar) setting of the parameter.

Condition 40
Native Language Parameter condition (typical): Prefer to use the native language setting of the parameter.

Condition 41
Most Frequent Parameter condition (typical, graded): Prefer to use the most frequent setting of the parameter.

It is an empirical question of considerable importance as to what weighting, if any, is applied to each of these conditions and in what circumstances. We need to know the relative importance of various kinds of triggering: of examples in the target language, of explanation, or of fortuitously confirmed use of a form by the learner trying to speak or write the target language. The place to seek answers to the questions raised is most likely to be in work in cross-linguistic influence (see Kellerman's proposals below) or in the error analysis tradition.

As Cook (1985) points out, these principles imply a more precise notion of hypothesis-testing than that held in earlier language acquisition studies: the child does not produce random hypotheses to test against actual use, but rather hypotheses that are compatible both with the data of language he or she meets and the possible forms of a grammar set by Universal Grammar. It also increases emphasis on lexis; what needs learning is not so much grammatical structures as how particular lexical items can enter into them.

On this basis, Cook (1985) speculates on differences between first and second language learning. The obvious difference is that second language learners already have the grammar of their first language, based on Universal Grammar with a particular set of values for parameters prescribed. In these terms, the key question is whether or not second language grammars are constrained by Universal Grammar in the same way as first language grammars: the question of whether second language learning recapitulates first becomes a question of whether the principles of Universal Grammar can still be applied and whether the triggering process assumed for first language learning is still available for setting parameters. We have already seen this in a similar question as to whether or not second language grammars (called by some interlanguages) are natural languages.

Cook cites two studies that he feels bear on this question. The first, by Schmidt (1980), argues that the utterances produced by second language learners in the study violated the rules of English but never the principles of Universal Grammar. The second, by Ritchie (1978), showed Universal Grammar principles also applying. A more recent relevant study is Mazurkewich (1984, 1985). who finds that both French-speaking and Inuit-speaking (Eskimo) learners of English similarly find unmarked English dative constructions easier than marked, suggesting that some universal rather than language-specific influences are work-ing. This leads Cook to the conclusion that the process is still open and that the strong version of the Critical Period Hypothesis does not apply. Differences between young first language learners and older second language learners call, therefore, for other explanations. There is evidence that second language development is affected by cognitive factors, such as explanation: older learners, especially in classroom situations, are likely to experience not just correction but also explanation. There is also some suggestion that 'channel capacity' needs to be re-established. The evidence of learning order is not enough, for the sequence might be affected by channel capacity rather than acquisition, and anyway, as Cook points out (echoing the comments cited in Chapter 1 from Gregg and others), the evidence of order of acquisition refers only to a few surface features. The fact that there is no reason for core (i.e. universal) elements to be learned before peripheral (*pace* Chomsky) also raises some doubts about the attractiveness of the markedness hypothesis.

There are scholars who do not share the enthusiasm of Eckman, Cook, and White for finding in core and periphery, in marked and unmarked, the solution to the problem of transfer. Kean calls for considerable caution:

> There is no such thing as an unmarked grammar for any natural human language... Because there are constraints on possible markedness relations, at no point in time will a simple comparison of marked/unmarked in the native language and marked/unmarked in the target language suffice to characterize the learner's options. (Kean 1986:89)

As a learner's grammar grows, the domains of transfer will change: markedness, then, is dynamic, and 'cannot solve the questions posed by transfer but only contribute to their solution' (op.cit.:90).

A question of considerable importance is also the domain of application of the conditions. Even if we accept the correctness of the Unmarked Parameter condition, we do not know how it interacts with the two competing conditions; nor do we know how widely it applies: there are relatively few items covered by Universal Grammar constraints. Even while the condition may be true and of fundamental importance in providing evidence for an innate language faculty, it remains to be shown how much of second language learning it affects.

Essentially, all of these proposals take the notion of contrastive analysis from its simple structural linguistic days, where structures in the learner's native language were seen as a direct cause of error in the target language or as an explanation for learning difficulty, through a transformational stage where hypotheses about the target language could be interfered with by rules of the first language grammar, to a position much more consistent with current generative theory.

An even wider perspective on transfer has been proposed by Kellerman and Sharwood Smith (1986), who suggest dealing with the general issue of cross-linguistic influence, which they define as 'the interplay between earlier and later acquired languages'. Their approach seeks to avoid the value judgements of such terms as transfer, interference, and facilitation, to subsume issues like avoidance, to deal with native language constraints on second language learning, and include within it larger language contact issues. One of the parts of their appeal I find most sympathetic is their 'plea for modularity, i.e. a differentiated approach to the various areas of language, given the apparent and hitherto underestimated degree of complexity of cross-linguistic influence' (Kellerman and Sharwood Smith 1986:7). While Lado's original presentation of the notion of contrastive analysis called for contrast in all areas—the cultural contrasts he proposed are most striking—current work has focused on one aspect, the acquisition of a limited number of syntactic features. The greatest importance of this restricted work is perhaps in making clear a difference between first and second language learning. While in the former much of the learning of syntax will be a result of the Universal Grammar (the exception is of course what Chomsky calls the peripheral grammar), in the case of second language learning there will be the additional influence of the parameters set for the first language. However, the model suggests, any difficulty this may cause will be alleviated by the availability of more advanced cognitive strategies.

The conditions looked at so far in this chapter are related to the innate learning strategies assumed to be common to all. Where there is more likely to be individual variation of the kind that will account for differences in speed or quality of learning is in the application of somewhat more conscious learning strategies. We might make this transition by looking again at Kellerman's interest in markedness.

There are, Kellerman argues, three constraints on the language learning process. The more the learner perceives distance between the target and native language, the less he or she will be likely to attempt to transfer. Secondly, the more marked an item is, the less transfer there will be. Thirdly, the learner's real or assumed knowledge of the target language will affect transfer.

Essentially, the first of his constraints proposes weighting for the two contradictory typicality conditions, the second adds grading to the condition, and the third moves us closer to the notion of conscious strategies.

The effect of knowledge of the first language on second language learning needs closer scrutiny: as Kohn (1986:32) concludes: '. . . transfer is in no way the monolithic process that error analysis has treated it as. Transfer assumes various functions in the developmental organization of interlanguage *knowledge* as well as in the *retrieval* of this knowledge in the production of interlanguage output.'

A similar argument for recognizing the complexity of transfer has been presented by Færch and Kasper (1987), who call for distinguishing its effects in learning, in reception, and in production. Transfer in production is particularly complex, being influenced by social and psychological factors. They consider the methodological difficulties involved in studying transfer with performance data alone.

The previous knowledge that a second language learner has, and in particular the knowledge of his or her first language, is a factor of potential importance in second language learning. It does not work directly or simply, and varies according to situation or stage of learning. While there is considerable value in comparing the two languages,[4] the complexity of the nature of cross-linguistic influence requires that we continue to attempt to distinguish the detailed working of the conditions listed above.

As I suggested earlier, the ordering of items in this book follows the possibility of manipulation and control by a language teacher. Like other capacities, a learner's previous knowledge of a first language is not under the control of a second language teacher, although it of course sets interesting challenges. The conditions looked at so far are conditions of the individual learner; the disciplines that have informed the discussion have been biology, psychology, and linguistics. Before turning to another individual phenomenon, the attitudes that a learner brings to the learning task, it is necessary to set the social context within which all language learning takes place. This will be the focus of the next chapter.

Notes

1   For discussion, see Spolsky (1979b).
2   In actual fact, the time or even likelihood of learning is not the same in each direction. It is often the case that speakers of one language take longer to learn another language than in the reciprocal case.
3   We say 'He is six feet tall', but not 'He is five feet short'.
4   A study like Rogers (1987) demonstrates the potential value of such comparison, as she shows how a specific problem (learning of grammatical gender in German) may be clarified by psycho-linguistic and linguistic analysis.

9 The social context

Social factors

Because language is primarily a social mechanism, languages are learned in social contexts. Even in the learning of a first language where the biological basis is important, there is strong influence from social factors concerned with the special relation of child and caretaker. For this reason, Bruner's (1981) suggestion to add to the Language Acquisition Device a Language Acquisition Support System was only partly facetious. One of the weaknesses of modern linguistic theory has been a self-imposed restriction to language out of context. Hymes (1972 and elsewhere) has continually stressed the social nature of language, and argues for a wider view of linguistics than one limited to the grammar of sentences:

> What is needed is a linguistics which can describe whatever features of speech prove relevant in the given case, and which can relate linguistic elements to each other in terms of relationships of role, status, task, and the like. Such a linguistics requires foundations in social theory and ethnographic practice (Hymes 1964a, 1974) as well as in practical phonetics and grammar. (Hymes 1985:12)

The process of first language learning can be better understood if the social dimension is included. Social factors have even more importance in the case of second language learning because of the greater complexity of the second language learner's social context and the resulting increase in its ability to cause variability. Part of this became clear in Chapters 2 to 5, where it was shown that the description of language proficiency requires attention to social factors, which are fundamental in accounting for variation in structural knowledge and which form the basis for a functional analysis.

In the model sketched at the end of the first chapter, the social context was assumed to influence second language learning in two indirect but essential ways. First, it plays a major role in developing in the learner the set of attitudes towards the language being learned, its speakers, and the language learning situation that, as will be set forth in the next chapter, are hypothesized to influence motivation directly. Second, it determines the social provision of language learning situations and opportunities of various kinds, which will be considered in Chapters 11 and 12.

It is important to note that the model claims that the social context is not directly involved in setting specific conditions for language learning. Its effect rather is indirect, and its conditions are conditions on the development of attitudes to learning and learning opportunities.

To understand these effects, a first task is to find a way to characterize the significant features of the social contexts in which more than one language is learned. One way to do this is to describe the general sociolinguistic situation of the learner and the learning. The range of possible aims for language education in a society is limited by the language situation, and the choice of aims is affected by a number of sociolinguistic pressures.[1] An overview of the linguistic situation is provided by setting out the number of languages in use in the community,[2] the number of speakers of each, and the number of bilinguals.[3]

Such a count is far from simple for it presupposes a decision on what constitutes a variety. Many cases are fairly simple: laymen and linguists alike will agree that Spanish and Italian are different languages, and will recognize differences between English and Friesian, or High German and Swiss German, or Classical Arabic and the local varieties. But what about cases where there are several dialects, or where the dialects are socially rather than geographically defined? Even where there is linguistic closeness and a fairly high degree of mutual intelligibility, the fact that varieties are recognizably different can be very significant socially. Linguists may discuss as much as they like whether Black English is a different dialect or the end-result of a post-creole continuum, or whether it is similar to or different from southern white American English, but the fact remains, as James Sledd (1969) pointed out, that whites can if they choose use it just like skin colour as a basis for discrimination.

To start, then, we assume that we will want data on all socially significant varieties. In a study of the sociolinguistics of an Arabic-speaking community in Israel, for instance, we are likely to try to distinguish between the various identifiable varieties of Arabic, noting city versus village dialects as well as the Classical versus vernacular diglossia. We could further ask whether the religious communities can be distinguished, as in Baghdad (Blanc 1964), by their dialect. Are there differences between the Arabic of Christian and Moslem Arabs in Jerusalem? We might want to see whether there are significant differences of admixtures of loan words from English, Hebrew, or Turkish, that identify social situation, age, or education, as has been shown to be the case in one Arab village.[4] The question of what is a significant variety is, then, an empirical one, to be decided for each community studied in accordance with the level of precision or sophistication of the study. To carry out our study, we will also have to decide what constitutes 'knowledge' or 'use' of a language, the difficulty of which was explored in earlier chapters.

The numbers of speakers of each of the varieties, both within and outside the community studied and whether as a first or second language, can be interpreted as a first criterion for the relative value of each language for communicating with other people. For example, the importance of English in the Old City of Jerusalem comes not from the number of first language speakers, but from the number of speakers of Arabic and Hebrew for whom it is the second language, from its use by outside visitors (tourists and pilgrims), and internationally.[5]

Condition 42
Number of Speakers condition (typical, graded): The number of people who speak a language as a first or second language influences the desire of others to learn it.

A first argument quoted in selecting a foreign language to be taught in schools, or in arguing for steps to preserve an immigrant language, is commonly the number of people who speak it.

A second criterion emerges from the relationship between the several languages in a community. The closer the relation between two varieties, the more chance of mutual intelligibility and the shorter the learning time for speakers of one language for the other. These relations may be either genetic, where two languages are derived from the same common ancestor, or a result of contact, where there has been extensive borrowing or shared linguistic and cultural features. This particular feature formed the basis for the Language Distance condition mentioned in Chapter 8.

A third criterion that is very important for second language learning is the kind of language involved. Three taxonomies are relevant. The first was proposed originally by Stewart (1968), who argued that one can distinguish between important kinds of language such as standard languages, vernaculars, classical languages, dialects, pidgins, and creoles by considering them on four dimensions: standardization, autonomy, historicity, and vitality. Fishman (1970) made clear that these dimensions are to be seen as attitudes rather than absolute properties.

Standardization refers to the belief by the community that there exists a set of norms for 'correct' use of the variety, and these norms are listed in the available dictionaries and grammar books. It assumes the existence of a standardized writing system for the variety. Autonomy refers to the beliefs held by the speakers that their language is an independent one, usually with a name of its own; it is not considered (nor does its name imply) a dialect of another language. Historicity refers to the belief that the language was not just recently invented, but developed in the historic past usually in association with the Great Tradition associated with the history of the people speaking the variety. Vitality refers to the belief in or existence of a community of people speaking the variety who have acquired it as their first language, their mother tongue in the strictest sense of the term. Using these four features, it is possible to set up a typology of languages according to attitude.

A standard language has all four attributes, and is the language usually associated with formal education and language teaching. The official languages of most countries are standard languages.

A vernacular language is autonomous, historic and vital, but lacks standardization. Its speakers recognize it as a separate language, and are surprised to find its relation to others; their traditions speak of its past; it is spoken by parents with their children; but it lacks a formal set of norms, a community-used writing system, dictionary, and grammar books. American Indian languages, such as Navajo and Tewa were vernacular languages by this definition; the speakers recognized them as separate languages, even though to ignorant outsiders they were all lumped together as Indian or considered dialects.[6] Because of their lack of standardization, vernacular languages do not have the prestige of standard languages. It is, however, very common for children to come to school speaking a vernacular and for the school to wish to teach them the standard language. When the school is prepared, for political, educational, or ideological reasons, to teach children in a vernacular, it is often necessary to work to standardize it.

A classical language has all the attributes of a standard language except vitality or native speakers. The most widely used classical language in the world today is Classical Arabic: it is in official use in Arab countries and in religious use throughout the Moslem world. Others are Latin, recently overthrown from its place in the Roman Catholic Church; Classical Hebrew (or, more precisely, Lashon Kodesh), the religious language of Judaism; Sanskrit, the language of the Hindu scriptures; and Geez, the language in which Ethiopian Christians and Jews read their Bible and say their prayers.

A dialect, according to this same model, is a vernacular language that lacks autonomy, and by definition it also lacks standardization.[7]

These are the main varieties of language that are educationally important; pidgins and creoles function within the system like vernaculars and dialects, and artificial languages like classical ones. These essential features lead to important implications for second language learning:

(1) Only a language with the feature of standardization can be (or will be considered a candidate for being) taught formally.
(2) Only a language with the feature of vitality can be (or is likely to provide opportunities to be) learned informally.

These can be translated into necessary conditions on learning opportunities.

Condition 43.
Standard Language condition (necessary): Formal teaching situations are possible only with standardized languages.

Condition 44
Vitality condition (necessary): Informal learning situations are possible only with languages with vitality.[8]

These conditions have an effect on the provision of learning opportunities. They also have significance for attitudes, but to see how this works, it is useful to note two other special taxonomies. The first is suggested by Stewart (1968) in noting special functions for languages that will determine the importance of learning and teaching them. Of special significance here are the following:

(1) an *official or national language*, used by law in defined political or cultural activities within a specific state
(2) a *regional language*, which has its geographical limits set within a political unit
(3) a *language of wider communication*, also called a vehicular language or a lingua franca, used for communication between linguistic groups.

Note that the first two kinds of language are likely candidates for formal teaching; the last kind is by definition a candidate for informal learning.

The second taxonomy is one proposed by Kloss (1968) in considering the possible role of a language according to its capability of serving the functions of a modern technologically developed society. He suggests the following six stages:

(1) a preliterate language, never or rarely used in writing
(2) an alphabetized but unstandardized language; usually the writing system has been developed by outsiders, and is not widely used
(3) a young standard language, recently standardized and used for mass education at the elementary level but not beyond
(4) an archaic standard language, which had its flowering in pre-industrial times, so that while it may have a well-developed capacity for religion, philosophy, poetry, etc., it lacks the vocabulary for modern science and technology
(5) a small-group standard language, used by a small community and, therefore, unlikely to reach full development
(6) a mature standard language, fully modernized, which may be used to teach all branches of science and technology at advanced stages.

There is in this typology one essential dimension, the degree of modernization, with two other confounding ones, literacy and traditional development. Literacy clearly tends to go along with modernization, although it is important to note that it is a much more complex phenomenon than is sometimes allowed (Spolsky 1986a). It is also noteworthy that modernization tends to go beyond literacy; witness telephones, television, and more recently, voice-controlled computers. Great Traditions which are associated with rich pre- or non-industrial societies have important educational consequences, especially when they set up tensions between the competing values of two second languages, the one tied to modernization and the other to the earlier Great Tradition.

To capture these various reasons for setting a value on a variety and so explain the social pressures that are likely to encourage it being taught and learned, I propose a set of conditions which work in conjunction with the Number of Speakers condition (which is specially relevant in the case of regional and other languages of wider communication):

Condition 45
Official Use condition (typical, graded): Prefer to teach or learn a language which is officially used or recognized.

Condition 46
Modernized Language condition (typical, graded): Prefer to teach or learn a language which is standardized and which has been modernized.

Condition 47
Great Tradition condition (typical, graded): Prefer to teach or learn a language which has a desirable Great Tradition (including a religion) associated with it.

Basically then, the social and political status of a variety in a community will be significant in determining goals and opportunities for learning and attitudes to the target language and its speakers. But individual attitudes to language learning have a much more complex basis, as we shall see.

The stylistic dimension

The description so far has shown the complexity of factors that can account for attitudes towards a language and those who speak it. It is useful to analyse situational facts, rationales, and operations concerned with second language teaching under various headings such as psychological, sociological, linguistic, economic, political, religious, or historical.[9] In most real cases, more than one of these factors will be needed to give a full picture of the major forces at work. There is reason to argue that any one of these factors might be an underlying reason for learning a language.

The approach so far has been social, and the effects have been generally social effects. This is why the last few conditions have been stated as conditions on a social decision to teach a language. Clearly, these social values lead to individual responses; learners either agree with or are not in harmony with the decision. Another way to look at it is to take it that there are two outcomes of the conditions; they explain provision of learning opportunities, and they contribute to individual attitudes.

When we consider individual attitudes to language learning, we need to have a more psychologically oriented view. In their original work on attitudes and motivation, Gardner and Lambert (1959) proposed to organize all the possible reasons one might have for learning a second language into two clusters, which they labelled instrumental and integrative. An integrative reason is when I learn a language in order to become like or even join the people who speak the language; all other reasons are instrumental. This dichotomy is very much in harmony with Guiora's suggestion discussed earlier that essentially divides languages into two: my native language with which I identify, and any other language.

Another approach to this question of attitude to language is summarized in a discussion by Bell (1984) of language style. Bell undertakes to deal with the basic issue of language variation. He points out that analyses of language variation have shown it to be accounted for on two dimensions, linguistic (for example, phonological or other constraints on the operation of a variable rule) and extralinguistic. It is the second dimension in which we are interested. It may be divided into the social axis, dealing with variations between speakers, and stylistic, dealing with variation within a speaker. The first of these has been extensively investigated, showing correlation of linguistic variation with the class, sex, age, and social level of the speaker. In the literature (as was noted earlier in discussing Tarone's work on stylistic variation in second languages), style has generally been assumed to be a matter of attention: in Labov's words: 'Styles can be ranged along a single dimension, measured by the amount of attention paid to speech' (Labov 1972:208).

There is, Bell points out, very little empirical support for this claim. In the main evidence cited in its support, Bell himself argues that the speaker's inability to monitor his interviewer was more important than his inability to monitor his own production. He claims, then, that attention is at most a mechanism; the crucial dimension is more likely to be concerned with the social situation and in particular the audience.

The model that Bell proposes is developed from what he calls a style axiom: 'Variation on the style dimension within the speech of a single speaker derives from and echoes the variation which exists between speakers on the "social" dimension' (Bell 1984:151). In certain situations, speakers shift styles so that they might sound like other people; when someone moves to another region, he or she might also make a more permanent change in speech pattern; and whole groups can shift their speech to sound like other people. The essential motivating force for these shifts is the social value assigned to a given variety or feature and to the group which uses it. From this, Bell shows how intraspeaker variation (style) can be derived from interspeaker or social variation: each group has its own identity, which has value assigned by itself and others; as a result, the group differentiates its variety of language from others; its language is subsequently valued by itself and others; and others can choose to shift towards the group's language.

In support of his model, Bell argues that stylistic variation appears always to mirror and never to exceed social variation. A feature that marks stylistic variation will be a less strong version of a feature that indicates social variation.[10] The axiom has other important consequences: in language learning, the range of styles depends on the linguistic range to which a child is exposed.[11] In language loss or death, the reduction of social variation leads to loss of stylistic variation. Monolingual style shift is analogous to bilingual code switch.

Having established the basic match between intraspeaker stylistic variation and interspeaker social variation, Bell goes on to argue that both must have a similar explanation. He proposes the notion he calls 'audience design', and suggests that there are four levels of hearer to be taken into account, ranging in salience from addressee through auditor and overhearer to eavesdropper:

> The proposed framework . . . assumes that persons respond mainly to other persons, that speakers take most account of hearers in designing their talk. The *speaker* is first person, qualitatively apart from other interlocutors. The first person's characteristics account for speech differences between speakers. However, speakers design their style for their audience. Differences within the speech of a single speaker are accountable as the influence of the second person and some third persons, who together compose the audience to a speaker's utterances. (Bell 1984:159)

Bell proposes that just as the audience forms a continuum of salience, so its influence varies in strength. There are two confounding factors to be considered later, the one called initiative dealing with attempts to redefine the social situation rather than respond to it, and the second concerning responses to non-audience factors such as topic and setting. But audience is the main force, Bell argues.

The evidence supporting this notion can be divided into two parts, Bell suggests: part from the work on accommodation theory of Giles and others and part from recent variationist studies. Speech accommodation theory was developed to attempt to account for changes in speech style in the course of conversations: it deals, then, directly with the issue of intraspeaker variation. As summarized most recently (Beebe and Giles 1984, based largely on Street and Giles 1982), it has the following half-dozen basic propositions:

(1) People will attempt to converge linguistically toward the speech pattern believed to be characteristic of their recipients when they (a) desire their social approval and the perceived costs of so acting are proportionally lower than the reward anticipated, and/or (b) desire a high level of communicative efficiency, and (c) social norms are not perceived to dictate alternative speech strategies . . .
(2) The magnitude of such linguistic convergence will be a function of (a) the extent of the speakers' repertoires, and (b) factors (individual difference and environmental) that may increase the need for social approval and/or high communicational efficiency . . .
(3) Speech convergence will be positively evaluated by recipients when the resultant behaviour is (a) perceived as such psychologically (i.e. as integrative); (b) perceived to be an optimal sociolinguistic distance from them; and (c) attributed to positive intent . . .
(4) People will attempt to maintain their speech patterns or even diverge linguistically away from those believed characteristic of their recipients when they (a) define the encounter in intergroup terms and desire a positive ingroup identity, or (b) wish to dissociate personally from another in an individual encounter, or (c) wish to bring another's speech behaviours to a personally acceptable level . . .
(5) The magnitude of such divergence will be a function of (a) the extent of the speakers' repertoires, and (b) individual differences and contextual factors increasing the salience of the cognitive or affective functions in (4) . . .
(6) Speech maintenance and divergence will be negatively evaluated by recipients when the acts are perceived as psychologically diverging (i.e. dissociative), but favourably reacted to by observers who define the interaction in intergroup terms and who share a common, positively valued group membership with the speaker . . . (Beebe and Giles 1984:8–9)

As can be seen, the theory is far from simple, and continues to be refined. There is a good body of empirical data supporting its main conclusions, derived, as Bell complains, from studies that are linguistically naive in their use of such parameters as speech rate, utterance rate, and unsophisticated ratings of accent.

There is considerably more linguistic sophistication in a number of recent studies Bell cites of the effect of addressee on the speaker's style. The most comprehensive is that of Coupland (1980, 1984), who attempted to provide solid linguistic support for Giles's accommodation theory. For this study, Coupland collected tape recordings of interviews of an assistant in a travel agency with fifty-two different clients. The assistant herself and the clients were all local. The clients varied in social background, sex, and age, and consequently also in the degree to which their speech was marked as regional. Coupland wanted to study the degree to which the assistant's own speech varied in response to the person she was speaking to. To do this, he quantified four locally significant variables (h dropping, -ng simplification, intervocalic t voicing or tapping, and final consonant cluster simplification). Analysis showed that the occurrence of these features was correlated with the social class of the client. It further showed that the rating for the assistant's own usage varied and correlated with the client she was addressing. Reanalysis of Coupland's data by Bell shows that the convergence is consistent and massive towards lower class clients (on average over half-way), but less consistent in the case of higher class clients.

One complex issue that Bell raises is whether the speaker is responding to personal characteristics of the addressee, an assessment of the general style level of the addressee's speech, or the level of specific linguistic variables. There is evidence of the first, but reason to suspect that all three are involved. He further assumes that the theory needs to be refined to allow for the status and solidarity dimensions of the various studies involving address systems.

Bell also considers the effect of non-audience features, in particular of setting and topic. There is good evidence that each has an effect, and their relation has been shown by Fishman's development of the construct of domain (Fishman 1972). Bell argues interestingly that these two features might be considered to be derived from the addressee; while they are in specific cases independent factors determining stylistic level, they may well gain their effect from their association with the personal factors. As Breitborde (1983:33) puts it: 'At a more abstract level topic and locale may themselves be manifestations or concomitants of a person's social status.'

The final dimension that Bell considers in his article is the contrast between style design that is responsive to changes in the extralinguistic situation (audience or non-audience), and style design that itself initiates a change.[12] Initiative design depends ultimately on the norms of responsive design; it is the marked case. It may also vary socially and personally. Initiative shift is interpretable (in terms of the normal system) but not predictable. One of the essential features of it is to address a person as though they were someone else. It is most obvious, Bell suggests, when the shift is towards an absent third person, labelled a referee. 'Referees are third persons not physically present at an interaction but possessing such salience for a speaker that they influence speech even in their absence' (Bell 1984:186). In referee design, the speaker chooses a style as though the referee were an audience. The shift may be towards the speaker's own group (ingroup) or towards a group of which the speaker is not a member (outgroup). Ingroup referee design involves the social psychological surfacing of conflicting socio-political situations; examples Bell mentions are Wales and Montreal. It is essentially a short-term confrontation, a challenge that if successful will end the conversation. Outgroup referee design occurs when a speaker shifts to a prestigious style (or language) for a short time for an immediate purpose (rhetorical effect, for instance); it can also occur on a long-term basis and become institutionalized. This last is the case, Bell suggests, with diglossia, where an outgroup variety (geographically distinct in the case, for instance, of Haiti and Switzerland, and historically distant in the case of Greek and Arabic) forms the prestige variety. This kind of long-term pattern, though becoming the norm (and not the usual marked case of initiative behaviour), is in every other way like the short-term patterns:

> It involves divergence from the addressee; convergence to an absent referee, symbolic of identification with an outgroup; agreement by both speaker and addressee on the status of the outgroup and its language; inconsistent adoption of the forms of outgroup speech . . .; and absence of feedback from outgroup speakers. (Bell 1984:189)

This notion of the importance of group membership is basic to the development of two other sets of theories by Giles and his associates: ethnolinguistic identity theory, and intergroup theory. Ethnolinguistic identity theory is an attempt to deal with language and ethnicity in a social psychological framework. It is summarized in Beebe and Giles:

> Individuals are more likely to define themselves in ethnic terms and adopt strategies for positive linguistic differentiation (for example, divergence and linguistic creativity) to the extent that they (1) identify strongly with their ethnic group, which considers language an important dimension of its identity; (2) regard their group's relative status as changeable and illegitimate; (3) perceive their ingroup to have high ethnolinguistic vitality; (4) perceive their ingroup boundaries to be hard and closed; (5) identify strongly with few other social categories. . . (Beebe and Giles 1984:13)

In such cases, then, one finds the emphasizing of ethnic speech markers and the creation of new ones; in the converse case, where each of the named values is weak or low, there are the conditions for linguistic assimilation with the dominant group. From these principles is derived the intergroup theory of second language acquisition. Individuals in whom the five factors named above are strong would be unlikely to achieve high proficiency in a second language, which would be seen to detract from their ethnic identity; they would, following Gardner, avoid informal learning situations and learn in the classroom formal aspects of the language. Individuals in whom the five factors have weak values would be likely to have integrative motivation towards the second language, to seek out opportunities for informal learning, to work to gain the social and communicative aspects of the second language. The features of the approach relevant to second language learning may be summarized in two complex conditions for linguistic convergence and divergence:

Condition 48
Linguistic Convergence condition (typical, graded): Prefer to learn a language when
(a) *you desire the social approval of its speakers, and/or*
(b) *you see strong value in being able to communicate with its speakers, and/or*
(c) *there are no social norms providing other methods of communicating with speakers of that language, and/or*
(d) *your learning is reinforced or encouraged by speakers of the language.*

Condition 49
Linguistic Divergence condition (typical, graded): Prefer not to learn a language if
(a) *you wish to stress your continued membership of your own language community, and/or*
(b) *you wish to stress your dissociation from speakers of the language, and/or*
(c) *you wish speakers of that language to learn your language.*

The acculturation model

In a somewhat different approach to the same issue, John Schumann has since 1975 been working on a model that tries to clarify the importance of both social and affective factors on second language learning. Schumann's work falls into two distinct parts, for, though connected, there are two separate claims: one concerns the analogy of second language learning to pidginization and decreolization, which I will talk about in Chapter 11, and the second, to be considered here, concerns a search for a social and psychological explanation of forces that determine how successful the process of learning can be. We look first, then, at the acculturation model without reference to the pidginization hypothesis, even though the latter is the process by which it has its effect.

There are, Schumann (1986) suggests, nine classes of factors which can influence second language acquisition: apart from social and affective factors, there are personality, cognitive, biological, aptitude, personal, input, and instructional factors. Social and affective factors cluster, he suggests, into a single variable which he calls *acculturation*.[13]

Acculturation is 'a[14] major causal variable in SLA [Second Language Acquisition]' and is defined as 'the social and psychological integration of the learner with the target language (TL) group'.[15] Any learner, he suggests, can be placed on a continuum ranging from 'social and psychological distance' to 'social and psychological proximity' to speakers of the second language, and 'the learner will acquire the second language only to the degree that he acculturates'.

There are two kinds of acculturation: type one involves social integration and sufficient contacts with the second language group, and psychological openness 'such that input to which he is exposed becomes intake'. Type two has 'all the characteristics of type one' except that the learner looks on the second language group as a reference group, one whose way of life he or she wants to adopt.[16]

Schumann discusses the social variables involved in acculturation in turn. The two groups involved (the second language learning group and the target language group) may be related in different ways. First is the factor of social dominance; a group that is dominant (politically, economically, culturally, technically) will tend not to learn the language of the group that is dominated. Similarly, the social distance caused by subordination (the lack of easy upward mobility identified by Joshua Fishman) will decrease the likelihood of the dominated group learning the language of the dominant.

There are next three integration strategies: assimilation, whereby the second language group gives up its own values and life style, and also learns the language of the target group; preservation, where it maintains its own way of life, rejects that of the other group, and so increases social distance and fails to learn the second language; and adaptation (in Schumann's earlier papers called acculturation), where there are varying degrees of mix and so varying degrees of distance and language learning.

The next social factor is enclosure, which seems to be the extent to which the two groups maintain separate social institutions ('churches, schools, clubs, recreational facilities, crafts, professions, and trades') or share them. Low enclosure (shared institutions) leads to increased opportunities for contact and language acquisition. (There seems to be no directionality in this factor.)

Another two factors affecting opportunities for contact are cohesiveness (different in an unexplained way from enclosure) and size. On the other hand, congruence or similarity between the two cultures will increase social contact and facilitate second language learning (again, with no notion of directionality). Positive attitudes between the two groups will make second language learning more probable. So will the second language learning group's intended length of residence in the country of the target language group.

The factors that Schumann considers are those generally discussed in the literature on language maintenance. The model is sparser than the

Kloss (1968) list of factors (most of which, like Schumann's, lack directionality); it is less parsimonious than Fishman's (the existence of interactive upward social mobility) and fails to take account of a great deal of more sophisticated work in the field.

Schumann suggests the main difference between social and affective variables is that the latter deal with individuals who may learn in spite of social conditions. He differs in this from Gardner, who, as we will see in the next chapter, wants to use social context to set attitudes which then determine individual motivation. Schumann discusses four factors. Language shock refers to the fear of appearing comic, infantile, ridiculous, and the loss of accuracy of expression and 'narcissistic gratification' available with the native language. Culture shock is 'the anxiety resulting from the disorientation encountered upon entering a new culture' and discourages 'the effort necessary to become bilingual'. Motivation is a complex construct, with integrative and instrumental motivations varying (as we have noted) according to setting. Finally, there is 'ego-permeability' as proposed by Guiora. 'In sum, if language shock and cultural shock are not overcome and if the learner does not have sufficient and appropriate motivation and ego-permeability, then he will not fully acculturate and hence will not acquire the second language fully' (Schumann 1986:384).

Schumann's acculturation model has as its main hypothesis that second language learning is just one aspect of acculturation; in an idealized model, one will learn a second language to the degree that one is acculturated. The causal chain may work like this:

> Acculturation as a remote cause brings the learner into contact with TL [Target Language] speakers. Verbal interaction with those speakers as a proximate cause brings about the negotiation of appropriate input which, then, operates as the immediate cause of language acquisition. Acculturation, then, is of particular importance because it initiates the chain of causality. (Schumann 1986:385)

The model, Schumann himself persists in claiming, deals only with second language acquisition 'under conditions of immigration where learning takes place without instruction' and so has nothing to say about 'language teaching'. Note, however, that in contrast to Gardner and Lambert's proposal that motivation is most important in deciding the level achieved, and Schumann's own work on pidginization, this paper (Schumann 1986) suggests that acculturation is only important as initiating the chain. The model also seems to take the Monitor Model as its basis, without any clear consideration of how it interacts with it.

Schumann describes recent studies to 'test the model'. There is the problem posed to both the acculturation and the Extended Monitor Model by a case described by Schmidt (1983) of a Japanese who emigrated to Hawaii where, as an artist, he had all the possible motivation, social and psychological proximity, and opportunities for conversation (including extensive interaction with English speakers); nevertheless, he developed a high degree of communicative competence but not 'comparable linguistic competence' (that is, he did not become a grammatical speaker). Another case study providing unclear evidence is an MA thesis by K.A. Kitch (1982), where an adult's language development seems to match psychological but not social distance, causing problems for the model which does not distinguish the two. An MA thesis by J.P. Kelley (1982) studies six Spanish speaking adults who came to the US as adults (20–34 years old), had lived here at least nine years, had little or no instruction, and a very low level of English. There was no relation (or perhaps a negative one) between acculturation measures and language proficiency.

A Ph. D. dissertation by Stauble (1981) compares six Japanese and six Spanish speakers of English; acculturation scores did not predict proficiency. Another Ph. D. dissertation by R. Maple (1982) explores the notion of social distance. A group of 190 Spanish-speaking students in an intensive language programme at Austin completed three questionnaires on social distance. The social distance variables, and also two other predictors 'social class and marital status' account for 15–25 per cent of the variation in gains over the course. Schumann is unhappy with these results, for they show the acculturation model seeming to work with a case for which it is not intended, where there is formal instruction and not informal interaction of immigrants. Further, Maple treats dominance as domination rather than as superiority. Finally, Maple fails to deal with psychological distance.

Considering these studies, and proposals by other scholars calling for testing of the model on a large sample, Schumann is finally pessimistic; he believes the model may be very difficult to test. There would be technical problems with the measures of acculturation and of language proficiency used, and with the statistical techniques. Finally, none of the models would be able to handle the dynamic nature of the process. The earlier version of the paper (1984) wondered whether this model, or any other social science model is in fact testable, and whether or not one can know if the ultimate truth is ever knowable; the 1986 version is cautious but more hopeful.

Schumann's acculturation model is important for its forthright attempt to show the relevance of social factors to informal language learning. It is handicapped by its lack of generalization to all kinds of second language learning and by its tendency to assume direct effect of the social factors on the learning process. I argue for indirect effects rather; effects in providing opportunities for learning that will be looked at in Chapter 11, and effects in the establishment of attitude and motivation that will be considered in the next chapter, at the end of which the implications of Schumann's proposals will be seen more clearly.

Notes

1   For more detailed discussion, see Spolsky (1978b).
2   Just as there is no required size for a speech community for sociolinguistic purposes, so a speech community for educational purposes is not limited. I have suggested (Spolsky 1974) that the minimum useful starting point is a community served by a single school; empirical evidence will permit building larger groups when they are significant.
3   Stewart (1968) proposed a language census that gives the exact or estimated number of speakers of all language varieties used in the community being studied.
4   See Amara and Spolsky (1986).
5   See Spolsky and Cooper (1986).
6   By the term 'community-based' I mean to exclude the writing system, dictionary, and grammar book that may have been developed by anthropologists, linguists, or missionaries for their own purposes, but that have not been taken over for extensive indigenous use. See Spolsky (1981).
7   It is necessary, then, to distinguish between dialects and standardized regional varieties of a language. This helps account for the discomfort caused to educational systems by linguists who argue for the acceptability of local standards. A school system that wants to teach what it considers to be standard English is not happy to be told that West Indian English or Singapore English or any of the other new Englishes (to use Kachru's term) deserves to serve as a model. (See, for example, Quirk 1987.)
8   Note the special exceptions in attempts to teach Classical Languages informally (for example, the Direct Method for Latin) or to teach vernaculars formally (for example, programmes in spoken Arabic).
9   I have suggested this in a model proposed for the description and evaluation of bilingual education, defined so as to include second language teaching (Spolsky, Green, and Read 1976; Spolsky 1978b).
10 Bell recognizes possible exceptions to this principle, one in hypercorrection where there is exaggerated style shift as a group tries to break out of its social class, and the other with certain 'hyperstyle' cases that co-occur with ritualized courtesy.
11 The fact that foreign language learners tend to be one-style speakers is a result of the limited social variation in their learning situations.

12 As he points out, this is equivalent to the distinction between situational and metaphorical switching in Blom and Gumperz (1972).

13 Somewhat confusingly, 'acculturation' is also *one* of the twelve factors listed as social factors; a footnote in the 1984 preliminary version of the paper suggests renaming acculturation on this chart adaptation, and this is done in the text of the 1986 version but not in the chart in Table 1.

14 'The' major variable in the 1984 version.

15 In the footnote in the 1984 version, it is also defined as 'social and psychological contact with speakers of the TL [Target Language]'.

16 See Spolsky (1969a) for discussion of the membership group—reference group distinction.

10 Attitudes and motivation

Language learning motivation

The analysis of social context in the last chapter makes it possible to return to the individual learner and ask how social effects are carried into language learning. The first connection is in the development of motivation. In a paper that sets out an important model for research in foreign language teaching that I used as the basis for a formula at the end of Chapter 1, Carroll (1962) suggested that the critical factors are aptitude, opportunity or method, and motivation, the latter predicting the amount of time a learner would apply to the task of language learning. Carroll's formula may be rewritten as a set of graded conditions:

Condition 50
Aptitude condition (typical, graded): The greater a learner's aptitude, the faster he or she will learn all parts of the second language.

Condition 51
Exposure condition (necessary, graded): The more time spent learning any aspect of a second language, the more will be learned.

Condition 52
Motivation condition (typical, graded): The more motivation a learner has, the more time he or she will spend learning an aspect of a second language.

The discussion of language aptitude in Chapter 7 led to the conclusion that while there is evidence for its relevance in a number of studies, it needs more precise qualification according to the goal of learning; there are different aspects of aptitude that are relevant to different situations and kinds of learning. Thus, it was divided into three more precisely stated conditions, dealing with the effect of sound discrimination aptitude on control of the spoken language, of memory on learning lexicon, and of grammatical sensitivity or analytical ability on the speed of learning grammar.[1] The Exposure condition, which will be discussed in Chapters 11 and 12, and the Motivation condition are similarly at present too grossly stated to permit empirical testing.

To be more specific about motivation, three questions arise: Where does motivation come from? Is there one kind of motivation, or more?

What parts of second language learning does motivation (of whatever kind) influence?

In one of the earliest statements on motivation in second language learning, Gardner and Lambert (1959) suggested that an individual's motivation to learn a second language is controlled by his 'attitudes towards the other group in particular and by his orientation to the learning task itself'. Of all school subjects, language learning is the one where attitude is specially relevant: Gardner points out that:

> Language courses are different from other curriculum topics. They require that the individual incorporates elements from another culture. As a consequence, reactions to the other culture become important considerations. Furthermore, because the material is not merely an extension of the students' own cultural heritage, the dynamics of the classroom and the methodology assume greater importance than they do in other school topics. (Gardner 1985:8)

For Gardner and Lambert, motivation comes from attitude. Attitude itself is to be measured by asking a subject to evaluate an object: '. . . from an operational point of view, an individual's attitude is *an evaluative reaction to some referent or attitude object, inferred on the basis of the individual's beliefs or opinions about the referent*' (op.cit.:9). In practical terms, then, an attitude is a construct derived from a subject's answers to a number of questions about an object. Its establishment is subject to all the normal worries of the validity of the instrument used and of the honesty of the subject's answers to the questions.

There are two significant kinds of attitude, Gardner believes: attitudes to the people who speak the target language, and attitudes to the practical use to which the learner assumes he or she can put the language being learned. Gardner suggests that the effects of the two kinds of attitude are different: 'whereas the first set of attitudes is fairly consistently related to achievement, the second shows a more variable set of relationships' (op.cit.:39).

From studies summarized in Gardner (1985), the measures most relevant to French proficiency are attitudes towards learning French and interest in foreign languages; the least relevant are evaluation of the French teacher and attitudes towards French Canadians. Overall, he concludes that: 'It seems clear . . . that attitude measures account for a significant and meaningful proportion of the variance in second language achievement and that some attitude variables are more relevant than others' (op.cit.:50).

Attitudes do not have direct influence on learning, but they lead to motivation which does: 'Motivation in the present context refers to the combination of effort plus desire to achieve the goal of learning plus favourable attitudes towards learning the language' (op.cit.:10). Motivation itself is a complex construct, as Gardner remarks: '. . . motivation involves four aspects, a goal, effortful behaviour, a desire to attain the goal and favourable attitudes towards the activity in question. These four aspects are not unidimensional . . .' (op.cit.:50). We might summarize this claim so far by setting a condition on attitudes leading to motivation, as follows:

Condition 53
Attitude condition (typical, graded): A learner's attitudes affect the development of motivation.

Just as there are two kinds of attitude, so there are also two kinds of motivation. Lambert describes the first of these like this:

> One would expect that if the student is to be successful in his attempt to learn another social group's language he must be both able and willing to adopt various aspects of behaviour, including verbal behaviour, which characterize members of the other linguistic-cultural group. The learner's ethnocentric tendencies and his attitudes towards the other group are believed to determine his success in learning the new language. His motivation to learn is thought to be determined by both his attitudes and by the type of orientation he has toward learning a second language. (Lambert 1967:102)

In a series of studies, collected in Gardner and Lambert (1972), a distinction was proposed between integrative orientation, characterized by those who learn the second language in order to identify themselves with the second language speaking group and ultimately join it, and instrumental orientation described as any more practical reason for learning. Gardner later has a modified definition:

> Integrative reasons are defined as those which indicate an interest in learning the language in order to meet and communicate with members of the second language community. Instrumental reasons refer to those reasons which stress the pragmatic aspects of learning the second language, without any particular interest in communicating with the second language community. (Gardner, Smythe, and Brunet 1977:244)

In Lambert and Gardner's earlier papers, it was originally held that integrative orientation was better than instrumental, or at least that it was necessary to achieve native-like proficiency in pronunciation and a native-like semantic system. Note that this is a further specification of the application of the Linguistic Convergence and Divergence conditions discussed in Chapter 9. The specific effect of integrative motivation, itself a product of integrative orientation or attitudes towards speakers of the target language, is set out in the following Integrative Motivation condition.

Condition 54
Integrative Motivation condition (typical, graded): Integrative orien-
tation, a cluster of favourable attitudes to the speakers of the target
language, has a positive effect on the learning of a second language, and
in particular on the development of a native-like pronunciation and
semantic system.

It should be noted that many subsequent studies have not, however, treated integrative motivation as limited to pronunciation and semantics, but have looked for influence on all aspects of second language learning.

The general conclusions of the research into the differential effects of integrative and instrumental motivations over the years are summed up in Gardner, Smythe, and Brunet:

> These studies were conducted in the context of traditional language programmes where students study the language as part of their standard school curriculum. In general, these studies are in agreement showing that measures of achievement in the second language are substantially related to measures of attitudes and motivation. Examples of such measures include attitudes towards French speaking people, the French language, the course and teacher, desire to learn French, and interest in learning French for either integrative or instrumental reasons. (Gardner, Smythe, and Brunet 1977:243–4)

There has been criticism of the work on motivation that it has depended on the use of factor analysis; studies by Oller and others using other techniques have not shown its existence.[2] Gardner, however, holds his position:

> In general, most but not all of the factor analytic studies support the notion of an integrative motive as being important in second language acquisition, while the multiple regression studies appear to cast doubt on this conclusion. . . Obviously, I am biased, but it is my opinion that the weight of evidence supports the generalization that an integrative motive does facilitate second language acquisition . . . (Gardner 1985:63)

He analyses studies starting with Gardner and Lambert (1959) and up to Lalonde (1982): 'Many of them either produce a unitary integrative motive factor or a set of factors which demonstrate some commonality between the three major components, integrativeness, attitudes toward the learning situation and motivation' (Gardner 1985:72). These three factors, then, turn out to share some variance in common with second language achievement. Gardner is not convinced by contradictory evidence, suggesting that it could result from failure to control for effects of training; he also sees methodological problems with multiple regression analysis. He concludes:

Based on the literature review . . ., it seems clear that achievement in a second language is influenced by attitudinal/motivational characteristics. Postulating that achievement in a second language is promoted by an integrative motive is not tantamount to saying that this is the only cause or predictor. Undoubtedly many factors operate in the development of second language proficiency. This is only one—but it and language aptitude are the only two individual differences which have been well documented to date as being implicated in the language learning process. (op.cit.:83)

When one looks not at the effect on language achievement (as measured by various kinds of language tests) but on morpheme development, the results are less clear, reflecting a critical difference between microlevel and macrolevel.

In any statistical study where we wish to interpret correlational results, we need to consider the question of causality: it is a serious error to assume without further checking that correlation means cause. If certain kinds of attitude are correlated with higher achievement, might not the direction of cause be from achievement to cause? Might not those learners with higher ability in a language consequently have better attitudes to the language and its speakers? Even if the main causal effect is from attitude to achievement, might there not also be a reciprocal flow from achievement to attitude? While one focus of research has been on attitude and motivation as a cause, they have also been studied as a result. Such studies ask, in other words, about the effect that a programme can have on attitudes and motivations, looking at non-linguistic outcomes of the learning process.

One early study (Lambert, Gardner, Barik, and Tunstall 1963) had shown some changes in attitudes in students on summer intensive French courses, with in particular increases in *anomie*. As the students' French proficiency increased, they became less certain of their identity, and subsequently stopped following the rule to speak only French.

Gardner, Smythe, and Brunet (1977) looked at a similar group—sixty-two Ontario high school students who had been selected after volunteering for an intensive five-week French as a second language programme in a residential environment (with weekends at home). The students were assessed on twenty-three different measures of attitude and motivation.[3] A large number of proficiency measures were taken,[4] on the basis of which the students were divided into three groups: beginners, intermediate, and advanced. The groups were found to vary significantly in attitude scores on six of the twenty-three measures: the intermediate students had the highest level of need achievement; the beginners were most and the advanced students least anxious; the beginners were more ethnocentric than the other groups; they also saw the course as more difficult. The advanced group saw more teacher rapport (there was in fact more conversation and less drill in this class). The intermediate students had the least interest in continuing and the least favourable attitudes to French Canadians. Looking at changes over the course, students tended at the end of the course to be more ethnocentric, less interested in foreign languages, and less integrative in their orientation. Second, they became less anxious in class, found the course less difficult, were more motivated to learn French, and made greater use of opportunities to use French. Changes in self-rating were interesting: they dropped in the second week, but showed recognition of improvement after that. The teachers reported continual improvement. The tests also showed considerable increase in achievement.

Gardner, Smythe, and Clément (1979) extended the 1977 study to a group of adult learners: a sample of eighty-nine Canadians and one of sixty-five Americans studying in five- and six-week intensive French programmes in northern Quebec. The design was similar: eighteen scales tested at the beginning and end of the course, two measures of satisfaction, and pre- and post-testing of oral expression and aural comprehension. After standardization, the variables were factor analysed, and the principal factors recognized for the Canadian sample were integrative motivation (favourable attitudes to learning French, a strong desire to learn French, favourable attitudes to bilingualism and French Canadians, integrative reasons for learning, and high need achievement, satisfaction with the programme and its outcomes, and French oral expression); French achievement (aural proficiency before the course and oral and aural proficiency after it), and anxiety (nervous in classroom and speaking French outside, highly self-critical, and integrative rather than instrumental reasons). For the American sample, the same factors emerged, but the first was not related to satisfaction with the course or with achievement in it; satisfaction with the course loaded on the second factor; and factor three is similar to the Canadian sample. In comparing pre- and post-test scores, there were decreases in anxiety, increases in oral and aural ability, and the Canadian students were more likely to think in French when speaking it. However, the Canadian subjects became less positive towards bilingualism, and the Americans, while having 'a greater desire to learn French' had less interest in learning French for integrative reasons, less favourable attitudes towards learning French and to French Canadians. The differences between the two groups were, it was hypothesized, to be explained socio-culturally: the American subjects were older, had had less time learning French, and came from a milieu where French Canadians were not a major group.

The general weight of these studies has been to suggest that while greater motivation and better attitudes lead to better learning, the converse is not in fact true: learning another group's language does not necessarily improve one's attitude to the group. Gardner concludes his analysis with a statement that 'changes in social attitudes assessed at the time may be greatest where the programmes involve novel experiences of rather brief duration' (1985:106). He suspects that it is the novelty of the programme rather than the process of learning a second language that motivates attitude change.

The socio-educational model

As I mentioned in the first chapter, Gardner has expanded on the work he began with Lambert and formalized it into what he now calls a 'socio-educational model' of second language acquisition with four variables summarizing individual differences: intelligence, language aptitude, motivation, and situational anxiety. How important each of these is depends on the beliefs of the community as to the values of language learning. While all are important in formal classroom learning, motivation and situational anxiety are dominant in informal learning contexts, outside the classroom (for example, going to a movie). Second language proficiency can develop in both contexts, but as motivation and situational anxiety will determine the extent to which students take advantage of the opportunity for informal contexts, their importance is increased (Gardner 1979).

Following this model, Gardner, Lalonde, and Pierson (1983) set out to investigate the causal aspect of attitudes in second language learning. According to Gardner's socio-educational model, a student's motivation is influenced by two kinds of attitudes. The first is integrativeness, now more precisely defined as 'a cluster of attitudes relating to outgroups and foreign languages in general as well as attitudes toward the specific language community and integrative orientations to language study' (Gardner, Lalonde, and Pierson (1983:2). The second is attitudes towards the language learning situation as a whole, including the teacher and the course itself. Motivation itself has three components: attitudes towards learning the second language, desire to learn the language, and effort made to learn the language. All three are involved if the student is 'truly motivated'. Achievement can influence attitude, but the 'primary causal relationship' is that achievement is the result of attitude and motivation. The socio-educational model further holds that 'cultural beliefs about the second language community will influence both the nature and the role played by attitudes in the language learning process' (op.cit.:3).

In the 1983 study, this last factor was controlled by carrying out the research in a region where the second language was not widely used; cultural beliefs of the subjects about learning the language were also tested. The study involved formulating the theory to make it amenable to causal modelling procedures. The technique that Gardner has chosen to use is the Linear Structural Relations analysis (LISREL) developed by

Joreskog and Sorbom (1978). The technique requires the researcher to carry out a maximum likelihood factor analysis and then check the significance of the factor loadings for the variables related to the concept; it sets up causal relationships among latent variables.

The reformulated socio-educational model postulated two latent variables (theoretical constructs), built on cultural beliefs: importance of language objectives and opportunities to use the language. These influence two attitudinal latent variables: integrativeness and attitudes towards the language learning situation. These in turn determine the individual's level of motivation. Motivation and situational anxiety determine second language achievement. In addition, initial proficiency is assumed to influence both final achievement and situational anxiety.

The study was carried out with 140 first-year French students at the University of Regina. Eighteen indicator variables were collected in questionnaires.[5] The measures were obtained at various times over an academic term. The final causal model supports the following con- clusions. The indicator variables do in fact group into the latent variables as hypothesized. There are three independent latent variables: importance of language objectives, opportunities to use the language, and initial proficiency. Importance of language objectives and oppor- tunities to use the language are both causally related to integrativeness, but only the first is causally related to attitudes to the language learning situation. Integrativeness and attitude towards the learning situation are, as hypothesized, causally linked to motivation, which in turn causes achievement. Note that attitudes affect motivation, but are not directly linked to achievement. Also, as hypothesized, prior proficiency affects achievement and situational anxiety. However, situational anxiety does not turn out to be a causal factor in final achievement. Another unanticipated finding is the reciprocal effect between achievement and motivation (but not prior achievement). The study as a whole is an important one in clarifying the model and in suggesting how precision can be added to the work. Gardner (1985) emphasizes the fact that his model is empirical and developing; he does not claim it to be true or final.

One issue of concern in some of the studies related to this work is in the definition of orientation. Clément and Kruidenier (1983) discuss some of the ambiguities in definitions of integrative and instrumental motivation: various researchers seem to classify reasons differently. There are also contextual or cultural differences, depending on social context, ethnicity, and familiarity with the target group. They therefore set out to clarify the definitions and so be able to reconcile earlier studies. They developed a questionnaire with thirty-seven orientation items from previous studies and gave it to eight groups of eleventh grade students selected for differences of setting (uni- or multicultural setting, with London and Quebec considered unicultural and Ottawa multicultural), language (anglophones and francophones), and official or minority languages being learned (French and English official, Spanish minority). Using factor analysis, they studied the responses of each group. Four orientations were common to all groups: 'Students learned a second language to achieve pragmatic goals (i.e., the instrumental orientation), to travel, to seek new friendships, and to acquire knowledge' (Clément and Kruidenier 1983:286). There were other factors important to specific groups. There was no support for 'the construct validity of a general integrative motivation'. Among franco-phones, it emerged coupled with a desire to become influential in one's own community; among anglophones it was found only among the dominant group in a multicultural setting. They conclude that there is no clear justification for belief in the universality and exhaustiveness of the integrative-instrumental distinction.

This argument is supported by research reported by Hidalgo (1986), who studied language attitudes of inhabitants of Juarez, a Mexican city on the border with the US, in which there was no evidence of distinction between integrative and instrumental motivation; Hidalgo argues that this is a result of the special social situation of the city. However, Ely (1986b) in a study of first year university students of Spanish identifies two influential attitudinal clusters, one identifiable as integrative and one as instrumental. A third cluster, learning because it is a requirement, does not predict achievement.

Another investigation of the model is provided by Genesee, Rogers, and Holobow (1983). They stress the social context of the relevance of integrativeness, and suggest adding to clarify its role a measure of the learner's expectations from the speakers of the target language. In their study, English-speaking Canadian students were asked both why they were learning French and why they thought French-speaking Canadians wanted them to learn French. Summarizing the conclusions of what is essentially a pilot study, they found that 'SL [Second Language] learners' perceptions of the TL [Target Language] group's support for learning their language is positively correlated with the learners' self-rated proficiency in the language and to their reported willingness to belong to social groups that include members of the TL group' (1983:220). The learner's own motivations were, however, the only predictor of performance in a listening comprehension test and the main predictors of performance in other tests.

In trying to pin down the directness of relationship between attitudes, motivation, and second language learning, Lalonde and Gardner (1984) collected data in six different Canadian regions over a two year period. In their study, they established three composite measures. The first is motivation, 'the individual's total drive to learn the second language . . . a combination of effort, desire, and affective reaction toward learning French'. The second composite measure is integrativeness, a positive orientation to French speakers and other groups. The third is attitudes to the learning situation, the learner's evaluation of the course and teacher. The three composites were generally good predictors of proficiency measure, with the motivational measure significantly better than the other two, thus supporting Gardner's claim that motivation is the more direct factor, itself influenced by the other two.

The work surveyed in this chapter sets the requirement for a different statement of conditions. Gardner's studies make clear that attitude has an indirect rather than a direct effect on second language learning. If he is correct, the model will be stronger if it allows for a two-stage effect, with attitude learning to motivation, and motivation to learning. In fact, I would argue for more levels: attitude is derivable in some measure from social context, and motivation is expressed in the learner's strategies or behaviours in a specific learning situation.[6] The outcomes of attitude conditions, this would mean, need to be stated as motivations rather than as linguistic outcomes. Thus, favourable attitudes to speakers of a language, its culture, and its country lead to integrativeness (a special kind of motivation), and favourable attitudes to school, to a language as a school subject, and to the person who teaches it, lead to positive motivation.

The question of attitude may provide an explanation of the age differences discussed earlier. An emphasis on affective factors like attitude and on personality offers an alternative hypothesis to those who argue that the explanation of differences between children and adults is a critical period, biologically determined. It has the decided advantage of taking a factor considered true of all children (for example, language ego-permeability as in Guiora) and suggesting that it is differentially true of adults; this is surely more easily credible than the notion of a language acquisition device that sometimes does not decay but usually does. These notions are clearly formulated by Taylor (1974), who argues that adult and child second language learners seem to use the same processes and strategies, if in slightly different mixes. Thus,

> There is no cognitive reason to assume that adults will be less efficient than children in language learning. In fact, as already suggested, it seems logical to assume that the adult's more advanced cognitive maturity would allow him to deal with the abstract nature of language even better than children. If we reject a hypothesis which calls for a cognitive deficiency in adults, we are left with the alternative of accepting a non-cognitive deficiency—one based on affective measures—to account for the lack of uniform success in adult second language acquisition. (Taylor 1974:32–33)

Attitudes, motivation, and acculturation

Gardner's model derives from empirical studies within the context of social psychology; Schumann's work described at the end of the last chapter is more based on research in sociolinguistics. A very interesting contrast between Gardner and Schumann is that each seems to want to restrict his work to dissimilar situations: Gardner's is presented as a model of school language learning and Schumann's as a potential model of natural second language learning.[7] But as I argued in the first chapter, this distinction is one that needs to be accounted for by a general theory of second language learning and not used as the basis for restriction of the scope of the theory. The two approaches do in fact fit together quite well. Even in the pure classroom learning situation, there are attitudes resulting from the presence of at least a stereotype of the other language culture (in the textual material for instance, or represented by the teacher); even in natural language learning situations, there are choices to be made of opportunities for language use, and interlocutors who attempt to teach.[8]

Gardner's model is a good starting point for the attempt to describe the conditions considered in this chapter. His model in its latest version includes a number of important constructs dealt with throughout this book: achievement, the complexity of which was discussed in Chapters 2 to 5; initial proficiency (the influence of first language knowledge was considered in Chapter 8); opportunity to use the language, which will be looked at in Chapter 11; cultural beliefs about the importance of language objectives, which were considered in Chapter 9 as part of the sociolinguistic context within which all language learning and teaching takes place; situational anxiety, which was discussed in Chapter 7; and finally the attitude to the language learning situation, which relates to attitude to teacher and school.

What Gardner labels integrativeness is similar in important ways to Schumann's notion of acculturation, which is the sum of a complex set of attitudes to the language (or variety of language) being learned, the social functions for which it may be used, the learner's views (whether based on experience or not) of the people who the learner believes (rightly or wrongly) use the language (natively or not), and the learner's belief of the effect on his or her own self-identification, character, or power, if he or she comes to use the language in a specific way.

In his description of the socio-educational model, Gardner (1983) adds the second language learning situation to the foreign language learning situation by adding to his model the notion of formal and informal language acquisition contexts. The model in this version is as follows. Cultural beliefs with a social milieu influence the development of two sets of attitudinal variables, the one towards the other language community (integrativeness) and the other towards the learning situation. These in turn influence motivation, which is itself composed of effort towards a goal, desire to achieve the goal, and positive affect towards the goal. Two individual variables, motivation on the one hand

and language aptitude on the other, interact with formal and informal second language acquisition contexts to lead to second language proficiency, the linguistic outcome of the process. Both aptitude and motivation are equally important in the foreign language classroom; motivation is likely to be more important in informal contexts. Besides linguistic outcomes, there are non-linguistic ones such as interest in learning the language, and desire to learn more.

Gardner reports that there is no clear evidence yet of the links between social milieu and the individual attitudinal variables. Nor has the full model been tested. Gardner refers in particular to the lack of testing in informal situations:

> . . . this book is concerned primarily with the student in the formal language class. It may be that the findings and conclusions discussed here are applicable to individuals who develop second language proficiency in any context, but the important point is that this generalization must be put to empirical testing. (Gardner 1985:4)

But besides the general test of the earlier version referred to previously in the chapter, he reports on studies supporting certain deductions to be made from the model. Studies by Gliksman (1976) and Naiman, Fröhlich, Stern, and Todesco (1978) have both shown that students classified as integratively motivated were more active (more likely to volunteer answers) in a foreign language classroom. Other studies he cites show that students who are integratively motivated are more likely to seek occasions for informal interaction (for example, taking part in excursions) and less likely to drop out of language classes. There have also been a number of studies on non-linguistic outcomes. Some earlier studies suggested that attitudes were in fact influenced by achievement: that in cases of low initial motivation and poor achievement, negative attitudes would be reinforced; that students who do well will have better motivation and students who do poorly will have less favourable attitudes. Gardner reports on a study he has conducted that contradicts these results: he found that while attitudes and motivation are in fact higher for the better student, and while as a general rule attitudes and motivation become lower in the course of instruction, the changes are not affected by degree of success. Thus, while there is evidence that higher motivation leads to increased success, there is neither evidence of the effect of success on motivation nor evidence that language learning leads to more positive attitudes towards the groups whose language is being learned.

Gardner's model is a major development in understanding the relation between attitudes and second language learning. Its greatest weakness is in not demonstrating the relationship between social milieu and attitudes, but this is because its basis is not sociolinguistics but social psychology. It is from the sociolinguistic factors listed by Schumann that we can expect to learn about the establishment of the social values that work in the model: it is sociolinguistics that should show the values established for the various varieties of language that are potential goals for a learner.

Social basis of motivation

While there is some serious question about the way to distinguish instrumental and integrative motivation, there remains basic value in the distinction. To see this, we might try distinguishing social from all other motivations. A language may be learned for any one or any collection of practical reasons. The importance of these reasons to the learner will determine what degree of effort he or she will make, what cost he or she will pay for the learning. A significant part of these reasons and of this potential cost involves socially determined factors: in other words, the social dimension may be seen as spreading itself over the other.

Let us take a simple example. I want to buy food regularly from a seller on my street whose native language is different from mine. If this were the only factor involved, I would probably be willing to learn the few words or phrases needed to make this regular transaction work; but as selling to me is likely to be more important to him than my buying from him is to me, there will be greater practical pressure on him to learn my language.

We could add to this simple model more buyers and sellers, and explore how this will increase the likelihood of buyer or seller learning the other language.[9] But as long as we restrict our attention to our simple model, with as driving force a simple economic transaction, we are dealing with a largely instrumental situation. Even here, though, the instrumental value of pleasing the other party—I am more likely to buy from someone with whom it is comfortable for me to talk, he is more likely to give good service to someone with whom he is comfortable— gives reason for convergence, bringing in the social dimension.

The social dimension becomes obviously important when the language choice is related to a wider social context (for example, my language is socially dominant, his is that of the ruled group) or when the social relation itself is valued as much as the practical business (for example, we are trying to be good neighbours or fellow-citizens as well as seller and buyer). And for either of us, the need to learn a new language is, as Guiora suggested, a challenging of our personal identity so that this will be added to the complex model explaining whether or not we will pay the cost.

It seems to me useful to see as underlying language attitude a set of norms for language choice which are themselves best represented by a set of preference rules: rules that apply typically but not necessarily, and the weighting or salience of which is dependent on situations and attitudes. There appear to be at least two necessary conditions for choice of language for communication:

(i)   Knowledge Condition on Language Choice (necessary): Use (speak, write) a language which you know.

(ii) Communication Condition on Language Choice (necessary): Use (speak, write) a language known by the person you want to communicate with.

While knowing a language is a gradient condition, that is to say, it is measured on a continuum (or perhaps, rather, on a number of continua) and not as a binary decision, the necessary condition for a well-formed linguistic interaction is that both speaker/writer and listener/reader can achieve a minimal threshold level of understanding. These two conditions explain why one of the first tasks that parents accept with a newborn child is teaching it their language, i.e. making sure that it can meet the Communication condition. Similarly, these two conditions explain why the continued presence of a significant monolingual in the home will ensure that other members of the family will know that language. In communication with oneself (counting, dreaming, writing notes), it is obvious that the speaker/writer has the fullest freedom. These two conditions translate into an instrumental language learning or teaching condition, as follows:

Condition 55
Instrumental Language Learning or Teaching condition (typical,[10] graded): If you need to speak to someone who does not know your language, you can learn that person's language or help that person to learn your language.

When the two necessary conditions on language choice have been met, that is, when the two interlocutors are (or can be expected to be) bilingual in the same two languages, other conditions apply. The first pair relates to a preference according to how well the language is known by each of them.

(iii) Topic Condition on Language Choice (typical): Prefer to use the language you know best for the topic concerned.

(iv) Accommodating Topic Condition (typical): Prefer to use the language that you believe the person you are addressing knows best for the topic being discussed.

Essentially, these two rules fall into two parts. First, they both assume that choice of language is influenced by amount of knowledge and ease of expression, which themselves vary from topic to topic (perhaps domain to domain) depending on the experience of the speaker and, at another remove, on the experience (cultural history) of users of the language as a whole. The second part, equally pertinent to our concerns, is the question of whose preference is to count. There will, of course, be cases where each user has (or can be assumed to have) equal and similar control of the two languages, but there will also be cases in which the two rules could lead to conflict. The resolution of this conflict is partly to be explained by the absolute and relative status of the two people concerned; it is partly to be explained by accommodation theory. The rules themselves are simple: the conditions that provide weighting for them are much more complex (see, for instance, Breitborde 1983; Genesee 1983).

The special relevance of these conditions for second language learning is in helping determine which party learns the other's language.

The next condition is a conservative factor:

(v)   Inertia Condition on Language Choice (typical): Prefer to use the language you used the last time you addressed this person.

To switch language use to a person you have regularly spoken to—a family member, a close friend—takes a major effort; thus, the weight of inertia favours conservatism: parents can be persuaded to speak a new language to their children more easily than they can be persuaded to use it to each other.

(vi)   Prefer a language that includes or excludes a third party.

There are conditions in which it is considered important to make it possible for a third party to be able to understand what one is saying or writing; similarly, there can be conditions that make it important to prevent a third party understanding. In other cases, this condition has no weight at all.

The final condition is a complex and important one: I am tempted to break it down into several, but prefer to try to treat it as a single rule, with the complexities in the weightings that determine its salience in a specific case.

(vii)   Social Advantage Condition on Language Choice (typical): Prefer to use a language that asserts the most advantageous social group membership for you in the proposed interaction.

Assume that both you and your addressee are equally bilingual; that it is a person you have not spoken to before; that there is no third party involved and that the conversation takes place in a society with at least two groups of uneven power, each with its associated language. If the interaction is between a member of the dominating group and of a dominated group, the Topic condition and the Social Advantage condition suggest that the comfort of the member of the dominating group will be served by using his or her language, unless he or she chooses to accommodate to the other party. Assume, however, a conversation between two members of the dominated group: in such a case, the use of the language of the dominant group will have nothing to do with comfort but will count as a claim to membership of that group and so to an advantageous status in the current situation. The working of conditions like these depends on the ideological values of both people involved and derives from general social values.

The model I am proposing for language choice is a competence model: a set of rules that underlies the understanding of a competent member of a speech community. In Chomsky's attempt to explain linguistic competence, this person was an idealized monolingual. In a socio-linguistic description, it is of necessity someone who shares not just the community's rules for forming sentences (linguistic competence in its narrowest sense) but its rules for language use (communicative competence). But knowing the rules is not the same as using them; there will in practice be cases where mistakes are made, or where knowledge is imperfect. In describing the rules of a speech community, there is another complication in that various members of the community will have different values and apply the same rules differently.

These rules describe for a given speech community its assumptions about appropriate language choice: it sets, in other words, what Genesee and Bourhis (1983) refer to as the situational norm. It sets expectations against which an actual performance is judged, and provides an ordered set of hypotheses to be tested in real life. If someone addresses me in a language I don't know, my first (and most charitable) guesses are that he thinks I know it or that he can't speak any other: once I have corrected the first, his persistence is judged to be because of the second, and if I later find that this is not so, I move on to a finer analysis.

But the various conditions themselves obtain their relative weighting in a number of ways. First, there is the question of the relative salience to the situation of the various domains or clusters of role relationships; is this a situation where it is appropriate/valuable to assert a role relationship expressed by choice of a certain language? For example, the foreign language teacher with a pupil outside class may choose to assert the teacher role by using the foreign language or the fellow-citizen role by using the native language. It is under this head that I would prefer to consider the importance of asserting ingroup membership. Second, there is the issue of the status of the language itself, a cluster of attributes as we saw earlier in this chapter arising in part from the functions with which the language is associated and in part from the status of the people who are assumed to use the language. Thirdly, there are the specific and immediate functional claims of the situation, as analysed by Scotton (1983) in her work on negotiation. For instance, in order to obtain a better price, the customer might choose to use the seller's language in contrast to the usual principle that sellers are assumed to accommodate to customers.

With this greater sophistication in understanding the social context of language choice, we may return to the issue of second language learning and summarize the conditions added in this chapter as follows. First, the effect of these language choice rules is to set values for second language learning:

Condition 56
Language Values condition (graded, typical): The social and individual values which underlie language choice also determine the value an individual assigns to the learning of a specific language.

These values translate into attitudes, and the attitudes lead to the development of the degree and kind of motivation that has such an important influence on the amount of effort a learner is prepared to make in learning a second language.

The attitudinal factor of course is not independent but interacts with the learner's personal abilities to determine the advantage taken of the opportunities presented for language learning and use. The original simple formula suggested this by considering linguistic outcome as the result of summing ability, motivation, and opportunity: the more of any one that is present, the less the others are needed. But attitude is not just additive; it is also focused in its impact. In Lambert's proposal, integrative motivation was especially relevant to the development of phonetic and semantic mastery of the new language. In the analysis of functional skills in Chapter 4, we saw also a potential relation between clusters of goals (referred to there as ideologies) and specific functional skills. In the case study in Chapter 13, this differentiation will be seen in practice.

It is the social situation, then, that indirectly affects second language learning by determining the learner's attitudes and motivation. The social context also determines the existence and kinds of situations and opportunities that are available for formal and informal second language learning. The next two chapters will look at the effect of these opportunities on language learning.

Notes

1   See Conditions 28, 29, and 30 in Chapter 7.
2   But it does in fact emerge in Ely (1986b), a study of first year university students learning Spanish, which makes use of factor analysis.
3   The measures were need achievement, ethnocentrism, French classroom anxiety, French Canadian attitudes, interest in foreign languages, instrumental and integrative orientation, parental encouragement to learn French, attitudes towards learning French, attitudes towards European French people, motivational intensity,

desire to learn French, orientation index (instrumental versus integrative), behavioural intention to continue French, opportunity for French outside the school, and eight measures derived from semantic differential rating of the concepts 'my French teacher' and 'my French class': evaluation of the French teacher, teacher-pupil rapport, student perception of teacher competence, student rating of teacher inspiration, evaluation of the French course, rating of difficulty of the French course, utility of the French course, and level of interest.

4 Students reported their own writing, understanding, reading, and speaking skills once a week; they were rated by their teachers at four different times on oral French skills and French aural achievement; they were tested in the first and last week of the course in a test that required them to produce a French response to each of twenty-five situations described in English; their taped responses were judged for accuracy and fluency.

5 These were interest in foreign languages, attitudes towards learning French, attitudes towards French Canadians, integrativeness, mo-tivational intensity, desire to learn French, French class anxiety, French use anxiety, French teacher evaluation, French course evaluation, self-report on French skills, teacher rating of French skills, a French screening test, French grades, student's perception of importance of course objectives, student's rating of importance of course objectives as perceived by administrators, opportunities to use French, and intentions to use French.

6 See the causal model for Hebrew learning proposed at the end of Chapter 13.

7 While this is still stressed in Schumann (1986), at the end of the paper he admits that it 'may also be applicable to other groups'.

8 Following Schumann's theory of pidginization to be discussed in Chapter 11, pages 173–8, it might be argued that pidginization results not just from a native speaker's absence or unwillingness to present a natural model, but rather by any available native speakers' assumption of the limited learning ability of the language learner, a sort of reverse Pygmalion effect. Thus, foreigner talk may be seen as a way of preventing someone learning your language or alterna-tively teaching him or her the limited variety he or she is capable of. All this will be dealt with later, when I consider the effect of the social context in providing opportunities for learning.

9 Cooper and Carpenter (1976) showed the effect of this principle in the Ethiopian markets, and it is further demonstrated in the markets of the Old City of Jerusalem (Spolsky and Cooper 1986).

10 It is a typical condition because there are other choices such as to seek a third person as an interpreter, to use gestures, to shop elsewhere, etc.

11 Opportunities for second language learning

Opportunities for learning

Whatever the language learner brings to the task, whether innate ability, a language acquisition device, attitudes, previous knowledge, and experience of languages and language learning, the outcome of language learning depends in large measure on the amount and kind of exposure to the target language. In Carroll's formula for language learning presented at the beginning of Chapter 10, this appears most simply as the factor of time, but at a more sophisticated level of analysis, it is not just time or amount but also the kind of exposure that is relevant.

Exposure to the new language is a necessary condition for learning. It was stated at the beginning of Chapter 10 as follows:

Condition 51
Exposure condition (necessary, graded): The more time spent learning any aspect of a second language, the more will be learned.

One case where this principle creates a problem for the second language learner is a context where native speakers are reluctant to use their language with non-natives. At times, the reluctance is almost a ban;[1] at other times, it is reported simply as a desire of native speakers to practise the foreign language themselves. Trosset (1986) observes that it is difficult for people learning Welsh as a second language, especially when they are still beginning their study, to persuade native speakers to speak Welsh with them. The next two chapters will not, however, try to establish the truth of the exposure condition, but rather to see how much more precisely it can be stated, and what specific factors besides the amount of exposure determine the successful learning of a second language.

A first step is to analyse the learning task. In a survey of the current state of understanding of second language acquisition in spontaneous or unguided situations, Klein (1986) presents a very useful discussion of the process from the point of view of the language learner. The second language learner, Klein says, has four essential tasks to perform: first, he or she must successfully analyse the speech input he or she hears into appropriate units.[2] Second, he or she must learn how to synthesize these minimal units into larger units. Third, he or she must learn how utterances are embedded in context (including of course non-linguistic context). Finally, he or she must learn to match his or her own present command of a language with the target aimed at.

Klein's tasks can be usefully restated as conditions under which exposure can lead to successful learning.

Condition 57
Opportunity for Analysis condition (necessary, graded): Learning a language involves an opportunity to analyse it, consciously or unconsciously, into its constituent parts.

This condition has already been noted as an outcome of learning, in the Analysed Knowledge condition presented in Chapter 2:

Condition 5
Analysed Knowledge condition (necessary, graded): As linguistic knowledge is analysed into its constituent parts, it becomes available for recombination; this creative language use may be enriched with unanalysed knowledge.

Note the last clause, which recognizes the potential value also of knowledge of unanalysed chunks. The condition also is expressed in the Discrete Item condition in Chapter 4:

Condition 16
Discrete Item condition (necessary): Knowing a language involves knowing a number of the discrete structural items (sounds, words, structures, etc.) that make it up.

In Chapter 7, it forms the basis for two special, language-related abilities. The first concerns the ability to recognize the sound units:

Condition 28
Sound Discrimination condition (necessary, graded): The better a learner can discriminate between the sounds of the language and recognize the constituent parts, the more successful his or her learning of speaking and understanding a second language will be.

The second specific ability was labelled grammatical sensitivity, and it includes the recognition of grammatical constituents and the rules for their recombination, thus overlapping with Klein's second task:

Condition 30
Grammatical Sensitivity condition (necessary, graded): Beyond the necessary minimum ability to 'derive a grammar' implicitly, the better a learner's ability to recognize constituents and develop or understand generalizations about recombination and meaning (whether from explicit or implicit generalizations, in whatever forms), the faster he or

she will develop control of the grammatical (and pragmatic) structure of a second language.

The second task for the learner according to Klein is learning how to recombine these units. I propose this as a condition of opportunity for synthesis:

Condition 58
Opportunity for Synthesis condition (necessary, graded): Learning a language involves an opportunity to learn how its constituent parts are recombinable grammatically into larger units.

To know a language, you must know the grammar, not necessarily consciously; that is to say, you must be able to put sounds together into words and words into sentences and sentences into utterances. In the early stages of learning, many learners (especially those learning informally) tend to use a number of pragmatic rather than syntactic principles for this recombination process,[3] but slowly the syntactic rules take over.

The third problem faced by the second language learner is what Klein calls embedding: learning to fit utterances into the appropriate context: 'Any utterance, whether belonging to a learner variety or to the target language, is embedded in the speaker's and hearer's informational set-up, composed of current perceptions, recollections of preceding events and utterances, and knowledge of the world' (Klein 1986:112). The context is complex and includes much redundancy. As linguistic competence increases, the learner is less dependent on contextual information. For practical purposes, contextual knowledge may be broken into knowledge of the world (which may vary from culture to culture), situational knowledge (perception of the visual environment, including gestures, facial expression, and deixis), and information gained from earlier utterances. Klein points out that this area, even more than syntax, suffers from lack of evidence on the relation between language and context. In this principle, Klein is combining in a single task the learning of meaning and use: the semantics, pragmatics, and sociolinguistics of the items:

Condition 59
Opportunity for Contextual Embedding condition (necessary, graded): Learning a language involves an opportunity to learn how its elements are embedded in linguistic and non-linguistic contexts.

This condition was an underlying element in the various conditions concerning integrated language and communicative functions discussed in Chapters 3, 4, and 5. It is involved in the notion of stylistic control and knowledge of appropriacy of variety.

The fourth problem faced by the second language learner is matching his or her performance with that of native speakers or other targets. Some language learners succeed in getting very close; the majority finish up with control of a variety that is recognizably distinguishable from native speakers of the target language. Klein points out a number of important issues. First, a distinction must be made between real discrepancy and perceived discrepancy: a language learner may not notice his or her variety is different from the target. This point is also made in a study by Yule, Yanz, and Tsuda (1985) who present some evidence of the complex relationship between a learner's confidence and accuracy. Conversely, the learner might notice the difference but not be able to overcome it. The problem is obviously compounded by the number of varieties that make up the target language.

The learner can carry out this matching in a number of ways: simultaneously, by monitoring; immediately after, by feedback; or later, by reflection. Monitoring or self-correction is common in first and second language use: it suggests a process of checking an utterance just before it is produced. Feedback occurs immediately after the utterance, and is provided by the hearer explicitly or implicitly. Remote, distanced reflection, such as checking a dictionary for pronunciation before starting a conversation, is more uncommon and likely to be associated with formal learning. The condition for matching may be stated as follows:

Condition 60
Opportunity for Matching condition (necessary, graded): Learning a language involves an opportunity for the learner to match his or her own knowledge with that of native speakers or other targets.

I have stated this condition using the term 'knowledge' in the generalized sense used in the formula in Chapter 1; it is most obviously relevant to observable performance, but refers also to receptive skills. It can, as has been discussed, be blocked or interfered with by internal causes (hearing impairment, lack of empathy) or by external circumstances (absence of native-speaking models, distorted foreigner talk).

Klein's four tasks are a good statement, from the point of view of an applied linguist, of the second language learner's task. There are, however, two elements that he takes for granted and leaves unstated, for they are true of all kinds of learning. The first of these is the remembering of the newly learned item. As Stevick (1986) sees it, the central issue in language learning and all other kinds of learning is to 'hold on to new words, new patterns, new skills, and new meanings'. I state this as an Opportunity for Remembering condition:

Condition 61
Opportunity for Remembering condition (necessary, graded): Learning a language involves an opportunity for new items to be remembered.

In Chapter 7 the relevance of memory as a special language learning aptitude was mentioned.

The second of the additional tasks that Klein does not include is the development of fluency and automaticity, discussed in Chapter 3. This refers to the opportunity for practice of the newly learned skills, or practice to maintain old ones.[4]

Condition 62
Opportunity for Practice condition (necessary, graded): Learning a language involves an opportunity for the new skills to be practised; the result is fluency.

Johnson (1986) has drawn attention to the value of the cognitive learning model described by Anderson (1980) for understanding the language learning process. In this model, the learning task is divided into three: a cognitive phase (developing and remembering the underlying, declarative knowledge involved in the first of the tasks described by Klein); an associative stage, where the declarative knowledge is transformed into procedural form, and where the learner starts to use the knowledge; and an autonomous phase, where the procedure becomes automated. It is the second two stages that are included in the Opportunity for Practice condition.[5]

The last six conditions (57 to 62) have been stated as necessary conditions. By this I am asserting that without them no language learning takes place, or that the outcome is not reasonably considered as second language knowledge.[6] It must be stressed that they are not sufficient conditions, for they work in conjunction with all the other conditions comprising the model as whole. They are also graded conditions: the more they are true, the more their outcome will be true.

These six conditions on learning opportunities will serve as a heuristic for analysing a number of central issues concerned with the values of formal and informal instruction. In this chapter I will first analyse the differences between formal and informal opportunities. I will then look at two specific problems with informal learning, firstly how it is possible for the learner to succeed with the task of analysis and synthesis in Klein's first two tasks, and secondly how it is relevant to the matching condition. In the next chapter I will ask a question most relevant to formal learning—What is the importance of comprehensible input?—which is basic to the third task. This will make it possible to consider the relative value of formal and informal learning opportunities, and in particular to look at language teaching in the light of the general theory being presented in this book.

Informal and formal learning

In the common view, there is a distinction to be made between what is usually called natural language learning, picking up a second language in the environment in which it is spoken from others speaking it with the purpose of using it to communicate, and formal or classroom learning, learning it in a situation where only one person (the teacher) has command of it, and the teacher is working to control the exposure so that it will lead to learning. Klein (1986) suggests the terms 'spontaneous' and 'guided' language learning. Others use the terms untutored and tutored; Long (1988) refers to 'instructed' (classroom) learning.

The distinction between the two is usually stated as a set of contrasting conditions. In natural second language learning, the language is being used for communication, but in the formal situation it is used only to teach. In natural language learning, the learner is surrounded by fluent speakers of the target language, but in the formal classroom, only the teacher (if anyone) is fluent. In natural learning, the context is the real outside world, open and stimulating; in formal learning, it is the closed four walls of the classroom. In natural language learning, the language used is free and normal; in the formal classroom it is carefully controlled and simplified. Finally, in the natural learning situation, attention is on the meaning of the communication; in the formal situation, it is on meaningless drills.

These seemingly categorical features turn out in fact to be better expressed as typicality conditions.[7] While they serve to show what is typical of the kind of learning they help recognize, closer analysis shows that they are in fact, all of them, conditions which contribute positively to second language learning.[8] We will look at them in turn, then return to some in more detail:

Condition 63
Communication condition (typical of natural learning, graded): The language is being used for communication.

The reason this condition favours learning is, as Klein (1986:21) points out, that 'The spontaneous learner is invariably under pressure to utilize his entire language potential in order to communicate successfully.' It provides, in other words, a necessary kind of practice. Varonis and Gass (1985) study the interactions between non-native speakers and show a process of negotiation of meaning that is a very valuable form of practice.

Condition 64
Learning Goal condition (typical of formal learning, graded): The language is being used so that it can be learned.

As the goal is learning, the tasks presented to the learner are smaller and more within his or her grasp, making it easier to analyse, synthesize, embed, and match, giving time for memory and opportunity for sufficient practice.

Condition 65
Fluent Speakers condition (typical of natural learning, graded): Many speakers in the environment are fluent and native.

As a result, the learner is exposed to a wide variety of forms and styles with which he or she can match his or her own knowledge.

Condition 66
Teacher Model condition (typical of formal learning, graded): Only one speaker (the teacher) is fluent; the majority in the environment (classroom) are not.

Two favourable results follow: the learner has time to get used to one style at a time, and there is no competition from other speakers better than the learners to make them feel inadequate.

Condition 67
Open Area condition (typical of natural learning, graded): The learning takes place in the open or in unconstrained areas.

The natural environment provides a multitude of contextual clues for understanding language in use, and makes it easy to see the rules for language use in different physical and social contexts.

Condition 68
Classroom condition (typical of formal learning, graded): The learning takes place in a closed physical space, a single classroom.

Controlled acoustics make it possible to hear better; comfortable physical surroundings make concentration possible; by judicious decoration, the classroom can be turned into a foreign culture island.[9] Di Pietro (1987) explains how full advantage can be taken of the classroom for regulated dialogues, which can be more effective than the free interchange in the open natural situation for developing ability to interact in the second language.

Condition 69
Uncontrolled Language condition (typical of natural learning, graded): The language is normal and uncontrolled.

The learner is exposed to a wide range of natural styles and registers; the language is normal and not bookish.

Condition 70
Simplified Language condition (typical of formal learning, graded): The language is simplified and controlled.[10]

The teacher can make sure that the language used is within the competence of the learner, and can see that new items are added only as fast as they can be reasonably expected to be learned; the simplification is particularly important for the analysis and synthesis tasks.

Condition 71
Comprehensible Input condition (typical of natural learning, graded):
The learner is expected to understand; therefore the speaker makes an
effort to see that language is comprehensible.

This condition should especially favour embedding. One can be said to
know a new item in a language only when one knows its meaning.

Condition 72
Drill Input condition (typical of formal learning, graded): The learner is
expected to learn; therefore ample practice is given to develop automatic
control.

Without practice, learning is likely to be haphazard and uneven; with it,
there can be systematic development of fluency and accuracy. This
condition therefore favours automatization.

As I explained at the end of the first chapter, typicality conditions are
a method of allowing for the fact that categorical judgements can be
made when all conditions are not in fact met; the decisions may be
weaker, but will still hold. We will not, then, be surprised to discover
that there are approaches to formal classroom teaching that argue for
imposing what I have called here natural conditions on teaching in the
classroom. Similarly, we need not be surprised to find that the next
sections will concentrate on showing that in one way at least natural
language learning situations are in fact quite constrained: in the social
control over the linguistic context. In other words, I will be looking at
various approaches which raise serious questions about the very
typicality of the Uncontrolled Language condition above, which holds
that controlled and simplified language occurs only in the foreign
language classroom.

The arguments will be considered that hold that in natural situations
too there is simplification and modification; that foreigner talk (to use
the term developed by Ferguson (1971)) is in fact typical of natural
learning. Thus, a process that Schumann (1978a) has likened to
pidginization turns out to be the result not just of inadequate language
learning (as in Schumann's model), but also of the nature of the sample
of the target language presented to the learner.

Pidginization and creolization

In 1973 Courtney Cazden began in collaboration with three graduate
students (Herlinda Cancino, Ellen Rosansky, and John Schumann), a
ten-month study of six native speakers of Spanish who were learning
English without formal instruction. During the period, samples of their
spontaneous and elicited speech were recorded and studied. One of the
subjects that Schumann worked with was a thirty-three-year old from
Costa Rica, and during the period of the study he showed very little

linguistic development. For example, while the rest of the subjects went through four stages in the development of the English negative, Schumann's subject did not go beyond the first; he did not move out of the first stage in wh- questions, his use of inflectional morphemes was poor, and his auxiliary verbs were not mastered. Schumann characterizes his English as 'reduced and simplified', and points out these specific features:

> a. . . . the negative particle remains external to the verb and is not placed after the first auxiliary element as required in well-formed English;
> b. . . . inversion is virtually absent in questions;
> c. . . . no auxiliaries except (possibly *is (cop)* [copula]) can be said to be *acquired*, and using a less stringent criterion only four auxiliaries (*is (cop)*, *am (cop)*, *can* and *are (cop)*) can be said to have *appeared*;
> d. . . . the possessive tends to be unmarked;
> e. . . . the regular past tense ending (ed) is virtually unmarked;
> f. . . . positive transfer from Spanish can account for the plural inflection being supplied 85% of the time, for *is (cop)*'s being correctly supplied to a greater extent than other auxiliaries and for *am (cop)*, *are (cop)* and *can* reaching criterion for appearance;
> g. and . . . the progressive morpheme *(-ing)* is supplied only about 60% of the time. (Schumann 1976b:393–4)

The criterion for *appearance* was that a form appear in obligatory contexts in three consecutive samples; the criterion for *acquisition* was that a form appear correctly in three consecutive samples in 90 per cent of the obligatory contexts.

Schumann considered three possible explanations for his subject's failure to develop. Ability was ruled out once it was shown that there was no evidence of 'gross cognitive deficits' and age was ruled out by the rejection of the critical period hypothesis. The explanation left was based on the observation that the subject's language contained several features of pidgin language and in particular the following forms that Schumann cites from descriptions of varieties of pidgin English:

(a) The uniform negative 'no' as in American Indian Pidgin English and English Worker Pidgin
(b) No inversion in questions as in Neo-Melanesian Pidgin and English Worker Pidgin
(c) No auxiliaries as in English Worker Pidgin
(d) No possessive inflection as in American Indian Pidgin English
(e) Unmarked forms of the verb as in English-Japanese Pidgin, American Indian Pidgin English, and English Worker Pidgin
(f) Deletion of subject pronouns as in English Worker Pidgin. (adapted from Schumann 1976b:394–5)

From this evidence, Schumann's argument goes like this. While language generally serves three functions, communicative, integrative, and expressive (Smith 1972), pidgin languages are generally restricted to the first of these functions. Pidginization therefore produces 'an interlanguage which is simplified and reduced'. Schumann explains this as a result of social distance; for the various reasons we have discussed when looking at Schumann's acculturation model, his subject was socially and psychologically distant from English, and so the pidginzation which, Schumann speculates, is the first stage of second language acquisition, persisted in his case.

In a later paper, Schumann (1978b) argues that the process he is describing is what Whinnom (1971) characterized as the secondary level of linguistic hybridization. Primary hybridization according to Whinnom is when a species language breaks up into dialects; secondary hybridization is the imperfect speech of second language learners in restricted contact with target language speakers, and tertiary hybridization occurs when to secondary are added two conditions, the absence of the target language as a norm, and the use of the hybrid (now a true pidgin) as a medium of communication among speakers of different languages. Even though he does not claim that his subject spoke a true pidgin, Schumann does claim that second language acquisition is secondary hybridization, that it is early pidginization. In the absence of the conditions necessary for tertiary hybridization it results not in a 'true pidgin' but 'in an interlanguage which is only pidginized' (Schumann 1978b:368).

On this basis, Schumann (1978b) responds to criticisms of his proposal by Flick and Gilbert (1976). Multiple first languages are necessary to tertiary and not secondary hybridization; many second language learners are already multilingual; secondary hybridization can be considered an individual phenomenon (we seem here to be touching on the basic issue of individual interlanguages); the absence of target language speakers as a correcting model is made up for by the social and psychological distance that makes the target language 'irrelevant input because it does not become intake. Hence, it ceases to be a real model of approximation and the learner's interlanguage fossilizes at the pidginized stage' (Schumann 1978b:371).

Schumann similarly answers criticisms by Meisel (1976). The absence of an admixture of languages is only relevant at the tertiary level; the absence of a norm is not serious because there are pidgins without norms; and social and psychological distance in some second language acquisition situations is enough to lead to pidginization if not to pidgins. The core of his defence is the distinction he makes between process and product:

> I would maintain that the critics of the analogy between second language acquisition and pidginization have equated the process of

pidginization with its end product, a pidgin language. The position
taken here, however, is that pidginization is a much broader process
than simply tertiary hybridization. The process of pidginization
begins when learners have to acquire and use a second language
under conditions of restricted social and psychological contact. These
conditions will produce an inter-language [sic] that is pidginized in
the sense that it is a reduced and simplified form of the target
language. (Schumann 1978b:373)

Schumann quotes Bickerton (1977) as seeing an analogy between
pidginization and second language acquisition, but considers that
Bickerton overstates the role of the first language.

Schumann (1978b) next considers his earlier (1974b) suggestion that
second language acquisition might also be thought of as analogous to
creolization. He now rejects this position, arguing that creolization is
language creation, without a target language goal,[11] while second
language acquisition is 'language acculturation', i.e. if there is acculturation, there is a target language goal. However, there is, he suggests,
following Bickerton (1975) and Stauble (1978), a closer analogy with
decreolization.

Stauble's paper is based on an MA thesis she did at UCLA. She starts
with Bickerton's suggestion that in the decreolization situation, where a
creole language is incorporating all the time more and more features
from the target standard language, there is a range of identifiable
varieties, called 'lects'; the full range, Bickerton suggests, consists of the
following: Basilect, Lower Mesolect, Mid Mesolect, Upper Mesolect,
Acrolect. The basilect is the closest to the creole, the acrolect the closest
to the target or standard language. The division of the mesolect into
lower, mid, and upper is Stauble's on the basis of Bickerton. It is
Bickerton's suggestion that the process of incorporating features is
similar to second language learning, and Stauble's concern in this study
is to see if this occurs in accordance with Schumann's acculturation
model. Bickerton (1975) describes the stages in the development of
negation in the Guyanese continuum. At the basilect stage, there is a
general negator *na* placed between the subject and the verb and
occasional variation with *kyaan* and *mon* ('can't' and 'mustn't') taken
from the target language. As the change from basilect to mesolect takes
place, *na* is further replaced by monomorphemic negators such as *en*
('ain't') and *doon(t)* ('don't'). Slowly, signs of post-verbal negation start
to appear. In the stage from mesolect to acrolect, the negative forms
start functioning as in standard Guyanese English, with the loss of *na*
and the post-verbal negation pattern with do-support. Stauble cites
Schumann as coining the terms Basilang, Mesolang, and Acrolang on
the analogy of Bickerton's -lect forms to refer to stages in second
language learning. In her study, Stauble reanalyses the data on negative
development in two of the Spanish ten-year olds in the Cazden *et al.*

(1975) study. She sees similarities: a pre-verbal negator in the basilang stage, model forms appearing but without their model function in the mesolang stage, and a gradual move to the standard in the acrolang stage. Following Bickerton's proposal to place languages along the continuum, she studies three adult Spanish learners of English and suggests on the basis of their negation development their placing along the basilang-acrolang continuum. She argues that this placing is a function of their degree of acculturation.

Schumann discusses this proposal, noting one problem: 'the basilect and the basilang are not really analogous because the basilect is a native language and the basilang is not' (Schumann 1978b:377). He recognizes by this that the basilect in Bickerton's model is learned as a native language; the basilang speaker on the other hand develops his or her own basilang by reduction and simplification. But the next stages are much more like decreolization: '. . . we see that secondary hybridization is parallel to the basilang of SLA [Second Language Acquisition]. Tertiary hybridization, creolization and the basilang phase of decreolization do not parallel SLA. And finally, the mesolect and acrolect phases of decreolization parallel the mesolang and acrolang of SLA' (op.cit.:378). Just as decreolization depends on 'language contact situations where there is progressive acculturation', so too one can argue that second language learning depends on 'social and cultural integration with the target group' (op.cit.:378).

In another study, Schumann (1980) studies the speech of seven Spanish speakers learning English (five of them from the Cazden *et al.* study) and looks in particular at relative clause development. His results agree with Kuno's (1974) hypothesis that centre embedding is difficult. There are signs of similarities with the sequence proposed for Hawaiian pidgin English.

In a further consideration of the pidginization hypothesis, Schumann (1982) looks in more detail at the early stage. He argues that pidginists (especially Bickerton and Odo 1976) see three main processes in pidginization: simplification, transfer, and relexification. He sees these three processes in second language acquisition: second language learners perform 'under the constraints of a general principle: *Keep L2 [second language] output simple* and its corollary: *Maintain your NL [Native Language]* to whatever extent possible' (Schumann 1982:338).

He summarizes Stauble's study of the development of negation as evidence of the parallel of second language acquisition with decreolization. He then cites a further study by Stauble and Schumann (in press) in which they look at verb phrase morphology, focusing on the proportion of occurrence of correct or incorrect morphemes in obligatory contexts; absence or low production of a morpheme is counted as evidence of simplification. He cites Schumann (1980) as evidence of the simplification of the relative clause. He looks at the relatively high proportion of non-syntactic or paratactic utterances in three speakers. He gives two examples of cases where negation shows transfer as well as simplification. Finally, he considers the question of relexification, defined by Bickerton as the speaker 'using his native tongue and relexifying first only a few key words' (1977:54). Schumann looks at some of the interviews from the Cazden *et al.* study to show some signs of relexification; the issue is left fairly open, for while there is a good deal of Spanish used by one subject in an early transcript and virtually none by the last, there is not clear evidence of development, and it is difficult to distinguish relexification from bilingual shifting. Finally, Schumann confronts the criticism of his hypothesis in a review of his book (1978a) in *Language*. The criticism presented there by Washabaugh and Eckman (1980) is that the analogy is not possible because of the lack of agreement among pidginists on the nature of a pidgin. Schumann agrees with their description of the state of the art in pidgin studies, but he suggests that it is reasonable to propose a move from analogy (second language acquisition is like pidginization) to icon: 'early SLA [Second Language Acquisition] *is* pidginization' (Schumann 1982:363). He concludes that 'a consensus about what linguistic phenomena constitute pidginization will only be possible when pidginists study pidginization in all its forms, and this includes basilang varieties of SLA [Second Language Acquisition]' (op.cit.:364).

Schumann's work puts the emphasis on the learner: because of social or psychological distance, the learner does not manage to acquire the target language properly. But the pidginization hypothesis is in fact potentially much richer than this, for it assumes the existence of a limited exposure to the target language; in the classic plantation situation, there was limited intercourse with native speakers of the target language, and most use of the target language with other non-natives. Any learning situation that leads to such limited exposure has necessary effects on the learning; only in a creolization situation (which, as Bickerton suggests, occurs only for a short period in a plantation situation where children learn a pidgin as their first language from pidgin speakers) does one expect major restructuring of the grammar as universals work unimpeded by locally set parameters. But it will always be the case that learners will learn the variety to which they are exposed rather than some idealized standard. If, then, the language to which learners are exposed in natural situations is regularly reshaped, we have a possible explanation for the way that simplification might work in two opposite directions, making learning easier but, at the same time, preventing learners from achieving native-like ability.

Foreigner talk

The notion of the existence of a set of simplified registers addressed to language learners and other 'imperfect speakers' (Cooper and Greenbaum, MS) was proposed by Ferguson (1964, 1971, 1975, 1981): these include *baby talk* (the variety of language spoken to babies and young children), *teacher talk* (spoken by teachers to their pupils), *foreigner talk* (spoken to people assumed not to understand the language), and varieties addressed to people who are sick or old or deaf, or to animals. A number of recent studies (see, for example, Waterson and Snow 1978) have shown that the language addressed to young children is simplified and more well-formed than Chomsky originally argued.[12] The most interesting explanations for the simplification are based on an interactionist model, with the speaker modifying and simplifying on the basis of perception of attributes in the listener (learner) such as linguistic ability and social status.

Cooper and Greenbaum set out to systematize the interactionist model proposed by Freed (1980, 1981) and Snow *et al.* (1981) within what they call an accommodation model, using this term somewhat differently, they say, from the way Giles does. Their use is broader:

> We define accommodation as the adjustment of speech in response to the mutuality which speakers perceive between themselves and their hearers. We suggest that there are four types of mutuality which are relevant: 1) verbal repertoire, 2) background knowledge, 3) solidarity or intimacy, and 4) power. Phenomenologically, these domains correspond to perceptions of knowing (verbal repertoire and background knowledge), feeling (solidarity or intimacy) and doing (power). (Cooper and Greenbaum 1987)

The register itself is defined, they suggest, by simplification and well-formedness. The typicality conditions for simplification are less complex syntax, shorter utterances, higher frequency lexical items, and slower speech. Well-formedness refers to 'the extent to which utterances are grammatically acceptable in terms of the surface structure of the normal adult vernacular'.

Cooper and Greenbaum describe how each of the causes have been shown to lead to simplified registers. They express these four conditions in their own words as follows:

1. Perceived commonality of linguistic repertoire leads to greater complexity and greater well-formedness.
2. Perceived commonality of background information leads to greater simplicity and greater well-formedness.
3. Perceived solidarity leads to greater simplicity and greater well-formedness.
4. Perceived commonality of power leads to greater well-formedness. (op.cit.)

They point out that these conditions may all be true and interact in various ways. It makes sense therefore to consider what happens when we try to restate them as preference conditions.

When speaker and listener share a verbal repertoire (i.e. are members of the same speech community), only sociolinguistic factors determine variety choice. If they do not, there must be some degree of accommodation, which may well involve selection of a third language. If the speaker observes that the listener is having difficulty, it is normal to modify and simplify the register, tuning it to the desired level. There is also evidence of moving away from well-formed speech in these cases. Following them, then, we would formulate two typicality conditions as follows:

(*a*) Simplifying Condition for Foreigner Talk (typical, graded): The more you perceive that your interlocutor does not share your variety and therefore might not understand your speech, the more you should simplify the register you use.

This condition under certain circumstances is strong enough to overcome the general requirement (itself a typicality condition) of using well-formed speech only.[13]

The second condition proposed by Cooper and Greenbaum concerns shared knowledge: the greater the amount of shared knowledge between speaker and listener, the shorter and simpler the utterance can be. Conversely, explicit conveying of necessary knowledge tends to lead both to more complexity in syntax and greater length of utterance. This may be stated also as a graded typicality condition:

(*b*) Matching Condition for Foreigner Talk (typical, graded): The greater the amount of knowledge perceived as shared by the interlocutor, the sparser (shorter, simpler) the expression; conversely, the more information to be conveyed verbally, the richer (longer, more complex) the expression.

The application of the solidarity principle to this issue can be variously considered. Cooper and Greenbaum suggest that informality is typically associated with solidarity. Now note that solidarity is in fact a feeling expressed by a greater degree of sharing: this includes shared knowledge and shared repertoire. Is it therefore needed as a separate factor? Only, I suspect, if we can postulate solidarity without the other two, or the other two without solidarity. Or perhaps we are dealing with a different dimension: in the two conditions so far discussed, we have talked about 'perceived' shared repertoire and shared knowledge; here we are concerned with a choice expressing an attitude, a kind of metaphorical extension of the two conditions. Tentatively, I express it as a typicality condition:

(*c*) Solidarity Condition for Foreigner Talk (typical): Prefer to express solidarity by acting as though there were shared repertoire and knowledge and therefore by simplifying.

The fourth factor proposed by Cooper and Greenbaum is status. Here, they observe that there appears to be evidence that speakers simplify their speech to the point of deformation when they perceive themselves as being of higher status than their interlocutors. This is true in many cases of foreigner talk, and implies a perception that the interlocutor has neither need, opportunity, nor perhaps even ability to learn the language properly. We may express this as a condition affecting in particular well-formedness.

(d) Distortion Condition for Foreigner Talk (typical): If interlocutors are perceived as being of low status, then simplify even if it involves distorting.

What evidence is there for the working of these conditions in second language learning? Two articles by Long (1983a, 1983c) summarize a number of studies of native speaker reactions to the speech of non-native speakers. Long has analysed the nature of interaction between native and non-native speakers, and proposes the existence of some fifteen different devices used by native speakers in order to help non-native speakers understand them. He divides them into 'strategies', which are devices used in order to avoid problems, and 'tactics', which are used to repair misunderstandings; a third group serves both purposes. To avoid confusion with the many other uses of these terms, I shall refer to them as planning devices, repair devices, and planning and repair devices. The fifteen detailed in Long (1983a) are as follows: I give first Long's title, then a rewording as a preference rule and discussion:

1 'Relinquish topic control'
(i) Topic Choice condition (typical): Prefer to allow the non-native speaker to choose the topic.

Long presents cases where native speakers modify specific questions by tagging on a phrase inviting the non-native to talk about something else. On closer analysis, the examples read as though they occur in one of two situations: where a tester is probing to encourage a student to talk on any topic he or she can manage, or when a native speaker is encouraging conversation.

2 'Select salient topics'
(ii) Salience condition (typical): Prefer topics that refer to things that are immediately present or clearly known to the non-native speaker.

Long points out evidence of both caretaker-child (Cross 1978) and native speaker-non-native speaker conversations (Long 1980, 1981) being more likely to have verbs marked for present tense.

3 'Treat topics briefly'
(iii) Brevity condition (typical): Prefer to switch topics often with non-native speakers.

Spending long on a topic is likely to test the non-native speaker's vocabulary and expressive powers to the limit; Long (1981) showed that native speakers were much more likely to continue a topic beyond a first mention with native than with non-native speakers.

4 'Make new topics salient'
(iv) Novelty Marking condition (typical): Prefer to mark clearly any new topic.

There are a number of devices Long points out used for this purpose, including use of frames such as 'OK', 'So', 'Now', and 'Well'; moving topics to the beginning or end of utterances; slowing pace, stressing key words, pausing before or after; using questions to make clear that the non-native speaker is expected to take a turn; leading in the new topic with a statement requiring confirmation.

5 'Check non-native speaker's comprehension'
(v) Checking condition (typical): Prefer regular checks that the non-native speaker has understood.

In Long's study, comprehension checks such as 'Right?', 'OK?', and 'Do you understand?' occurred much more often with non-native speakers than with native speakers.

6 'Accept unintentional topic switches'
(vi) Accepting Topic condition (typical): Prefer to accept the non-native speaker's choice of topic even if it is an inappropriate response to a question.

This is a repair technique equivalent to the first planned technique.

7 'Request clarification'

I am not sure that this is a relevant condition, for it refers, Long says, to the fact that native speakers are more likely to ask non-native speakers than native speakers for clarification. But it is surely obvious that it will be more difficult to understand non-native than native speakers: it is not so much a special as a general condition of such interchanges. Similarly, I suspect with the next case:

8 'Confirm own comprehension'

Long says that native speakers are more likely to use confirmation checks (repetitions of a key word or two from the previous statement, followed sometimes by the word 'Right' and with rising intonation) with non-native speakers than with native. Once again, I suspect that the cause is likely to be the existence of uncertainty rather than an expectation that it will occur. The final repair device (if that is an appropriate term for a decision not to repair) is similarly difficult to accept:

9 'Tolerate ambiguity'

These are cases, Long says, that are difficult to quantify and that occur in conversations between native speakers as well when an interlocutor chooses not to clear up something that is unclear.

The last six devices are much more precise.

10 'Use slow pace'
(vii) Slowing condition (typical, graded): Use a speed of speaking that is considered suitable for the non-native speaker's level of understanding.

We have here one of the identified features of foreigner talk. Others follow:

11 'Stress key words'
(viii) Stress condition (typical, graded): Prefer to exaggerate sentence stress patterns.

12 'Pause before key words'

Perhaps this is a combination of the last two: exaggerated suprasegmentals with slower speed will lead to increase in the length of pauses.

13 'Decompose topic-comment constructions'

This is the device referred to earlier where a new topic is introduced in a question calling for some response before a comment is made about it.

14 'Repeat own utterances'

15 'Repeat other's utterances'

Both of these devices are, Long reports, significantly more common when a native speaker is talking to a non-native than to another native. They are in fact likely to be quite different in function and goal, and cannot be combined. The partial or complete repetition or paraphrase of one's own utterance is an obvious device to achieve comprehension: it follows from a general conversational maxim for quantity (see Grice 1975):

(ix) Redundancy condition (typical, graded): Prefer to increase redundancy through repetition, paraphrase, illustration, or other device, the more you consider that your interlocutor's lack of shared language or knowledge will decrease the chance of ready comprehension.

It is the same principle that explains repetition in scholarly writing and in teaching.

The second device appears to be the basis for Cazden's classic observation of the use of repetition by caretakers (and particularly of repetitions with correction or expansion) as a primary though probably unconscious teaching device. It might be expressed as follows:

(x) Expanding Correction condition (typical): When speaking to interlocutors whose speech is incorrect, prefer to repeat their utterances with correction.

It is interesting to note that Long's devices do not include the breaches of well-formedness, the distortions and violations of necessary conditions, that Cooper and Greenbaum and Schumann refer to as critical features of foreigner talk. This is presumably because of the special conditions in which he gathered his data, for such distortions only occur, he argues, when two or more of the following four conditions are met:

(1) the non-native speaker has very low proficiency
(2) the native speaker believes he or she is of higher status than the non-native
(3) the native speaker has considerable foreigner talk experience
(4) it is a natural (non-laboratory) conversation.

Long (1983c) points out that there is evidence of all kinds of native speakers—children as well as adults, all classes, with and without foreigner talk experience, teachers and lay people—using these devices. There has been some work on what triggers such speech. Long discusses some research which adds up to a claim that there are at least three factors involved: the ease with which the native speaker can comprehend the non-native speaker's own speech, the nature of this speech, and the apparent level of the non-native speaker's comprehension. Gass and Varonis (1985) have studied the modification of speech by native speakers speaking to non-natives, showing that the native speaker was more likely to modify his or her speech if he or she had difficulty in understanding the non-native; if the non-native speaker expressed difficulty in understanding, the natives also modified their speech.

At the beginning of this chapter, I listed the six basic conditions to be met by opportunities for second language learning and pointed to a number of conditions that favour language learning in informal and formal settings. The chief advantage of the formal setting seemed to be in the control over presentation, the possibility of adding new items step by step and then practising them. In the rest of the chapter, I discussed what is one of the disadvantages of the informal setting, the exposure to uncontrolled language, and noted that in fact there is a great deal of control provided by generally established rules for talking to foreigners and exemplified in native speech with non-natives. This general fact may be set out as a Foreigner Talk condition:

Condition 73
Foreigner Talk condition (typical, graded): Conditions of speech addressed by native speakers to non-natives (foreigner talk) lead to modification in the structures and frequency of language that form the basis for input in natural learning situations.

Schumann's likening of second language learning to pidginization has drawn attention to one of the real dangers of natural learning; as explained in the Cooper and Greenbaum model, the distortion used in foreigner talk to some foreigners serves as an effective way to prevent them learning to speak.

At the same time, it must again be stressed that the interactive nature of second language learning makes it necessary to call attention again to the connection between outcomes and opportunities: only informal learning exposes the learner to a sufficient range of variation in language use to permit easy natural communication. But for many learners, the only learning opportunity is formal instruction, which will be the topic of the next chapter.

Notes

1   When a Pueblo Indian language was first formally taught at the University of New Mexico, it was with the understanding that only Pueblo Indians would be permitted in the classes.

2   The condition is simplified in learning the written language, for writing separates out many units, but it is still there.

3   For example, they seem to use a topic-comment structure rather than a subject-predicate one (Givón) 1979). Klein (1986) lists eight such pragmatic rules he has identified in second language speech: given information before new, theme before rheme, semantic association, consistent serialization, orientational elements first, events in natural order, modality by intonation, and rheme marked by intonation.

4   Expressed in this way, this condition might be seen as broadening a theory of second language learning so as to make it a potential theory of second language loss; this issue is discussed in more detail in Chapter 14.

5   McLeod and McLaughlin (1986) draw attention to suggestions that improved performance may come from restructuring of the components rather than from automaticity.

6   It might be what I have called (Spolsky 1968) 'language-like behaviour', such as the parrot-like recitation of unanalysed chunks of the language.

7   For example, Kramsch (1985) shows how discourse in the classroom extends along a continuum from natural to instruc-

tional. She argues that the 'microworld' of the classroom can be adapted to productive social interaction.

8   To say this is not to deny that there exist negative effects of the various listed conditions. There can be bad teaching as well as good; there can be misdirected activity as well as well-directed. But looked at carefully, studies that show inadequacies of any one condition are usually showing that it is not sufficient. Only when one is committed to a simple ideology does any use of a typical condition seem wrong. Thus, for instance, Pica (1987) is interesting when she points out the way that unequal participant relationships lead to limitation in interactions between students and teachers; wrong when she suggests that language is learned only in natural social interaction.

9   Teachers forced to teach foreign languages in noisy, uncomfortable classrooms provide evidence that this is a typicality condition.

10   But not distorted; see discussion of foreigner talk later in this chapter.

11   But see Bickerton (1977).

12   Chomsky (1986) now argues that in spite of it being well-formed, there are critical generalizations not derivable from even well-formed sentences.

13   This seems to be a typicality condition that controls the application of necessary conditions.

12   Formal instruction

The nature and effect of input

One of the more important effects of the Chomskyan revolution in linguistic theory on first and second language learning theory was to turn the applied linguist's attention from the nature of verbal input to the internal processes. The arguments put forward by Chomsky and his followers that simple imitation and practice of surface structures was not enough to account for language learning but that there must be some kind of internal, preprogrammed language acquisition device were quickly accepted. For some time, then, language learning theory concentrated on the nature of the internal device, the processes involved in developing a grammar from an undifferentiated body of raw data of the natural language.

A number of reasons lie behind the modification of this approach: the difficulty and inconclusiveness of the approach itself; the gap between those concerned with theoretical constraints on the form of natural languages and those concerned with accounting for the learning of normal languages; the growing evidence of modifications and regularizations in the forms of language addressed to first and second language learners, and in second language learning theory and practice, a vogue for communicative approaches with its consequent emphasis on language learning as an interactive activity. The model implied by this approach is a more complex one than either the simple pre-Chomskyan view of language learning as a matter of internalizing externally provided patterns, or the simple early generativist view that all the work would be done by an internal device without outside help. It involves finding a place for both kinds of process in a consistent and complex model and not just a facile eclecticism.

Two articles set out evidence on the issue. Landes (1975) summarizes research on first language learning, showing how the initial emphasis on innate universal principles in the work of scholars like Lenneberg (1967) and McNeill (1970) led to a 'naïve' assumption that children hear 'a random, often ungrammatical sample of adult utterances' from which they could not possibly derive a grammar without extensive preprogramming. Landes cites research showing that at least until a child is ten, parents and teachers modify their speech in various ways: there is, for instance, a larger proportion of interrogatives; utterances are shorter; sentences are less complex; lexicon is more restricted; and a variety of 'training' strategies appear, including modelling, corrective feedback, and expansion. Landes (1975:376) concludes: 'it is clear that adults are not only sensitive to and affected by the need to communicate with their children, but that interaction patterns between parents and offspring change with the increasing language skills of the child.'

In the second article, looking at the issue of second language learning, Wagner-Gough and Hatch (1975:297) argue for more attention not just to input but to the communicative process as a whole: data used in research has been limited to specific forms being learned (as in the morpheme order studies) and has lost sight of the relation between form and function in natural communication. They summarize early findings from research that looks at the wider view:

1. The frequency of forms in speech addressed to the learner influences the language he produces.
2. A grammatical form can communicate just about anything the learner wants it to in communication. The learner may produce grammatical forms without a clear notion of their function in speech.
3. The flow of speech in discourse may provide the learner with some of the larger units which he incorporates for sentence construction.
4. The nature of language addressed to young children may be very different from that addressed to the older learner. (Wagner-Gough and Hatch 1975:298)

Input theory is summed up by Schachter (1983). Given that a learner has the capability and the motivation to learn, she asks, what else is needed? There are four proposed kinds of input: simplified, comprehensible, negative, and sufficient. *Simplified input* is a notion developed from studies of caretaker speech with first language learners, teacher talk with students, and native speaker talk with foreigners. The alterations made vary, but they are all likely to include a slower rate of speech, fewer idioms and pronouns, shorter and less complex sentences, and morphological stripping.

The general claim is summarized in the Simplified language condition set out in the last chapter:

Condition 70
Simplified Language condition (typical of formal learning, graded): The language is simplified and controlled.

The simplification makes it possible for the learner to recognize the units and to see how they are combined and used.

Schachter does not believe that there exists evidence that the presence of these features facilitates second language learning or that their absence impedes it. Krashen (1980) sees values in such codes:

If caretaker speech is helpful for first language acquisition it may be the case that simple codes are useful in much the same way. The teacher, the more advanced second language performer, and the native speaker in casual conversation, in attempting to communicate with the second language acquirer, may unconsciously make the '100 or 1000 alterations' in speech that provide the acquirer with optimal input for language acquisition. (Krashen 1980:14)[1]

Schachter sees this notion of carefully structured presentations to the learner, albeit unconscious, as very similar to the notion of careful grading of presentation help by the Audio-Lingual Method and its proponents like Fries. It seems attractive, but there already exists counter-evidence in the first language learning research of Elinor Ochs (1982) in Western Samoa, Bambi Schieffelin (1979) among the Kaluli in New Guinea, and Shirley Brice Heath (1982) in a south-eastern US Black community. In none of these cases is caretaker speech reported: Samoan adults do not consider children capable of communicating and make no effort to adjust to them; the Kaluli use adult speech to their children; and the mothers in the south-eastern community do not talk to their children until they can take part in normal conversations. There remains no evidence, Schachter concludes, that simplified input is necessary to first language learning, and therefore no reason to claim that it is necessary to second language learning. But we must point out that saying that something is not necessary or sufficient does not rule out the possibility that it is typical and valuable.

Comprehensible input, however, Schachter does consider necessary, so much so that she satisfies herself with stating that without it, there can be no language learning.

But when her claim is made more precise, it seems more modest:

> I do not want to be understood to be claiming that in order for people to learn a language they must understand each and every word in each and every utterance they hear. If this were the criterion, no one would learn. What I do mean is that in order for learners to incorporate a structure or lexical item into their productive capacity they must have understood it as meaningful in some way. (Schachter 1983:181)

Unanalysed chunks might, for example, be learned without precise knowledge of their structure or full knowledge of their appropriate use. Put in this way, the claim seems to be little more than that some meaning (however slight) must be attached to forms. Or the requirement could be met by knowing that this is a potentially meaningful form. Schachter believes that simplification is one way to make comprehension easier; others are pauses, repetition, and enriched context.

Negative input is defined as information provided to the learner that an attempt at communication has been unsuccessful. She quotes Vigil and Oller (1976), who distinguish between affective feedback (information of approval or disapproval) and cognitive feedback (information of understanding or lack of understanding); the former she considers not a necessary condition for language learning. Negative cognitive feedback (input), however, Vigil, Oller, and Schachter agree is necessary: 'unless learners receive appropriate negative input fossilization will occur' (Schachter 1983:183). There are many kinds of negative input: explicit correction of error (rare), confirmation checks, clarification requests, and clear evidence of failure to understand. The phenomenon is complex,[2] and there has not yet been conclusive evidence.

The final requirement is *sufficient input*, but there does not seem to be evidence of how much is enough. The best indications we have are studies of the effect of school programmes. Thus, Baetens Beardsmore and Swain (1985) report that French immersion programmes in Toronto offering 4500 hours of classroom contact achieve similar results of complete working second language fluency to European school programmes with 1500 hours of classroom contact supplemented by the French social context of Brussels.[3]

Ellis (1981), like Landes, is interested to survey work on the relevance of input in first language learning in order to speculate on its relevance in second language learning. He argues that only an 'inter-organism' approach will prove of use to the teacher. Research in first language learning has shown the existence of special varieties of language addressed to children: in place of the view proposed by Chomsky that input was degenerate, analysis of caretaker speech has shown not just a good proportion of well-formed sentences, but also various methods of simplifying and regularizing language presented to children. However, it has not been demonstrated that this has direct and obvious effects on morphosyntactic development, where universalist and innate order notions seem to hold sway, certainly in so far as order of learning is concerned. There are, however, studies, one by Cross (1978) and one by Ellis and Wells (1980), suggesting that the speed of learning a first language is related to the amount and kind of input children receive from their mothers.

Krashen deals with input in what he labels simply 'the input hypothesis':

> Children progress by *understanding* language that is a little beyond them . . . That is, a child who is at a stage i can progress to stage $i + 1$ along the 'natural sequence' (where i and $i + 1$ may be a block of structures; more correctly the child who has just acquired the members of i can then acquire a member of $i + 1$) by understanding language containing $i + 1$. (Krashen 1980:11)

In this view, caretaker speech or other simplified input may be useful in providing the next item to be learned in an appropriately understandable form.

A critical feature of this hypothesis is that it bases second language learning on listening and not on speaking; the child or learner's speech only has a role in helping the interlocutor adapt his or her presentation to be comprehensible. The main observation in support of the hypothesis is the effectiveness of a silent period: the existence of a period of time in first language learning where the child does not speak, and the effectiveness of teaching methods that do not require speaking.

One of the most outstanding of these is Asher's Total Physical Response (Asher 1964, 1981, 1984). Asher believes that people fail to learn foreign languages because of the 'unbearable stress' produced by 'left-brain strategies' in the foreign language classroom. His 'fundamental discovery' comes from observing first language learning before and not after the child starts speaking.

> The critical period to investigate is the period of silence from birth to the appearance of talk. Silence is difficult to study because most linguistic techniques are focused upon the analysis of talk. 'Talk' is the primary subject matter of linguistics.
>
> During the silent period in infant development, there are three important clues. The first is that *we cannot teach an infant to talk.* Children can talk when they are *ready.*
>
> Secondly, children become ready to talk only after they have acquired a rather intricate map of how the language works . . . The home is an 'acquisition-rich environment' in which there is a maximum understanding of the spoken language in transactions between the caretakers and the child. Note that these transactions do *not* demand speech from the children. (Asher 1981:325)

The foreign language classroom on the other hand is 'acquisition-impoverished' and requires the child to speak. Adults can learn foreign languages quickly, Asher says, by his method which involves the instructor telling the class to do things. Of course they will have a foreign accent. Abstractions like 'Good morning. It's a beautiful day today. How are you feeling?' should be postponed until 'a more advanced stage' of learning when the phonology and morphology have been 'internalized without stress using semantic contact that is related to physical reality'.

Another method based on a similar claim is Terrell's Natural Approach (Krashen and Terrell 1983). Its primary principle, that comprehension precedes production, came from Terrell's experience learning and teaching Dutch, but came to be influenced by such ideas as those of Asher (as cited) and Krashen. Krashen and Terrell (1983:78) believe that this silent period for young children could be from one to six months.

There is, however, some doubt about these claims. Gibbons (1985) points out that the available evidence is inconclusive; a number of studies point to silence of one to two weeks rather than the months suggested, and there is some question on what counts as silence; some seem to include in it the routine use of patterns. The evidence of the value of silence for adult learners is also unclear, for there are no controlled experiments on the topic. Gibbons himself investigated a group of young children, recent immigrants to Australia, and found a very wide range (from 0 to 56 days, with the mean about 15 days) in the time before they were reported to be willing to try to speak. He argues that the silence can be explained by lack of understanding or by cultural patterns, and sees no support in it for the comprehensible input hypothesis.

What kind of evidence could contradict the $i + 1$ hypothesis? As Gregg (1984) points out, the claim is confused by lack of clarity: it is not clear, for instance, whether $i + 1$ refers to the learner's competence after stage i or the next structure to be acquired. Chaudron (1985) argues that the process by which input becomes intake needs to be more carefully delineated and tested empirically. White (1987) shows that there are cases where the development of grammar in a learner can be shown to be internally driven rather than the result of context or meaning. She further draws attention to some potential dangers of simplified input which can lead to incorrect generalizations. With more precise specification of language knowledge, she argues that it should be possible to identify the kind of input that will lead to learning.[4] She calls, then, for a tightening up of the hypothesis.

Essentially, therefore, the general question of the effect of comprehensible input needs tighter formulation. Consider how it applies to comprehension rather than production (including arguments for a silent period). If the cases cited by Schachter are correct, someone will have to show how those children learned their languages without either simplified or in fact any input addressed to them. It is perhaps easier to explain the case of people who live all their life in a foreign environment without learning the language by saying they never received comprehensible input. But there is need to make clear if the claim is that silence is necessary or desirable, or that speaking is not necessary or not desirable. The claim seems to apply mainly to morphosyntax; if to phonology, then, not to pronunciation. It says nothing about the learning of pragmatic or sociolinguistic rules, and like most of Krashen's other claims, avoids considering applicability to the learning of vocabulary (where it does seem to fit.) The hardest part is to decide what is a structure or block of structures; unless this is defined, the hypothesis is vacuous.

At this stage, then, I satisfy myself with the modest statement of the condition derived from natural learning and stated in Chapter 11 as follows:

Condition 71
Comprehensible Input condition (typical of natural learning, graded):
The learner is expected to understand; therefore the speaker makes an
effort to see that language is comprehensible.

The value of formal instruction

A disinterested observer, when he finds language teachers wondering whether there is any way to teach a foreign language, might be forgiven for wondering whether they have been contaminated by the deconstructionism that has so charmed their literary colleagues. The popularity of the notion that teaching does not work and that only natural learning is possible does certainly seem like one of those aberrations that sometimes afflict academic minds. Nonetheless, there is value in occasionally pretending to be a young child looking at a naked emperor, and, in this case, in asking whether or not formal instruction makes any difference to second language learning.

The question can be critical for it confronts the core of the extended Monitor Model, with its initial major claims, namely that only 'informal' learning (dependent on innate language learning processes) leads to 'real' language proficiency. But it must first be pointed out that we only have to deal with this issue if we want to consider second and foreign language learning in a single model. If we give up the notion that theory must control practice and focus all our attention on what happens in the classroom, we would have no doubt that teaching is necessary. If on the other hand we look only at the development of bilinguals under natural conditions, we could be forgiven for assuming that teaching is irrelevant. In a general theory, then, we set out to explain the particular contribution of each.

Nonetheless, the question formally posed by Upshur (1968) as to whether teaching makes any difference is an important and non-trivial one, but it is not a simple one. As Long (1983b) points out, it has generally been taken for granted that instruction helps, with the result that he could find only four studies that directly set out to compare the language learning of students with and without instruction. The comparison is not simple to make. There are, he suggests, a number of more specific questions that make up the larger one: one could ask about what is learned through instruction alone, or how effective instruction is compared to what he ingenuously calls 'simple exposure to the second language' (Long 1983b:360); or one might compare instruction and exposure alone to various combinations of each. Conclusive research would need to consider the relationship between instruction alone, exposure alone, and various combinations of the two; it would need to deal with the process of learning itself (such as the sequence of learning certain forms described by Felix (1981)), the speed of learning, and the level of proficiency attained. Long himself takes the view that 'a definitive answer . . . requires use of a true experimental design, that is, (minimally) an experimental and a control group, plus random assignment of subjects to each' (1983b:361). On this basis, he sees the need for sixteen possible comparisons, ranging from comparing a group that receives only instruction with a group that receives no instruction (or exposure for that matter), to comparing groups that receive varying amounts of both.

Even the complex research design that Long proposes would probably be inadequate, for it controls only for *amount* of instruction and of exposure, and does not consider *kind* of instruction or exposure; it uses matching populations, but leaves open the question of generalizability to other kinds of learners open. It is the very complexity of the issue that explains why we make so little progress in spite of a good number of small studies; this is no doubt why Strevens (1988) considers the value of teaching to be 'undemonstrable'.

In spite of this difficulty, there is in fact research showing evidence for the value of instruction. Long (1983b) cites four studies, Upshur (1968), Hale and Budar (1970), Mason (1971), and Fathman (1975), that set out specifically to compare the relative effectiveness of exposure with and without instruction, with the total time held constant. Upshur studied foreign law students in a seven-week summer programme at the University of Michigan. He found no significant differences in performance[5] between those who took a course in English as a second language while taking courses in law and those who did not take the English as a second language class. Long sees problems with the study: the groups were not matched (the students who did better did not take the course); the pre-test was probably too easy for the group that did not take the English course; and the group that received instruction in fact showed higher gain scores. Thus Upshur's conclusion that there is no benefit from instruction is only supported weakly if at all.

In a second study, Mason (1971) also looked at foreign students at an American university. He compared the scores in English tests for students who took the full load of academic courses with those who took a reduced academic load and in addition had special English courses. While Mason found little difference between the treatments, Long argues that there is an advantage on the structure test (the formal language section) for the group that received instruction. This suggests that we are perhaps dealing with a not uncommon phenomenon in the field: results that are predictable not so much from the hypothesis as from the instrument used. In any case, we can sum up by saying that these two studies show that it is not easy to show the value of separate English as a second language classes for more advanced students in English-speaking universities.

The Fathman study and that by Hale and Budar were conducted in a different context, dealing with the question whether to keep students with limited English proficiency in normal schools or classes (an approach called mainstreaming) or whether to put them together in special schools or classes (a pull-out programme). Hale and Budar looked at high school children in Hawaii. They compared two groups of non-English-speaking children. One group was placed in schools where the large majority (110 to 1) of pupils were middle-class and English-speaking; this group was given no additional English instruction. The second group was placed in lower-class schools with a higher density of non-English speakers (1 in 25); this group received special English as a second language instruction. After a year or more, the group that received no instruction did better in standard tests than the instructed group. The difficulties with the comparison are fairly obvious. As Long points out, the conditions are very different; the children in the second group were reported to speak their native language most of the time when out of class, so that there were major changes in the amount of exposure even if we ignore the contaminating socio-economic factors.

Fathman used an oral production test to check the ability of a group of foreign children in Washington schools to produce 'standard English morphology and syntax'; the structures tested were ones looked at especially in first language acquisition studies. She found no evidence of differences in rate of learning between children who were in schools with structured English as second language programmes and those who were not. It is not clear, however, that the existence of such a programme guaranteed access to it, nor that there was in fact no formal instruction in the other schools. As Long points out, older children in the English as second language schools who had been in the US one year only had a higher mean test score than those in the non-ESL schools. Long concludes from these four studies that while there is no evidence of differences between programmes with and without instruction, there is evidence of benefits for students with lower proficiency, for whom, he suggests, a second language classroom might provide the best kind of exposure.

Long (1983b) goes on to cite another six studies that, while not designed directly to deal with the issue, provide clear evidence of the value of adding formal instruction to informal exposure. Three studies by Krashen and others[6] all showed that instructed adult learners of English did better.[7] The study by Carroll (1967) of American university students learning foreign languages, while showing the importance of natural exposure to the language, shows clear effects of formal instruction. Brière (1978) shows the advantage of instruction for children learning Spanish as a second language in Mexico, and Chihara and Oller (1978) report similar results for adults learning English in Japan.

Research on the question has continued, and Long (1988) summarizes it. Weslander and Stephany (1983) have shown that children in Iowa public schools with limited English proficiency benefit from 'pull-out' formal English as a second language instruction. Gass (1982) shows evidence of the value of instruction in the learning of relative clause formation by adult university students. Long also cites work by Zobl (1985) that shows how instruction, by controlling the proportions of marked and unmarked data bearing on an item (here the learning of English possessives by French adults) leads to more efficient learning.

These results, then, support the general view that there is benefit in formal instruction. In trying to understand why this is so, Long (1988) suggests that formal instruction provides options in two significant areas, options in the manipulation of input, and options in the production tasks set to learners. In the former, there are options in sequencing of presentation, frequency and intensity, and salience; in the latter, the learner might be expected to avoid error, or carry out tasks which encourage them to take risks. One key question, then, is how differences in these options might lead to differences in language learning.

The question is investigated by Pica (1985), who studied eighteen adults, native speakers of Spanish, learning English in three different contexts. Six learned only through formal classroom instruction, six were picking up English only through everyday social interaction, and six received a combination of formal instruction and social interaction. Data were collected in informal conversations to study the development of control over some selected English morphological patterns, in particular the indefinite article, the plural -s, and the progressive -ing. In analysis of the use of the indefinite article a, there was no significant difference in the sequence of production accuracy. This, she argues, is related to the complexity of the grammatical distinctions and the fact that the instructional programme did not cover all aspects of it. In the case of plural -s, a relatively simple item and more easily and adequately covered in instruction, there appeared to be good evidence that the instruction-only group achieved higher levels of accuracy. Finally, in the case of the progressive -ing, instruction appeared to have led to inaccurate over-use.

Pica's study is important in showing, at the microlevel of the learning of individual items, the possible effects of instruction. Lightbown (1983) also presents evidence of over-use of certain forms (for example, the various English -s morphemes) by French students, which she attributes to drill, but as time went on these 'side-effects' wore off and the correct forms were established.

These studies are concerned with the possibility of instruction making fundamental differences, at the microlevel, in the learning of individual morphological items. The question is an interesting one in that it is focused on the possibility of there being different processes involved in natural and tutored learning. But if our interest is on the macrolevel, that is in the development of specific or general language proficiency, there is much better evidence of the value of instruction. Long (1983b) summarizes eleven studies, six of which showed faster development in the case of children and adults receiving formal instruction, two of which were ambiguous or favourable to instruction, and three of which showed only minor or no advantage for instruction. Long (1988) cites two new studies that provide further support for the case that formal instruction is the most efficient way for adults at least to learn a second language. He concludes that '... formal SL [Second Language] instruction has positive effects on SLA *processes*, on the *rate* at which learners acquire the language, and on their *ultimate level of attainment*' (1988:135). While instruction does not seem to change the sequence of learning certain grammatical items, it seems to be a *sine qua non* for reaching the full competence of a native speaker.

One might add to these Cooper's finding that formal instruction in Hebrew (which usually means attendance at an ulpan) is the best predictor for Hebrew language use and proficiency.

The studies we have looked at confirm the obvious truth that language learning does take place through formal instruction. Why this should be a surprise will be clear only if one takes the view of the extended Monitor Model that real learning (earlier acquisition) depends on exposure and cannot come from formal learning. One answer proposed by Long is to modify Krashen's definition of learning, to include not just knowledge of 'easy', 'low-level' rules, but also 'the ability to improve SL[Second Language] performance in language-like behaviour in general' (op.cit.:378). Long goes on to point out the influence of the task: 'Language tests of all kinds probably encourage the use of this ability' (loc.cit.). We will return to this point. In his summary, then, Long finds that the attack on instruction is not proven.

The evidence thus supports a view like that propounded at the beginning of Chapter 11. While there are great advantages in the conditions associated with informal language learning, there are also great advantages in the conditions of formal instruction. Each also has its limitations. If there is a restriction in time available, formal instruction appears to be more efficient. There is reason to believe that it is of particular value in the early stages, and it is of obvious benefit in developing control of the formal aspects of language. But formal instruction by itself is limited, and leads typically to limited outcomes.

The approach from teaching

Within the literature that we have been surveying, there is little demonstrable effect of teaching on learning. One reason is surely that much of the research, as Strevens observes, derives from a theoretical paradigm that has already made up its mind that teaching is unimportant. Another reason is the very complexity of the language learning situation, and the difficulty of observing other than minor effects. The practical research problem is simply described. I can, with a small captive audience, attempt to set up a controlled experiment of the learning of a limited segment of language in which my main manipulation is to alter something in the method of presentation. But, as this book has been arguing, the experience of the new language (the presentation) is only one part of a complex set of conditions. The amount of control needed, therefore, would leave a very limited and doubtful experiment, or at least one of very limited generalizability. In a non-experimental design, such as that presented in the next chapter, we will see that it is difficult to describe the learning experience with any degree of precision; one can categorize it as natural or formal, with some general label for kind of learning situation (visit, residence, kind of school) and with some rough quantification of the time spent in each environment. These variables do have some effect on the model, but the study did not make possible an examination study of the complex variations in teacher-controlled experiences that form the basis of informed language teaching.

An attempt has been made by Spada (1987) to study the interaction of instructional approaches with second language learning. Spada compared three classrooms in all of which the teachers used a communicative approach. By observing sixty hours of classroom instruction in each, she was able to show quantifiable and qualitative differences in the implementation of the methodology. One class, for instance, spent much more time on form, while the other two spent more time on function. In one, there was twice as much student-teacher conversation as in a second. Similarly, there was variation in the amount of time that the students spent listening and writing. Having established that there were differences in the instructional situation, she was interested to study the effect on the students' learning as measured by seven different proficiency measures. She found significant differences in the effect of instructional differences on listening and speaking tests when comparing two classes with the third, although there was the possibility of a problem in the scoring of the speaking test. The amount of time spent listening did not account for the difference, which appears to be explained rather by the fact that the teachers of these two classes presented listening material in carefully organized and adjusted chunks, while the class which did not improve had all its practice with natural unadjusted passages. Spada is cautious in her conclusions, pointing out that the sample size is small, the time-range of the study short, and the observed differences often not statistically significant. The difficulty of obtaining evidence of the effect of changes in instruction is clear when one considers the results of even such a well-designed and meticulous study as this one.

An alternative approach, then, is to fall back on what Strevens calls postulates: propositions which are 'self-evident' but perhaps not experimentally demonstrable. Strevens sets out six postulates:

1. The manner of presentation of language input to a learner affects comprehension and therefore learning.
2. A language learner's progress is affected by a large number of features, principally in three sets:
(i) features of the individual, particularly his/her previous experience and profile of language abilities;
(ii) the learner's intentionality or *volition*;
(iii) features of human language learning in general, notably intelligence, memory, and a range of mental processes for learning.
3. Language is comprehended and learned not as discrete, atomistic items presented one at a time in sequence . . . but as a varying flux of sensory data in three modes: *complex*, *multiple*, and *gradual*; so that 'having learned an item of language' has many different manifestations.
4. Comprehension . . . and learning stand in a complex relationship . . . learning is initially only receptive . . .
5. Gaining practical command of a language . . . requires multiple presentations . . . as well as multiple opportunities for the learner to practise . . .
6. Where 'informed language teaching' produces effective language learning, the wide range of teaching/learning techniques and methods employed have developed through reciprocal awareness of how learning can be shaped and managed as a consequence of deliberate teaching . . . (Strevens 1986:2–3)

The issues in the first four postulates have already been discussed. It is the last two that focus on the teaching and learning process. The complexity of possible control of classroom learning conditions is obviously vast. Without even starting on such issues as differences in method, materials, and syllabus, there are an enormous number of options in class size and homogeneity, lesson time and frequency, disciplinary framework and physical arrangement. And even when overall method has been specified by a set of materials, there remains, as Stevick (1986) has dramatically demonstrated, a huge combination of potential choices in presentation, all ways of making it possible for the learner to 'hold on to new words, new patterns, new skills, and new meanings', which he sees as the central issue of language (and any other kind of) learning. His book describes thirty-three options for teaching material at the various levels, ranging from 'Should the students write in their books?' through 'What should the teacher assume about the students' ability?' to 'Should activities that involve spontaneous language be tape-recorded?'. In each case, he shows significant reasons, in appropriate circumstances, to use the two or more possible answers to the options, and throughout he encourages choosing various combinations. 'Remember that the real flexibility and power in the use of these options comes when you use more than one alternative of each option in various combinations in successive steps of your technique' (Stevick 1986:67).

Putting this together with Strevens's last two postulates, we might state a generalized condition for learning in formal situations as follows:

Condition 74
Formal language Learning-Teaching condition (typical, graded): In formal language learning situations, multiple opportunities to observe and practise the new language can be provided. The more these match other relevant conditions (the learner, the goals, the situation), the more efficient the learning will be.

The most important element in this general statement is the notion that formal language teaching is not so much good or bad as it is appropriate or inappropriate.[8] An analysis of a teaching method in terms suggested in the general theory could provide some measure of appropriateness. Most likely, while it would not show any single correct method of teaching, it would show that certain approaches are likely to be inefficient or ineffective in certain situations.[9] Appropriate formal second language teaching would not only provide the best set of opportunities, but would do this in a way that exploits previous knowledge, recognizes language differences, takes advantage of individual student capacities, respects learners' personalities, and benefits from positive attitudes and minimizes negative ones. One can only echo Strevens's call for teaching to be informed by knowledge of the conditions of language learning. As Candlin and Widdowson (1987) put it, advances in language teaching are not dependent on the imposition of fixed ideas or the promotion of fashionable formulas, but arise from 'the independent efforts of teachers in their own classrooms' exploring principles and experimenting with techniques.

Notes

1   Note that optimal input is the $i+1$ of Krashen's theory.
2   Birdsong (1987) suggests that the effect of negative input should be considered a learner-specific rather than a general issue, or in my terms, that it should be expressed as a typicality and not a necessary condition.
3   This issue is discussed again in Chapter 13.
4   See Chapter 8 for a discussion of triggering.

5   The test used was the Michigan Test of English as a Second Language.

6   Krashen, Seliger, and Hartnett (1974); Krashen and Seliger (1976); and Krashen, Jones, Zelinski, and Usprich (1978).

7   There is disagreement between Krashen (1985:26–31) who argues that this happens only at the beginning stage and Long (1986) who cites Krashen, Jones, Zelinski, and Usprich (1978:260) to the effect that the results of these studies led them to conclude 'that formal instruction is a more efficient way of learning English for adults than trying to learn it "on the streets" '.

8   Cf. Sharwood Smith (1985), Bialystok (1985), both of whom see evidence that research supports a much wider range of methods than was once thought to be the case.

9   For one account of a development of a principled second language pedagogy, see Prabhu (1987).

13   Testing the model

Testing a preference model

In proposing a general theory of second language learning, my aim has been a model which will account for generalizable differences in individual achievement; a model which will explain why, in certain circumstances, some learners do better than others. I have argued that this can be achieved by a preference model, with the generalizations presented as preference rules or conditions, some of which are necessary but most of which are graded and typical. In Chapter 1 I first presented a set of informally stated conditions derived from my reading of current research, and in the rest of the book, I have summarized the arguments for them. In this chapter I will discuss evidence from a case study for a number of the conditions that I have been discussing.

The case study dealt with the learning of Hebrew in a Jewish school in a diaspora community.[1] It is far from a thorough testing of the theory, which, as I acknowledged in Chapter 1, is not stated formally enough for such testing, but it will give some idea of its general value and indicate how further verification might be attempted.

Researchers often work in situations that do not permit them to test a full and complex model of second language learning. The restricted definitions of what I have labelled K, the second language learner's knowledge of the language he or she is learning, have hindered comparisons across studies, and the limitation of much research in the interlanguage or second language acquisition tradition to the learning of comparatively few morphemes and features of sentence syntax has put a major constraint on its generalizability. Even scholars who take the wider view of second language learning often accept such limitations, as witness Gardner's reluctance to consider informal learning and Schumann's complementary reluctance to consider formal learning.[2] The school I chose to study gave me the chance to look at the two together, for its pupils had a wide range of experience with Hebrew and knowledge of it. A number were native speakers; others had lived and studied in Israel for a year or more; many had made long or short visits. The majority had had various amounts of formal instruction in Hebrew, some at the school and some before they came there, giving a wide range of proficiency that was an enormous challenge to the Hebrew teaching staff.

The school, then, was a good place to test a theory which claims to be general and aims to include (and so be able to distinguish between) formal and informal learning, to recognize different outcomes of learning, to provide for different kinds of learners, and to deal with different levels of specificity. The testing was limited by the usual methodological and time problems, and in particular, in the absence of a statistical technique to explore the effects of a preference model, I have used correlational models. Nor did I manage to gather all the data needed: information on IQ and the age of beginning to learn Hebrew is missing, and I have no detailed microlevel language learning results to report. The study does, however, make it possible to check the relative weight of a number of the conditions proposed in the model and so to see ways of testing and refining the claims of the general theory.

To establish the correctness of a model of the kind I am presenting, there are two separate tasks: to show the correctness of individual conditions or rules, and then to establish the correctness of the set of conditions as a whole. An empirical claim is considered correct when it is shown that it cannot be falsified. A theory, or any individual rule in it, is generally[3] considered to be falsified by the existence of a clear counter-example. There is no problem about how this applies to necessary conditions, whether graded or not. If a case is found in which the condition should apply but does not, or a case where the strength of the condition should affect the strength of the outcome, but does not, this case constitutes a counter-example that challenges or falsifies the condition. For example, if it were to be proposed that normal hearing is a necessary condition of second language learning, the existence of successful deaf learners would show the proposal to be wrong. Similarly, if it had been suggested that language aptitude is a graded necessary condition rather than a graded typicality condition, the lack of correlation between aptitude and Hebrew learning found in this study would be counter-evidence. Examples of adult second language learners with perfect accents make it impossible to consider youth a necessary condition even for learning pronunciation.

With typicality conditions, disconfirmation is more of a problem. Seeing that there is no claim that they work all the time, is there any way to falsify them, or are they so powerful, so unfalsifiable, as to be useless in constructing an empirically verifiable theory? First, a typicality condition is wrongly labelled if there are no known cases where it does not apply: that would make it a necessary condition. Secondly, it has no claim on typicality if it does not apply in a reasonable number of cases. The term 'typical' suggests in fact that it should usually apply, but the existence of a number of counter-examples does not falsify a typicality condition but rather shows that it is correctly labelled. The important effect of typicality conditions, subject to testing, is that they strengthen the likelihood of an outcome; they are not necessary but additive. They are not absolute, but lead, as Jackendoff pointed out, to stronger judgements. Thus, when one says that normal hearing is a typicality condition for second language learning, one is claiming that learners with normal hearing will typically, other things being equal, learn better than those with hearing impairment. Setting language aptitude as a graded typicality condition says that students in whom some aspect of aptitude is highly developed will learn faster than others. However, the fact that typicality conditions are additive means that the effect of any one condition can be masked by the strong influence of other conditions; thus aptitude might be masked by attitude or learning opportunity. The interesting question about typicality conditions that calls for empirical testing is their weight: when are they powerful enough to mask other conditions? How do they contribute to a complex outcome?

In this chapter I will only touch on this latter question, which relates to the question of how to test the model as a whole. To answer this, we need to ask how a preference model might work, how its various rules and conditions go together and produce results, or better, explain the results that we might expect to observe. The most useful analogy I can think of is an expert system; this will be discussed in the last chapter. In the meantime, I will use statistical techniques to explore the claims of the model.

Defining the outcomes

One of the most important emphases of the general theory that I have been presenting is the need to define outcomes clearly. The first twenty conditions were concerned with this issue. In Chapters 2 to 4 I argued that any general theory of second language learning must start by assuming that language proficiency is a complex phenomenon: to use any single measure for the criterial outcome leads to distortion. In the case study, then, to capture the wide range of proficiency, I used different assessment instruments, including examinations, interview tests, and self-reporting.[4]

The self-assessment questions, which cover many different skills (see Table 1 in the Appendix), were particularly useful in investigating the differences in proficiency. There was a high correlation between the functional Hebrew language skills claimed by the pupils, as Tables 4 and 6 in the Appendix show, but the fact that the correlations are not higher draws attention to the existence of differences in the pattern of proficiency of the population, differences in their control of the various skills. Part of this is the result of the difference between productive and receptive skills (Conditions 8 and 9); part the result of differing control of formal and informal skills. That we find these differences is to be interpreted not as a weakness of measurement but as a strength; the differences represent not just 'noise' (some of which arises from problems of reliability and validity in the instrument) but also underlying variation in the make-up of individual proficiency. They provide support, in other words, for the basic claim in the first twenty conditions setting out the complexity of second language knowledge. In looking at the influence of the various factors in the study, it will be important to be clear which aspects of linguistic proficiency are being considered as relevant outcomes. In practice, I will distinguish a number of specific clusters of skills: particularly useful for the study are Hebrew-speaking proficiency, Hebrew-reading proficiency, and Hebrew religious language skills, although others will be mentioned.

Ability and personality

The study casts no light on the issues covered in Conditions 21–26, concerned with physiological and biological differences. There was no effect shown for sex on the various Hebrew proficiency measures, nor was any effect apparent for age or form (grade).[5]

The study did, however, produce some evidence on Condition 27, the Intelligence condition, which proposes a relation between intelligence and school-related second language learning. The evidence is only indirect, as no IQ measures were available, but it is plausible to use scores in examinations in other school subjects as a possible indicator of what I will call school-related intelligence. Table 3 in the Appendix shows the correlations among some examination results. It can be seen that the Hebrew examination correlated significantly with the French examination; its correlation with the English, mathematics and even the Jewish Studies examinations, however, was quite low. In contrast, the French examination correlated highly with the four other examination results. This may be used to argue at least weak support for the correctness of Condition 27.

French at the school is taught as a purely academic subject; success in learning it correlates highly with success in other school subjects, which is itself usually predicted by intelligence tests, and, as shown in this study, by aptitude measures. The social and attitudinal factors relevant to language learning are in this case outweighed by the academic emphasis.[6] In a Jewish school, Hebrew, by contrast, is much less an academic subject: there are strong attitudinal influences, and even the formal teaching is affected by values concerned with informal use.

The difference in the relevance of ability to Hebrew and French learning is even more obvious when one looks at the effect of language learning aptitude. In Chapter 7 arguments were made for Condition 29, Memory condition, and Condition 30, Grammatical Sensitivity condition. In the case study, these specific aspects of language learning aptitude were measured by two different tests given to all fourth year pupils. One was the number learning section from the Elementary

Modern Language Aptitude Test;[7] the other was the York Language Aptitude Test. The number learning task correlated with the York test (r=0.65), but the level of the correlation confirms that each taps different abilities. The two parts of the aptitude test correlated well with French examination scores, as is shown in Table 7 in the Appendix, confirming that the tests are tapping two of the important components of language learning aptitude, and that they are in fact good predictors of achievement in formal foreign language learning. There was, however, no significant correlation between the two aptitude tests and any of the measures of Hebrew achievement or proficiency.

For the Hebrew examination, the correlation between the York test and the Hebrew examination score (r=0.26) and that between the number learning and the Hebrew examination (r=−0.06) are not significant; the York test in fact had a slight negative correlation with the various self-assessment measures. The case study, then, produced no evidence for the effect of the measured kinds of aptitude on learning Hebrew, even Hebrew achievement as tested formally in the second term examination, supporting the claim that these conditions are typical and not necessary.

How might the difference between the cases of Hebrew and French be explained? Several possible explanations come to mind. There is a difference in teacher characteristics: the French teachers are native speakers of English trained to teach French as a foreign language in a secondary school, and it is to be imagined that they would stress the formal skills that the aptitude tests are designed to measure. The Hebrew teachers are native speakers of Hebrew with training as teachers but not as teachers of Hebrew as a foreign language; their approach might well stress other abilities. Second, the pupils' exposure to French has been almost entirely formal, and in a classroom, where the particular aptitude skills are important. There will also be a greater homogeneity in the amount of time they have been learning the language. The pupils' exposure to Hebrew varies considerably both as to time and kind; many have exposure to informal language use. Third, the pupils' attitude to French is likely to be simpler and more instrumental; while attitudinal factors are still likely to exist, they are generally weaker than in the case of Hebrew. The pupils' attitude to Hebrew is complex, and involves integrative as well as instrumental values. Whatever the explanation, it is clear that while aptitude is important for the learning of a foreign language in formal classroom situations, it loses this importance when there is major variation introduced by such variables as time and kind of exposure and attitude.

This demonstration is important in the way it supports the preference model. Language aptitude, the theory claimed, is a typicality condition. In the case study, it is relevant to second language learning in certain circumstances (the learning of French in normal foreign language classroom conditions) but it is not as important in the learning of Hebrew where other factors outweigh it.

Anxiety

The study included some questions about learning strategies and behaviours, but these are better interpreted as motivation, for they refer to willingness to work hard at language learning rather than differentiating between learning styles. It did not focus on general personality factors—Chapter 7 showed the difficulty of formulating workable personality conditions. There is, however, considerable evidence of the effect of anxiety, as set out in Condition 33, the Second Language Learning Anxiety condition.

The responses to questions about anxiety on the questionnaire correlated negatively and strongly with the self-report measures, as can be seen in Table 8 in the Appendix. There was further evidence of the effect of anxiety in the high negative correlation between the anxiety measure and the interview scores. The small but important group of pupils who are embarrassed to speak in class, who are afraid that others will laugh at them, have a serious impediment to their language learning that shows up not just in oral active skills but also has effects on understanding and reading. Again, the condition meets the requirements for a typicality condition: in certain cases, it is a significant explanation, but in others it is not.

Attitudes and rationales

The model I have presented claims that social context affects second language learning in two ways, through attitudes and through the provision of opportunities for learning. It further claims that attitudes have their influence through the development of motivation (Condition 53). In the case study, attitudes were investigated by asking three sets of questions: questions about attitude to Israel and Israelis, questions about goals and rationales for learning Hebrew, and questions about religious orientation. There were also more direct questions about motivation (attitudes to Hebrew language learning and learning behaviours).

The overall attitude of pupils in the school to Israelis, represented to them by some of their fellows, is mixed; a third are positive, a third negative, and a third more or less balanced (see Table 9 in the Appendix). On the other hand, the pupils are very favourably inclined towards Israel. The majority see it as the centre of Jewish life and want to visit it; a good number see it as the best place for Jews to live and want to live there themselves for at least a year (see Table 10 in the Appendix). One reason for keeping these two sets of attitudes distinct was to allow for differences in attitudes to the country itself, Israel, and to the people from there (some of whom form a distinctive community in the school). The two measures are, however, summed up in a combined measure, integrative orientation.

Attitudes are also revealed by the reasons given for learning a language (see Table 11 in the Appendix). A factor analysis including the integrative attitude factors suggested the existence of three clusters of goals. The first of these is an integrative cluster, the second might be considered instrumental-educational, and the third religious-ethnic. This division may be considered a test of the relations between rationales and goals in Hebrew learning discussed at the end of Chapter 4. In Spolsky (1986b) I suggested that one might find Hebrew learning goals divisible into a large number of rationales. In this case, there appears to be support for a more parsimonious clustering, but in other Jewish schools in the diaspora more or different clusters probably emerge.

The third attitudinal measure in the study was a question on religious orientation; again, as Table 12 shows, the pupils represent a wide range of observance.

The three attitudinal measures (integrative orientation, amount and kinds of rationales, and religious orientation) all turn out to have high correlations with Hebrew language learning, but they appear to be more indirect in their effects than the motivational measures provided by attitude to Hebrew learning and learning behaviours.

Hebrew learning attitudes (see Table 13) and learning behaviours (as dealt with by Conditions 52 and 53) were examined by a number of items on the questionnaire, and composite measures were calculated. The relations among these various factors are suggested by a multiple regression analysis.[8] Three factors enter into the final equation:

Attitude to Hebrew = integrative goal + integrative orientation + good learning behaviours or strategies

The equation accounts for over half of the variance. Note that integrative orientation is itself a composite of attitudes to Israel and to Israelis. Anxiety is independent; so is age, religious observance, and time lived in Israel. Similarly, the good learning behaviours are themselves predictable, although the equation has an interesting turn to it. The first factor to enter and the most powerful is the general attitude to learning Hebrew. The second is form (grade), and it has a strong effect when treated negatively (lower forms report better learning behaviours). The third is the integrative goal cluster.

Another way of looking at this question is to consider the correlations among the various attitudinal measures, set out in Table 15 in the Appendix. The table shows that while situational anxiety is largely independent, there is a solid correlation among the three measures of learning strategies, attitude to Hebrew, and integrative orientation.

They add up in some ways to motivation: the attitudes to Israel and to Israelis, significant by themselves and together as contributors to learning, generally enter into the multivariate analyses as part of the learning strategies which they lead to or the attitudes transferred to Hebrew and learning it. However, as Gardner found, they show up in a factor analysis; the second factor in the analysis was most closely associated with the integrative orientation composite, although the principal attitudinal measure loading on the first, proficiency factor, was learning strategies.

An interesting point deserving of further analysis is the effect of sex on attitude. While there are no significant differences between boys and girls on the various combined self-assessment measures, girls in the study showed more favourable attitudes to Hebrew, to Israel, and to Israelis.

The effects of attitudes

The correlation of the various measures of Hebrew language proficiency with the various attitudinal measures is one way of exploring the effects of attitude on second language learning. It must be noted that there is no a priori way to decide that the effect is not in the opposite direction (namely, that high achievement leads to good attitudes) or that it is not to be accounted for by a third unknown factor causing the two of them to co-vary. But one can rely on other longitudinal studies such as those of Gardner cited earlier, which show that attitudes do not generally seem to change (and seldom to improve) as foreign language learning continues.

For 101 pupils in the lower forms, both Hebrew examination scores and attitudinal measures are available. The highest correlation ($r = -0.48$) is with the composite of the items I have labelled situational anxiety. There is also a weaker ($r=0.25$) correlation with the composite of attitudes to Hebrew and learning it. There is no significant correlation with any of the integrative measures or with the strategies and behaviours, nor is there any significant correlation with the number of rationales provided for learning Hebrew nor its components.

These results are intuitively satisfying and agree with the discussions in earlier chapters: school-related attitudes and behaviours are significantly related to the school-related learning that is tested in formal examinations. It shows further that the general attitude measure is likely to be closer to the motivation claimed in the model as the more direct cause.

When one looks at Hebrew functional proficiency derived from the self-assessment instrument, attitude to Hebrew and learning it is an important predictor, as shown in Table 14 in the Appendix; all correlations are strong and clear.

Weaker than the attitudinal measures but still significant is the effect of religious observance on functional Hebrew skills. The correlation set out in Table 16 in the Appendix shows an uneven but interpretable pattern. As expected the strongest effect shows up on proficiency in religious language skills and on the reading skills within which the three religious items occur; it is not significant in its effect on the understanding skills. This pattern becomes clearer when we look at the effect on the individual self-assessment items. It is statistically significant in only seven items. First, as one would expect, there is a highly significant correlation with the specific religious skills; other significant items are some elementary skills. The picture is convincing: first, the religiously observant pupils are the most likely to have developed the special religious skills, and secondly, those pupils who are observant are most likely to have received (at this school or elsewhere) an elementary Hebrew education.

The goals clusters also show effects on the Hebrew language proficiency developed, as Table 17 in the Appendix shows. There are also revealing relationships between individual goals and individual self-assessment items. In the majority of the cases, the correlations are significant. The results are less clear for four goals (to be educated, to train the mind, for examinations, and to read literature) with some items, but for these goals the correlation with the other twenty-eight items is highly significant. The two goals with the highest correlations are 'because it is important to my career' and 'because it is our language'. Note that learning Hebrew for a career, as Anisfeld and Lambert (1961) pointed out many years ago, is not in this case an instrumental factor, but an integrative one. In their study, it was interpreted as referring to an intention to work in a professional role in the Jewish community; here it is more likely to reflect intention to live and work in Israel. The second goal is also an integrative one, showing a high degree of identification with the language. A second pattern shows explainable high correlations between the other two integrative goals, to meet Israelis and to talk to people, and the social skills: introducing yourself, understanding native speakers, and understanding easy news on the radio; they also correlate very highly with reading a simple story (a major school activity).

The analysis supports the following view of the effect of attitudes and motivation. There is an independent factor, situational anxiety, that accounts for poor learning in the case of a small but important cluster of learners; this effect is clearest at earlier stages and in formal learning. There are a number of attitudinal factors—attitudes to Israel and Israelis, reasons for learning, religious orientation, as well as more general attitudes to learning Hebrew and ways of going about learning it—that affect the learning in two ways. First, they influence the development of motivation, which is an important explanation of success or failure; their influence is in this way general. Second, they have more specific effects, so that attitudes appear to carry into particular motivations (Condition 54, for instance): thus, religious orientation and goals predict the acquisition of religiously-relevant skills, integrative attitudes and goals predict social and communicative skills, and academic goals predict academic skills.

Opportunities for learning

So far in this chapter, evidence has been presented on the complexity of learning outcomes (K in the formula), the effects of some aspects of ability (A), and the nature of attitude and motivation (M). The fourth cluster of conditions to look at are those concerning learning opportunity (O), and in particular the application of the Exposure condition:

Condition 51
Exposure condition (necessary, graded): The more time spent learning any aspect of a second language, the more will be learned.

The best opportunity for learning Hebrew is in Israel where it is the dominant language. The pupils at this diaspora school have three kinds of experience in Israel: some were born there, some moved there at a later stage in their life, and many have made visits. The correlation of time in Israel with the composite self-reported skills is shown in Table 18 in the Appendix. All these correlations are high except for that between the score for the religious items and visits to Israel.

The effect of living in Israel on Hebrew proficiency needs no explanation. The effect of visits to Israel might be less obvious. A single, short tourist visit does not necessarily lead in itself to significant language learning; its effect is more likely to be indirect, through improved attitude and increased number or strength of rationales. A large number of visits, however, suggests some regular place to stay, such as a relative, with increased opportunities for language use, with relatives or friends.

Even leaving native speakers out of consideration (as in Table 19 in the Appendix), the importance of untutored exposure to Hebrew is clear from the study. A school programme with limited hours has little chance of competing. As other research has shown, tutored instruction needs to reach a high number of hours before it can approach the effect of long periods of natural exposure: the Canadian French immersion programmes provide about 4,500 hours of classroom contact, and the European School in Brussels, operating in a French context, provides 1,500 hours to non-French-speaking pupils in order to reach a high level of working proficiency (Baetens Beardsmore and Swain 1985).

What effects of formal instruction showed in the study? Detailed information on formal Hebrew learning was collected in the interviews. Four types of formal instruction were identified:

(a) Time spent at a school in Israel
(b) Private tuition (usually for bar mitzvah)
(c) Time in weekend or supplementary Hebrew classes
(d) Time in a Jewish day or boarding school (including this one).

For the sample of pupils I interviewed, which included native Israelis and others who had attended school in Israel, the correlation between Hebrew proficiency (as shown by their score in the interview test) and time spent in an Israeli school was high (r=0.69). Omitting the pupils with Israeli experience, the correlation of the total of the other three kinds of formal Hebrew instruction with Hebrew proficiency was also high (r=0.58). Of the three kinds of non-Israel formal experience, time in a Jewish day school was the only one to appear important; private tuition and time in weekend or supplementary classes had no clear influence on proficiency, but did have a marked negative effect on attitude to learning Hebrew.

The amount of time involved in each of these kinds of experience varies disproportionately. All instruction in Israeli schools is in Hebrew, meaning that the pupils receive at least 1,000–1,200 hours of instruction and exposure per year. Private tuition for bar mitzvah is unlikely to come to much more than a total of 80 hours, and is quite restricted in focus. The supplementary Hebrew classes meet for about two hours a week; there might be an addition for exposure to Hebrew in religious services, but at the same time a need to subtract for the fact that much of the time is spent on religious instruction rather than on Hebrew. Eighty hours a year of instruction in Hebrew, then, is probably a generous estimate for the normal Jewish religious school. The Jewish day schools the pupils had attended do not generally teach Jewish subjects in Hebrew; many of them probably do not even teach Hebrew itself in Hebrew, but through English. The amount of exposure to Hebrew and instruction in it in the day schools to which these pupils went might generously be estimated at 200 hours per year. Thinking about these figures, it is obvious why the time spent in Israel emerges as such a strong factor in the study. The figures also make clear the great potential of immersion programmes. The Jewish day schools in Canada with a double immersion programme in Hebrew and French studied by Genesee (1987) can make it possible for their students to have accumulated 3,000 hours of Hebrew instruction by the end of the fifth year: Jewish day schools in Latin America have similar high exposure to the language. But many European Jewish day schools offer no more time for Hebrew than for other languages, with not surprising results.

The case study did not look at the effect of kind of exposure, but illustrates the relevance of learning opportunity and in particular the effect of the amount of exposure to the language. Natural exposure and the kinds of major increases possible with immersion programmes would clearly seem to be ways of overcoming the effects of variation in ability and motivation.

A causal model

While the notion of cause and effect is by no means clear to philosophers, the working scientist, as Davis (1985) points out, finds it a necessary assumption. It is reasonable and desirable to try to connect the various factors involved in a general theory of second language learning into some kind of causal chain. At the very least, this will add to our understanding of the phenomenon, and it may well have additional benefits in the possibility of suggesting modifications of practice.

As Davis makes clear, the logical establishment of causality in the social sciences cannot depend on statistical techniques alone. Denied the ability of the experimental scientist to manipulate events, we can still find general principles for causal ordering and statistical evidence for the goodness of fit of the model. But the logical ordering must come first.

The Hebrew learning study was designed to provide data (through answers to questionnaires and scores in tests) representing a number of identifiable constructs. The most relevant of these are the following:

– Hebrew language proficiency (divisible into such components as reading, speaking, understanding, for religious, academic, or socio-communicative functions)
– native language
– good learning behaviours or strategies
– attitude to learning Hebrew or motivation
– language learning anxiety
– integrative orientation (divisible into attitude to Israel and attitude to Israelis)
– goals (divisible into Integrative, Educational, and Religio-ethnic goals)
– formal hours of Hebrew learning (distinguishable as in a day school or a supplementary school)
– time spent living in Israel
– time spent visiting Israel
– time spent in an Israeli school
– degree of religious observance
– success in academic school subjects.

In sorting these into a general model, a first question is which factors are likely to come at the end of the chain (i.e. not be a cause of any other) and which are likely to be original (i.e. have no other causes within the system). This establishes three groups:

(1) Only as a result:
    Hebrew language proficiency (divisible into components)

In spite of the possible logic in the claim that proficiency leads to better attitudes and stronger motivation, longitudinal studies (Gardner 1985) suggest that this is not the case. However, there are grounds for believing that low proficiency (poor academic results) increases language learning anxiety.

(2) Only as a cause:
      language aptitude
      native language
      formal hours of Hebrew learning (distinguishable as in a day school
        or a supplementary school)
      time spent living in Israel
      time spent visiting Israel
      time spent in an Israeli school
      degree of religious observance
      success in academic school subjects.

Because the pupils studied are not independent adults, we assume that the decisions where to live, what school to go to, when to visit Israel, how often to go to synagogue, were likely to have been made by their parents. We treat these factors as causes therefore.

(3) Both cause and result:
      good learning behaviours/strategies
      attitude to learning Hebrew and motivation
      language learning anxiety
      integrative orientation (divisible into attitude to Israel and attitude
        to Israelis'
      goals (divisible into integrative, educational, and religio-ethnic
        goals).

Many of these are likely to be influenced by the previous set of factors. The strength of religio-ethnic goals, for instance, can be seen to result from the degree of religious observance, for a pupil who is religiously observant is likely to value religious or ethnic goals for learning Hebrew. Similarly, a pupil who has lived in Israel is likely to value integrative goals. A pupil who has been academically successful is likely to have developed good learning behaviours. There will also be interactions, causes, and effects, within this cluster: goals may be assumed to cause attitudes, attitudes to lead to motivation, and motivation to cause good learning behaviours.

On the basis of this general analysis, I would propose a model that looks something like that shown in Figure 13.1. The model is to be read as follows. As a result of factors external to the model (native language, social situation, parents' attitudes, personal characteristics), the individual learner enters the model with four relevant factors: a degree of religious observance, a cluster of abilities, time spent in a Hebrew-

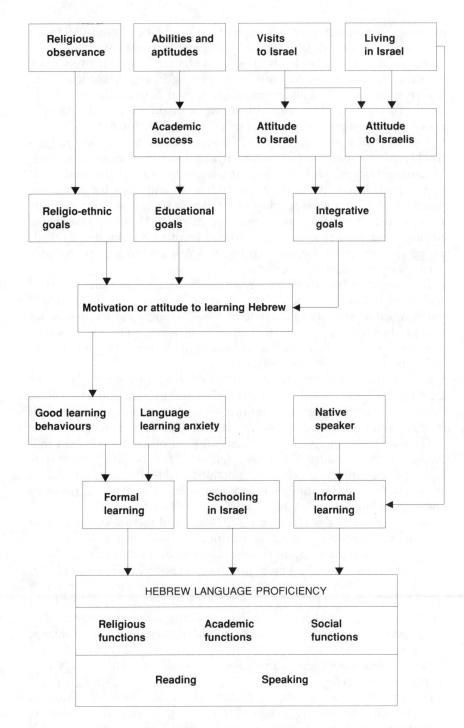

Figure 13.1   A proposed causal model for Hebrew learning in the case study

speaking environment (in the home as a native speaker, or in Israel living or visiting) and a possible tendency to language learning anxiety.

Being a native speaker leads directly to Hebrew language proficiency for social functions, as do visits to and living in Israel. Proficiency in academic functional skills depends on formal learning, either inside Israel or outside it. This formal learning is made more probable by a high degree of religious observance or as a result of living in Israel.

A pupil with a high degree of religious observance will have religio-ethnic goals for learning Hebrew, which lead to a more positive attitude to learning Hebrew, stronger motivation, good learning behaviours, and higher proficiency, particularly for religious and also for academic functions. A high ability pupil, with academic success in other subjects as well, will have academic goals for learning Hebrew, favourable attitudes and good motivation, and good learning behaviours; depend-ing on the amount of formal learning, this will lead to high proficiency particularly in academic functions.

Time spent in Israel will lead to more favourable attitudes to Israel and Israelis, and so to the development of integrative goals. This will result in better attitudes to learning Hebrew, stronger motivation, better learning behaviours, and so to higher proficiency especially in social functions, but above a critical level (where the learner plans a career in Israel), in academic functions as well.

Some learners will be inhibited in their learning by strong language learning anxiety; this will be reinforced by failure. The model assumes facilitation in the learning situation; a good learning experience will increase. and a bad one decrease, the development of proficiency.

The model also suggests that specification of outcomes will lead to a change in the conditions that are relevant; for example, when our interest is in explaining religious functional skills, the relevant factors are likely to be motivation, religio-ethnic goals, anxiety, and religious observance, but not, for example, time spent in Israel.

The correlations described so far give a useful picture of the factors that account for second language learning in this case. Pupils are more likely to develop (or to claim to have developed) functional proficiency in Hebrew if they have had more untutored exposure (by living in Israel or visiting it), if they are more religiously observant, if they have positive attitudes to learning Hebrew, if they have positive attitudes to Israel and Israelis, if they want to develop an Israeli accent, if they are not afraid of using Hebrew in class, if they have good language learning strategies, and if they see many reasons for learning Hebrew. But how can we decide the relative weight of these various conditions and the way that they are interrelated?

Put in these terms, one approach is to see how the various correlational (and putatively causal) factors are related. If two factors that cause a result are themselves closely related, their additive effect is less. The more independent the factors are, the more likely that their effect will be cumulative. A statistical technique that explores this specific relationship is multiple regression analysis. In multiple regression, the contribution of a number of variables to accounting for a selected dependent variable are checked, one by one, and entered into the final equation in the order of their importance.

The differences between the various composite skill measures may be analysed by looking at the various combinations of other factors that seem best to account for them. We would expect to find that the relative weight and even the actual make-up of the explanatory factors would vary. I take first the overall score, the sum of all thirty self-assessment items. As this item is the one with the highest variance, it should be possible to reach the highest level of explanation with it. I analyse first a group of pupils for whom I have Hebrew examination scores, 101 pupils in the lower forms. In the analysis, I tried fourteen possible predictors for overall proficiency:

Age, form, Hebrew examination score, years lived in Israel, religious observance, recent use of Hebrew, visits to Israel, goals, attitude to Hebrew, attitude to Israel, attitude to Israelis, anxiety, good learning strategies, and integrative orientation.

Five of these items entered the final regression equation before the limit (.05) was reached. Their combined correlation (multiple R) with the dependent measure is 0.73; this accounts for about half of the variance. The five factors in the equation, in order of entry, are:

Good learning strategies, years lived in Israel, anxiety, attitude to Hebrew, form (grade).

Note that all of the pupils in this analysis have had formal Hebrew learning in the school (otherwise there would not be a Hebrew examination score for them). The major differences among them are school-related: strategies, anxiety, attitudes, the form they are in. Time spent in Israel is, however, a significant factor; even though it enters the equation second, it has the highest beta[9] and highest level of significance. Thus, even in this group, natural learning opportunity is very important.

A second interesting analysis is to look at the variables which account for the Hebrew examination score, which, as noted earlier, was correlated with the self-assessment measures but not closely related to it. There is a small group of pupils, mainly in the junior forms (first to fourth inclusive), on whom there are available four examination scores (Hebrew, English, French, and mathematics) as well as full questionnaire data. A multiple regression analysis selects as the first variable accounting for the Hebrew examination score the score on the mathematics examination, this accounting for 20 per cent of the variance; adding to this good learner strategies, raises the multiple R to .58, meaning that between them the two variables account for a third of the variance. None of the other variables (including age, English and French examination scores, time in Israel, sum of self-assessment items, religious observance, or any of the attitudinal measures) enter into the equation. Thus, for this group the two best predictors of the Hebrew examination score are probably general school ability and motivation (represented by the learner strategy items).

The next analysis looks at 223 pupils and considers the variables accounting for Hebrew proficiency as claimed by pupils' own reports. The first item to enter the equation is the time that a pupil has lived in Israel. The second item to be added is the sum of positive attitudes to learning Hebrew, the measure I argue is close to motivation. The third variable added (with negative effect) is the sum of the language learning anxiety items. The final equation includes five variables; between them, they correlate (multiple R= 0.84) with overall proficiency, accounting for a quite high 70 per cent of the variance.[10] The five variables, in order of importance, are:

Years lived in Israel, attitude to Hebrew, anxiety (negative), degree of religious observance, number of visits to Israel.

Interpreting this analysis cautiously, it might be claimed that those pupils in this school who have lived longest in Israel, where Hebrew is spoken, are most likely to claim ability to function in the language.[11] Once this period of living in Israel is taken into account, the next most important variable is motivation. When the effect of these two variables is held constant, the third critical variable is the inhibiting effect of language learning anxiety. The fourth variable is degree of religious observance, represented by the regularity of attending synagogue; it accounts in particular, as noted earlier, for the religious self-assessment items. The fifth variable is visits to Israel.

It is interesting also to note the variables that do not enter into the equation, either because they have no effect or because they are already included in some way (through high correlations) in the other variables. In this case, the variables excluded by the analysis were attitude to Israel, attitude to Israelis, integrative orientation, and the goal clusters. Note that each of these has already been shown to correlate significantly with overall proficiency; their exclusion from the equation must result from the fact that they are included in (highly correlated with) other more powerful variables, in this case the general attitude or motivation measure.

Limited as these analyses have been, the case study has provided useful support for the model, and has given a first indication of how to go about testing it. In particular, the case study has justified the claim in the theory about the need to specify outcomes, and has shown the effect of a number of important typicality conditions, especially those concerning aptitude, anxiety, attitudes and motivation, and learning opportunities. In the next chapter, I will consider some of the ways it might be possible to overcome some of the methodological problems found in testing the theory, and how the theory itself might be refined.

Notes

1   For fuller details on the school and the methodology and for statistical tables, see the Appendix.
2   See Chapter 10.
3   As I mentioned earlier, Kuhn has drawn attention to the fact that normal science is not in fact quick to change when it finds counter-examples, but tries rather to patch the theory. But normal scientists speak as though we are always ready to modify our theories.
4   The reliability and validity of the self-assessment are discussed in the Appendix.
5   To see if this is the result of including native speakers in the analysis, these correlations were recalculated on only those pupils without extensive natural exposure to Hebrew (including in other words all who claimed it as a native language, or who claimed to have learned it from family members before going to school, or who reported that they had lived in Israel for more than two years). The correlations were only slightly higher, and still not statistically significant.
6   One might contrast their importance in Canada, where social conditions lead to the relevance of attitudinal factors to French learning.
7   After this had been given to some of the pupils, scoring showed that it was too easy, so a more difficult version (but not as difficult as the equivalent test in the MLAT) was developed and used with the rest of the students; only results of this second version are reported.
8   I have used Stepwise Multiple Regression, although it might be argued that hierarchical multiple regression would give more reliable results.
9   Beta is a partial correlation, with the effect of other measured variables taken into account.
10 Regression statistics provide a number of measures of relationships. The multiple R is the correlation of the variables in the equation with the dependent variable. R^2 is the percentage of variance accounted for by the equation; it is this figure that I generally cite.

An R^2 of .50 might be interpreted by saying that if we had only the variables in the equation, we would be half-way to predicting the dependent variable. In these terms, we might say that in this case, the amount of time a pupil has lived in Israel explains half of the variation in his or her knowledge of Hebrew. Our aim in the study is obviously to see as high an R^2 as possible; we will then have a reasonable hypothesis about the nature of the independent variables, the influence of which accounts for the dependent variable.

11 Because many of the native speakers do not learn Hebrew at the school, not all of them completed all parts of the questionnaire; as a result, this analysis does not express their influence on the model.

14   The form of a general theory

Choosing a model

In statistical studies such as the one reported in the last chapter, the focus of attention is necessarily on groups of learners. It must not, however, be forgotten that we are in fact trying to understand what happens to individual learners, each of whom, on the basis of individual ability and motivation, undergoes a large number of specific learning experiences and develops a personal level of knowledge and skill. The study of groups makes it possible to recognize the existence of common factors, which must then be applied to the individual again. Second language learning is essentially an individual process, however much it is socially relevant and derived. While it is true that *langue* is a social phenomenon, it ultimately exists in the brain and mind of each individual speaker. There is another sense in which interest in the collective may draw attention away from the individual, and this is by concentrating on the macrolevel of the summed knowledge and skills concerned with functional language use; this macrolevel knowledge depends ultimately on the microlevel learning of individual linguistic items and structures.

The significance of a concern for the individual is twofold. First, it is a reminder of the dangers of collective approaches to language testing and teaching; at the simplest pragmatic level, individualization permits greater precision in assessment and greater efficiency in teaching. Second, it raises interesting questions about the best model in which to present a general theory. If the focus is to be on the individual learner, the most appropriate model would seem to be one that works at the individual level. Even if we want, then, to look at groups, starting at the individual level should help allow for the necessary attention to individual differences. I want, therefore, to explore the possibility of using an individually focused model, one that will respect the demands of both the macro and microlevels.

In the course of this book I have presented a number of rules or conditions which I propose are basic postulates or hypotheses in a general theory of second language learning. These conditions were listed in the first chapter, argued for and exemplified in the course of the book, and some of their interactions displayed in the last chapter. I also proposed that they form a preference model. The preference model has been presented informally as a competence model; I have on occasions referred (not necessarily positively) to processing models. Essentially, my goal has been to understand rather than replicate; I want to account for learning rather than explain how to teach. The very basis of this book is the belief that there are in fact a very large (perhaps unlimited) number of ways to learn. My claim throughout the book has been that the preference conditions I have been stating model the underlying system and account for it without making particular claims as to how it works. Obviously, there would be no more sense in claiming that every learner sits there with a preference model in his or her head than there would be in a claim that speakers of a language proceed to apply the rules of a transformational grammar as they speak and understand. The model is a formalization; it substitutes reality, and claims that the actual process must involve at least something as complex as this system.

In Chapter 13 I discussed the problem of establishing the correctness of a preference model, and suggested that a useful analogy is an expert system. Expert systems, as developed in Artificial Intelligence research, seem to be consistent with the needs of the preference model I have been proposing.

Expert systems are models developed in the course of computer research into artificial intelligence that attempt to emulate the activities of human experts in solving complex problems. Let me give a simple, non-computational example of how an expert (that is, someone with experience) goes about diagnosing a non-functioning system. When my computer suddenly stops working, I check out a number of possible causes in turn, depending on my experience and expertise. If the lights in the house have also gone off, I am fairly sure that the problem is lack of electrical power. If the computer stops while it is daytime, then, my first step might be to check whether the lights work. If they don't, I need to follow up on the electricity problem (check my fuses, check with the neighbours) rather than worry about the computer. Underlying the action I take is a set of beliefs about the nature of the system I am dealing with: a necessary condition for the computer to work is electricity; if the computer doesn't work, one cause might be lack of electricity; if the house lights work, there might be another cause why the computer is not receiving electricity. And so on. An expert (especially one who uses a computer in a city with regular power cuts) quickly develops a more-or-less efficient system of checking out causes and trying remedies.

The more elaborate the problem, the more complex the expert system. One area that has been fairly well studied is that of medical diagnosis, where there are computer programs that lead through the steps of a diagnosis.[1] Expert systems are important in being able to deal with the uncertainty that occurs at two levels.[2] The first level is the accuracy of knowledge of the present situation. In the power failure I attempted to reduce this uncertainty by checking whether or not other lights work, but I still cannot be sure that power is getting to all necessary parts of the computer. In the diagnosis there may be certain relevant information that is hard to measure accurately, or hard or even impossible to obtain. This means that the first part of a conditional statement in a rule system will usually need to be qualified with a probability statement:

If I know *with a specified degree of probability* that X is the case . . .

rather than the more simple condition in the form

If X is the case . . .

In an expert system, corresponding to the requirements of typicality conditions, the second part of the rule is also to be stated as a degree of likelihood:

If the car won't start, and the fuel gauge is on zero, and I can't remember when I last bought fuel, the chances are very good that it is out of fuel.

As a failure in the car's electrical system would produce the same result, a wise driver checks it (to reduce uncertainty on the condition) before setting off to buy more petrol. There might be other causes of failure, but this evidence would usually be enough to lead to action, which itself is a way to produce more evidence.

The important feature of expert systems is that they are designed to deal with cases of uncertainty, with fuzzy situations. They work by gathering as much information as possible and then making a decision. They allow for the fact that results have multiple causation, for stronger and weaker judgements, for formal systems that remain open to modification.

The general theory of second language learning that I am proposing in this book consists of a set of preference conditions which, I suggest, might go together somewhat as the rules of an expert system do. We might think of our problem as a predictive one: what are the chances that a learner will develop a new linguistic behaviour? The theory shows how we might determine which pieces of information are relevant to that understanding. The more information available, and the more precisely the outcomes can be specified, the more accurate the prediction can be.

Let us try a couple of examples. To predict the likelihood of a specific item being learned to a criterion level by an individual, the simple model proposed by Carroll and summarized in a formula in Chapter 1 might be enough. The formula $Kf = Kp + A + M + O$ said that future knowledge and skills (in this case a criterion level control of a specific item) depends on present knowledge and skills, ability, motivation, and opportunity.

Can the formulation be improved? The additive nature of the formula misses some key features that have been found important in this book; the characteristics of typicality conditions in particular. Stating the formula on the basis of conditions, it is better presented as something like this:

$$P(CK) = K(R_{21-74})$$

The probability P of a change C in knowledge K of a second language (as specified in Conditions 2–20) is a function of present knowledge as modified by the application of R to the other Conditions 21–74.

In order to make the prediction more accurate, we need a precise specification of the outcome, a method of assessing present knowledge, information on the ability and motivation of the learner, and a notion of how much and what kind of opportunity can be given. The interactive nature of the model claims, for instance, that less able learners will need more motivation or opportunity; that while there is a wide choice of possible opportunities, learners will be more or less successful according to the kind of ability and kind of motivation; that some kinds of learning opportunity may well reduce motivation.

In considering the macrolevel of developing functional skills in a defined domain, the degree of specification of ability, motivation, and opportunity becomes more critical, for these conditions apply over a larger number of individual learning events. Social context will have more effect on the kinds of motivation that will keep the learner active and the kinds of opportunity that will be available, and the ability effects will be magnified and so differences in make-up will become more critical.

The expert system analogy makes it possible also to think about an application of the general theory to the specific problem of planning for language learning. Consider, for example, a desire to achieve different results in the school studied in the last chapter. The statistical model offers a false trail in its assumption of the low level of relevance of formal instruction. A more detailed analysis that revealed the existence of various groups of pupils is more in line with the implication of the preference model. Using the present level of Hebrew knowledge of the pupils as a criterion, three distinct populations emerge: a group with little or no knowledge, a group with native knowledge or naturally acquired fluency, and a group with formally acquired skills. Each requires different treatment. The group with no Hebrew is most likely to benefit from an intensive programme that will enable them, as soon as possible, to function alongside the third group. The pupils with native or natural fluency need rather an academically focused programme to develop their control of formal literate Hebrew. The group with formally acquired skills will presumably benefit from tighter focusing of their continuing formal programme and the search for time and space for informal learning. Of critical importance for the non-native speakers and those who have not lived in Israel is a concerted attempt to raise the status and value of the language. Especially relevant to the native speakers is concern about their religious orientation. Another sub-population that needs attention is the pupils with high levels of anxiety, who need an approach that will permit a level of satisfying achievement.

A generally stated set of goals like these is of course no more than a strategy: the specific tactics call for the devoted work of informed language teachers, capable of controlling their own pedagogy, as Widdowson has described them:

> The teacher, I have argued, needs to ask why he follows certain routines, or otherwise these routines are simply empty ritual, gestures in the void. He must be able to formulate problems based on an analysis of short term and long term objectives and then be able to test out solutions through teaching activities. Every teaching experience can be considered as an experiment whereby the teacher first undertakes a conceptual analysis of the problem he wishes to solve, then designs activities in the classroom by way of trial solutions, controlling the variables as best he can. (Widdowson 1984a:33)

The theory I have been presenting suggests the basis for the 'conceptual analysis' and begins to identify the variables which can be controlled and those which need to be taken into account. It suggests the additive value of many different kinds of intervention; it also suggests criteria for finding more appropriate and so more efficient modes of intervention, and the possibility of counter-productive activities, such as teaching techniques which may seriously reduce motivation in certain circumstances.

Beyond the preference model

The preference model highlights the problem of relating the learning of individual items to the learning of more general abilities, a distinction that I have referred to as micro and macrolevel learning. An analogy that might help clarify this issue is the problem of modelling weather. The development of television weather reporting has given all of us a view of weather changes as a matter of macrolevel processes: we see on the screen clouds and rain moving in broad sweeps. But there are recent suggestions that the more generalized models fail to predict with accuracy because they do not capture the minute changes in each tiny sector that make up the broader picture. Scientists are said to be working on models that permit the study of liquid flow not as a generalized process but as the result of changes in individual cells. The complexities involved in weather are easy to imagine: local conditions partly determine local weather, and in their turn affect neighbouring cells; this is passed on further as general conditions which in turn affect local cells.

There are two scientific models currently being developed that offer considerable promise. One is in the area of fractal geometry, where work by scholars following Mandelbrot (1974) is opening up new vistas for study not just of physical phenomena but of diffusion among human beings.[3] The second is the work in what is called Parallel Distributed Processing (Rumelhart and others 1986), which already is challenging basic assumptions in the area of language learning. While it is risky to be premature, it is worth considering briefly the implications of this potential revolution, which, Sampson (1987) argues, may well lead to a paradigm change as great as, or greater than, that launched by Chomsky's *Syntactic Structures*.

Proponents of Parallel Distributed Processing (called 'connectionism' by some) set out to build a model for human cognition on the basis of the complexity that is now known to exist in the brain. Just what possibilities this gives is revealed by the following account, taken from *The Economist*:[4]

> The brain is getting more complicated. Ten years ago scientists had a fairly simple picture of how it worked. The business of the brain, they believed, was conducted through circuits made of neurons which talked to each other via ten chemicals called neurotransmitters. Neurotransmitters are released at the ends of nerves and push electrical signals across junctions to neighbouring nerve fibres. The new picture is messier but more fruitful . . .
> Several tools have helped remap the brain and, in particular, its system of chemical locks and keys . . .
> The first lesson from such experiments (and others) is that each neuron can be linked to many others. In fact, each of the 100 billion nerve cells in the brain may form connections with up to 10,000 of its fellows. The brain is thus composed of a switchable network of neurons; it is not a vast electrical circuit with just one connection between each pair of neurons . . .
> The brain, it turns out, has not ten but around 100 different neurotransmitters . . .

> (*The Economist*, 26 December 1987)

The proponents of Parallel Distributed Processing argue that the generalizations, rules, and axioms with which we have become accustomed to work are gross and approximate ways of dealing with the outcomes of processes made up in fact of large numbers of microscale elements, which themselves are not conceptually interpretable. The processes themselves involve large numbers, varying in non-binary ways, and made up of individual events that are stochastic in nature; they occur in large networks, which, as the description of the brain above suggests, may be variously connected internally to each other or externally, receiving input from the outside world or sending output to it. A network learns a new behaviour pattern by changing the 'weight' of its various connections on the basis of patterns received from input to it. These patterns of 'weights' rather than the fixed connections determine the new pattern of behaviour.

The model is very complex. By some, it is considered as a direct application of the brain model; more generally, it is assumed to be based on what is called the brain metaphor, so that it does not directly depend on the neurophysiological evidence. The model has been used to explore a number of different questions. One of those most interesting to linguists is a study of the learning of past tense forms of English verbs. In this study, which requires a 460-member phonetic feature coding system, the input is paired base forms and past tense forms; high and low frequency verbs were input in 200 training cycles, by the end of which the model is claimed to be able to generate 91 per cent of the correct features of low frequency verbs with which it had not previously been presented. Its responses were always plausible (if not always correct) and mirrored in a number of ways the behaviour reported for children learning English as a first language.

Sampson is excited to note that these results are achieved without the rules proposed by competence models; they reflect much more closely the performance of normal speakers of a language. While he does not claim that this model is a disproof of the rule-based model, and points out that work on the PDP model is in its very early stages, it does seem to offer a strong potential challenge, and show the nature of a model that will account for performance without postulating competence. The argument is one that students of the history of language teaching theory might find somewhat familiar. The theoretical failure (and practical problem) of the Audio-Lingual Method was its inability to show how to move from learned sentences to creativity; this was one of the best arguments for the post-Chomskyan language learning models (for example, Krashen's championing of what he labelled acquisition, the first-language-like internalization of rules). Current language theories have so far failed to show how to go from competence to performance; how to relate structural knowledge and rules to functional language use. Parallel Distributed Processing offers, then, a possible model for developing the kind of performance grammar that many scholars call for. Its implications for second language learning theory are potentially immense.

Consider how this would work. While a generalized functional ability is developing, it is developing through the addition of individual items. A first critical question is what is meant by an 'item'. In pre-Chomskyan days, linguistic items were fairly easily defined (phonemes, morphemes, structures); generative grammar has led to a major emphasis on the grammatical rule and its parts as critical items to be learned, and on more complex phonetic and lexical features as part of the knowledge base. Work based on Parallel Distributed Processing approaches suggests an even more complex composition of linguistic knowledge (witness the 460-member phonetic coding system mentioned above). There is no fixed order in which most individual items are learned,[5] although it is affected by previous knowledge, ability, and the particular kind of exposure. The likelihood of learning a new item is affected in turn by the degree to which the last item learned satisfies, encourages, reduces, or maintains the motivation that led to the learner's first exposure. Thus, each individual act of learning combines into the broader level of functional skill development. The preference model is one attempt to capture this enormous complexity. It goes, I believe, a useful step beyond the binary models that allow only for necessary conditions in capturing the complexity of one aspect of human behaviour. But it too is, in the microscale terms of the Parallel Distributed Processing paradigm, just a broad generalization, albeit more within our conceptual grasp than the complex mathematical models that one day might come to bridge the gap between competence and performance, between the macrolevel of our observations and the microlevel of the underlying systems.

Extension of the theory to language loss

A number of studies have raised the question of the relation between a theory of language learning and a theory of language loss. In modern linguistics, studies of language loss tend to be derived from Roman Jakobson's proposal (1941) that loss (in particular in the case of aphasia) is a mirror image of acquisition. Studies of language loss have followed a number of paths: some, close to Jakobson's formulation, look at loss of language knowledge and skill as a result of trauma or age. The focus here is individual; the concern usually being with the first language (but with a steady interest in the relative loss of first and second language). A somewhat different set of studies is concerned with language loss as a result of language shift: working in anthropological or sociolinguistic frameworks, studies chart the changes in the linguistic repertoire of a community and the way in which languages are lost or maintained. Again, the emphasis tends to be on loss of first languages and their replacement by a second. A third area of interest, and the one most relevant to our present interest, is a series of studies on the loss of language skills in second languages.[6]

The issue can be best expressed in terms of the formula given earlier:

$$P(CK) = K(R_{21-74})$$

Note that this formula refers to change and not just learning; it allows in other words for forgetting as well. There are two ways that language attrition might be dealt with. One is to propose that Condition 62 be modified.

Condition 62
Opportunity for Practice condition (necessary, graded): Learning a language involves an opportunity for the new skills to be practised; the result is fluency.

The modification required would be to make this a condition on maintaining knowledge as well as on learning. But I think this misses some of the complexity of the issue, for in fact evidence suggests that the way items are lost relates to the conditions set for the model as a whole. I would, then, propose that second language attrition be accounted for by adding to the theory of second language learning an Atrophy condition, as follows:

Atrophy condition (necessary, graded): Second language knowledge is forgotten if it is not used.

It is important to be clear on the nature of the claim. First, it assumes the same complex definition of second language knowledge that we discussed in Chapters 2–5 and summarized in Condition 20. The analysis of loss of language skills will require the same careful specification of what is being lost as the study of language learning.[7] Secondly, it is neutral on the underlying process involved in forgetting. It is a competence rather than a processing claim, and does not make any pre-empirical claim that forgetting is either loss of underlying knowledge or loss of access to that knowledge; rather, as in the parallel specification of second language knowledge, it assumes that the theory will need to account for such differences specifically. Thirdly, it claims that the same factors that account for differences in individual second language learning will also be required to account for differences in individual second language attrition—the same clusters of conditions concerning previous knowledge, ability, personality, motivation, and opportunity will be involved.

Note that the claim that second language attrition mirrors second language learning is not a claim for reverse order, except for those aspects of second language where order can be established for learning. It is a claim, rather, that is subject to the same empirical testing as the general theory presented in this book, and suggests the possibility of using evidence from second language attrition to test both theories at once.

Conclusion

The principal task that I set myself in this book has been to identify the criteria for a formal, general model that will account for known facts about second language learning of all kinds and to use such a model to explore the interaction of conditions relevant to the process. The model that I have presented has been general in its coverage: it has aimed to encompass all kinds of second language learning, whether by children or adults, formally or informally. As a result, it has shown some of the important distinctions that can be made within a general theory between such special situations. It has stressed in particular the need to be precise in defining the outcome of second language learning, showing that differences in goal or outcome make fundamental differences in the working of the model. The model has shown the interaction of a large number of conditions, and thus overcome the weakness of simpler and more restricted models. It has shown that the relevant conditions are of two main kinds, some necessary and most typical, working in other words as the rules of a preference model which, I have argued, is the best model to depict the nature of second language learning. Finally, it has emphasized the need to place a model of second language learning within a social context, for individual learning is indirectly but strongly modified by the working of social factors.

The establishment of this general theory has no direct applications in second language pedagogy, but is tested by practice and has important implications for it. Essentially, it may be said to establish a principled theoretical basis for an informed eclecticism in second language pedagogy. Eclecticism without explicit criteria is anarchic and irresponsible. Eclecticism judged only pragmatically runs the risk of developing into dogmatic orthodoxy. The general theory I have been presenting provides criteria for developing practices in an eclectic way and for accounting for the success and failure of the practices in varying conditions. The principles it has established, then, can inform a reasoned eclecticism of method and approach.

The task I undertook was to set out a model for planning and evaluation of research in second language learning, and through it to highlight the state of present knowledge and the areas still requiring more detailed research. The use of the model enabled us to be much more positive than scholars often are about the present state of our knowledge. Thus, while I agree with McLaughlin (1987) that 'At this point, research and theory cannot act as sources of prescription about teaching procedures', I do not agree that this is because of 'too many gaps in our knowledge', but rather because, as I have argued earlier, no theory of second language learning can be translated into a prescription for teaching. There are gaps in our knowledge to be filled, but it is the nature of science that uncertainty continues, that new knowledge leads to new questions and uncertainties.

In the course of the book, I have drawn attention to this developing knowledge. The scholars who work in the interlanguage or second language acquisition tradition are making major contributions to our understanding of the learning of important parts of language, just as those who work in the social psychological paradigm are helping us understand the relevance of individual difference in motivation and other variables to the development of language proficiency. If the present study has focused attention on one crucial need, it is for studies that will relate these two trends. Just as interlanguage researchers have recognized the need to deal with variability, so must they continue to explore the relevance of their model to areas of second language learning other than morphology and syntax, and to the complex set of skills that makes up communicative competence. The model that I have been exploring assumes that these various studies can be integrated: that the sum of our knowledge of second language learning is in fact greater than its parts.

Notes

1 One of the best known is MYCIN, developed by E.H. Shortliffe in 1974 as a rule-based computer system to help doctors select appropriate anti-microbial therapy.
2 See Cohen (1985) for a detailed discussion of one way to deal with this problem.
3 For example, Robert May is applying the model to the field of epidemiology.
4 This enormous complexity might be usefully compared with the somewhat simple and almost mechanical neuropsychological models mentioned in the Introduction and in Chapter 6.
5 If there is a natural order, it is limited in its scope.
6 See Lambert and Freed (1982), Weltens, de Bot, and van Els (1986). Van Els (1986) suggests a four-way classification into research concerned with loss of first and second languages in first and second language environments.
7 Ginsberg (1986) discusses this issue when describing the complexity of skills to be tested in the Language Skills Attrition Project.

Appendix

Case Study: Hebrew in a Jewish school

The case study

The case study was carried out in a Jewish boarding school in a diaspora community and focuses on the learning of Hebrew. The pupils at the school include a number of Israelis who are native speakers of Hebrew, and also a number of native speakers of other languages who have lived in Israel for various amounts of time. The pupils reveal a wide range in their linguistic backgrounds, in the degree of Jewish religious identification (ranging from non-orthodox to orthodox), and in academic ability (including at one extreme a group with specific learning disabilities and at the other pupils already admitted to leading universities).

Most of the data were collected through questionnaires, which were completed by 293 pupils (a quarter of them girls) out of the total of 321 enrolled in the school at the time. The grade level of the pupils ranged from first to upper sixth form, and their ages from 10 to 18. After the questionnaire had been analysed, a random sample of fifty pupils, stratified to represent different levels of Hebrew knowledge, was selected to be interviewed and tested individually.

Overall, the pupils demonstrate considerable linguistic sophistication; they know twenty-two different languages. All of them know English,[1] 40 per cent claim Hebrew, a third French, and 10 per cent German. While only twenty-six pupils included in the study are native speakers of Hebrew, another thirty-one have heard it used around them before they first started school, and a further thirty-seven claim to have learned it from friends or relatives outside school. Thus, a third of the pupils in the study have been exposed to Hebrew in natural learning situations.

English is the only language of instruction in the school, including in language classes, and the language normally used between teachers and pupils and among pupils, but nearly a quarter of the pupils report that they use another language as well when speaking with their friends at school.

In the questionnaire, pupils were asked to report their Hebrew skill by checking one of three columns ('Cannot do it', 'Can do it', or 'Can do it well') for thirty different items, ten each for speaking, understanding speech, and understanding written Hebrew. Another section of the questionnaire presented the students with a list of ten possible reasons for learning Hebrew.

The questionnaire asked a number of questions about attitudes to learning Hebrew, to Israelis and to Israel, and about the learning strategies pupils followed. Another set of items dealt with characteristics of the anxious learner; this seemed to affect a small proportion (10–15 per cent) of the pupils.

Another question asked was about the strength of a pupil's personal religious commitment. While the school is strictly orthodox in all its practices, and while the parents of most pupils (88 per cent) belong to a synagogue, only a small proportion of the pupils reported themselves as being fully observant.

The reliability and validity of self-assessment

The main method of gaining information on the pupil's Hebrew language proficiency was a self-assessment form. Pupils were asked to report their functional proficiency in Hebrew by checking one of three columns ('Cannot do it', 'Can do it', or 'Can do it well') for thirty different items, ten each for speaking, understanding speech, and understanding written Hebrew. The items were selected to cover a broad range of communicative skills and more or less ranked in presumed order of difficulty.

Table 1 (see page 235) shows the kinds of items included, the degree of difficulty (mean score) of each item, and its discriminating power (the correlation of an individual item with the total score). The self-assessment battery as a whole forms a reliable measure; Cronbach's alpha is 0.982, theta is 0.985.

There is evidence also on the validity of the self-assessment.[2] Because of the way the items are worded, there is little difficulty in deciding about face or content validity: any reader can judge whether or not they constitute a reasonable description of linguistic outcomes for learning Hebrew.

It is also desirable to establish concurrent validity,[3] that is, validity by correlation with other methods of judging the pupils' knowledge of Hebrew. To do this, a number of test items were included in the interviews conducted with the stratified sample of pupils. In the interview, pupils were assessed on their ability to perform fourteen of the tasks named in the self-assessment items.[4] I graded their performance on a three-point scale like that used in the self-assessment items:

0 — could not do it
1 — could do it with difficulty
2 — could do it easily.

The correlation between the total interview test score[5] and the total self-assessment score was very high (r=0.92). Correlations of individual items on the interview with the equivalent self-assessment items were also high, ranging from r=0.89 for the counting items to r=0.57 for prayer-book reading. Generally, the more specific the item, the better the correlation. The self-assessments were slightly more cautious (mean 10.98, S.D. 8.61) than the interview test (mean 12.56, S.D. 8.78). A scatter-plot showed that two of the pupils had overclaimed and one had underclaimed. The interview test score correlated about as well with the total self-assessment score as did the various clusters of self-assessment items with each other (see Table 2 on page 236).

A further measure of Hebrew proficiency was provided by examination results at the end of the first term for pupils in the first four years. The correlations among first-term examination scores for some of the pupils are shown in Table 3 (see page 236).

For one third of the pupils (103), in the first four forms, we can compare the Hebrew examination score[6] with the combined self-assessment measures.[7] In all comparisons, the correlation is significant. The self-assessment scores correlate as well with the Hebrew Examination as the Hebrew examination does with any other examination (see Table 3).

It is possible, therefore, to interpret the self-assessment scores as being reasonably representative of the pupil's actual functional ability in Hebrew, and to base much of the analysis on the self-assessment scores.

Notes

1 Some were receiving instruction in English as a foreign language, but all of these were also expected to take classes taught in English.
2 Other studies which have shown the validity of self-assessment of language proficiency include von Elek (1982), Oskarsson (1984), Oscarson (1988 MS), and LeBlanc and Painchaud (1985).
3 For a discussion of the concept of validity, see Bachman (forthcoming).
4 Marked with an * in Table 1.
5 The interview test was reliable (Cronbach's alpha is 0.949, theta is 0.951).
6 It must of course be noted that the examination grade is a restricted measure: it is an achievement rather than a proficiency measure, and measures just those aspects of the course that the Hebrew teacher has selected to emphasize. It is not surprising, therefore, that the correlation of the teacher's grades with the self-reported proficiency scores of the same pupils students is not high.
7 The correlation of the Hebrew examination grade with individual self-report items is significant at the .001 level in only three cases—describing future plans, understanding written directions—and at the .01 level in thirteen (including the first six speaking items); it does not reach statistical significance in the other fourteen cases.

Tables

Skill	Mean score	Correlation with total
Speaking		
Count to 10*	1.49	0.60
Introduce self	1.15	0.77
Describe self*	0.97	0.83
Give date*	0.91	0.78
Ask directions	0.83	0.84
Describe picture*	0.63	0.89
Future plans*	0.47	0.89
Describe school	0.46	0.88
Present argument	0.28	0.79
Discuss politics*	0.27	0.75
Understanding		
Simple questions*	1.38	0.72
Slow speech*	1.02	0.83
Telephone (slow)	0.80	0.87
Easy news	0.68	0.90
Announcement	0.65	0.89
Song	0.48	0.83
Fast speech	0.47	0.87
Film	0.44	0.87
Radio news	0.42	0.86
Native speakers*	0.39	0.85
Reading		
Prayer book*	1.26	0.59
Letter	0.86	0.85
Signs	0.86	0.86
Easy stories*	0.75	0.86
Bible*	0.56	0.81
Newspaper headlines*	0.54	0.89
Directions on package	0.38	0.83
Rashi commentary**	0.36	0.71
Newspaper article*	0.34	0.85
Novel	0.27	0.79

Notes
*Tasks named included in interview test
**Eleventh century French Jewish commentator

Table 1   Can–do (self–assessment items)

	Interview score	Self–assessment score			
		Speak	Understand	Read	Total
Interview	1.00	0.93	0.90	0.84	0.92
Speak		1.00	0.94	0.85	0.96
Understand			1.00	0.89	0.98
Read				1.00	0.95
Total					1.00

Table 2   Correlations of the interview test and the self–assessment

	Jewish Studies	Hebrew	English	Maths	French
JS	1.00	0.24	0.42**	0.20	0.39**
Heb		1.00	0.12	0.22	0.34**
Eng			1.00	0.29**	0.30**
Maths				1.00	0.24**
Fr					1.00

Note
**Significant at the .001 level

Table 3   Correlations among end–of–term examinations

	Speak	Understand	Read
Speak		0.93	0.90
Understand			0.92

Note
The correlations in this table are for the full population; if we restrict the comparison to those who have not had any untutored exposure (omitting, in other words, those who have been exposed to Hebrew at home or as a result of living in Israel for more than a year), the correlations are naturally lower—about 0.84), but still show the same pattern.

Table 4   Correlation among the self–assessment claims

Grouped skill	Mean	SD	LQ	Median	UQ
HSpk	7.5	6.2	2	6	11
HUnd	6.7	6.6	0	4	10
HRd	6.2	5.9	1	3	8
HProf	20.4	18.2	5	15	29

Note

HSpk   The sum of the speaking items
HUnd   The sum of the understanding items
HRd   The sum of the reading items
HProf   The sum of all the items

Table 5   Means, standard deviations, medians, and lower and upper quartiles for grouped skills (self–assessment scores)

	HSpk	HUnd	HRd	HProf	HAcad	HRel
HSoc	0.97	0.96	0.91	0.97	0.93	0.82
HSpk	1.00	0.93	0.90	0.97	0.94	0.84
HUnd		1.00	0.92	0.98	0.94	0.84
HRd			1.00	0.97	0.92	0.91
HProf				1.00	0.96	0.82
HAcad					1.00	0.82

Note

*The four defined in the note to Table 5 and in addition:

HAcad   The sum of the three items (future plans, simple questions, directions on package) most related to proficiency in Hebrew for academic purposes
HRel   The sum of the four items (date, prayer book, Bible, and Rashi commentary) most relevant to religious functions
HSoc   The sum of the eight items most related to social or communicative purposes

*Table 6   Correlations among the various self–reported skills**

	French examination	
	First term	**Second term**
Numbers memory (22 cases)	0.69**	0.47
York test (41 cases)	0.75**	0.72**

Note
**Significant at the .001 level

Table 7   Correlations of aptitude measures and French examination scores

	Anxiety
HSpk	−0.43**
HUnd	−0.41**
HRd	−0.37**
HProf	−0.43**
HAcad	−0.39**
HRel	−0.33**
HSoc	−0.29**

Note
**Significant at the .001 level

Table 8   Correlations of anxiety with self–assessment scores

Statement	**% No**	**% Maybe**	**% Yes**
They are sociable, creative	25	49	26
I'd like to know more	26	36	39
Want to speak their language	40	27	33
They should learn English	16	29	56
They want to emigrate	40	50	11
They are considerate	31	55	14

Table 9   Attitudes to Israelis

Statement	% No	% Maybe	% Yes
The best place for a Jew	20	34	45
Centre of Jewish life	9	22	69
Want to visit	9	12	79
Want to live there for at least a year	31	29	40

Table 10   Attitudes to Israel

Statement	% No	% Maybe	% Yes
To speak to Israelis	24	26	50
For my future career	55	30	15
To meet people	26	25	49
To be knowledgeable	19	37	44
To know Jewish history	26	39	34
It's our language	26	32	43
To pray in it	23	31	46
To train the mind	24	38	38
For examinations	48	25	27
To read Hebrew literature	44	31	25

Table 11   Goals and rationales for learning Hebrew

Frequency	%
Never	4
Less than once a month	33
At least once a month	25
Once a week	8
Several times a week	4

Table 12   Reported synagogue attendance

Statement	% No	% Maybe	% Yes
It's good	24	38	38
Hate it	64	23	13
Enjoy it	39	36	25
Prefer another subject	23	29	49
It's important here	16	27	57
A waste of time	68	22	10
Will continue after school	37	29	34
It's dull	48	28	24
Will give up after school	43	32	25
Love it	51	33	17

Table 13   *What do you think about learning Hebrew?*

	HebAtt	SabAtt	IsrAtt	IntegOr
HSpk	0.50**	0.33**	0.41**	0.42**
HUnd	0.51**	0.37**	0.41**	0.41**
HRd	0.49**	0.33**	0.39**	0.42**
HProf	0.52**	0.37**	0.42**	0.44**
HAcad	0.47**	0.33**	0.40**	0.41**
HRel	0.42**	0.26**	0.38**	0.36**
HSoc	0.55**	0.35**	0.41**	0.43**

Notes
HebAtt   Attitudes to learning Hebrew (see statements in Table 13)
SabAtt   Attitudes to Israelis (see statements in Table 9)
IsrAtt   Attitudes to Israel (see statements in Table 10)
IntegOr   Integrative orientation (SabAtt + IsrAtt)
**Significant at the .001 level

Table 14   *Correlation of attitudes and linguistic outcomes*

	Goals	HebAtt	IntegOr	GLS	SitAnx
Goals	1.00	0.66	0.63	0.63	−0.18
HebAtt		1.00	0.64	0.64	−0.20
IntegOr			1.00	0.52	−0.16
GLS				1.00	−0.22
SitAnx					1.00

Notes

GLS   Good learning strategies, such as 'I answer questions in class', 'I do my homework regularly'

SitAnx anxiety such as, 'I am nervous when the teacher calls on me in class', 'I don't like to speak in class'

Table 15   Intercorrelations of the attitude measures

	Religious observance	
	Full group	**Without 'natural' groups**
HSpk	0.19*	0.33**
HUnd	0.13	0.28**
HRd	0.22**	0.43**
HProf	0.18*	0.37**
HAcad	0.17*	0.32**
HRel	0.35**	0.48**
HSoc	0.17*	0.29**

Notes

Full group = 225 pupils (those who completed all parts of the questionnaire)

Without 'natural' groups = 183 pupils (i.e. excluding those who have been exposed to Hebrew in natural learning situations)

*   Significant at the .01 level

**   Significant at the .001 level

Table 16   Correlation of degree of religious observance and self–assessment measures

	InteGl	EdGl	EthnGl
HSpk	0.49	0.28	0.36
HUnd	0.54	0.31	0.38
HRd	0.49	0.31	0.38
HProf	0.52	0.31	0.38
HAcad	0.49	0.29	0.37
HRel	0.42	0.28	0.38
HSoc	0.53	0.31	0.37

Notes
InteGl = Integrative goals
EdGl = Educational goals
EthnGl = Religio–ethnic goals
All correlations in this table are significant at the .001 level.

Table 17   Grouped goals and self–assessment items

Self–assessment measure	Time living in Israel	Visits to Israel
HSpk	0.63**	0.38**
HUnd	0.67**	0.41**
HRd	0.69**	0.28**
HProf	0.68**	0.37**
HAcad	0.67**	0.37**
HRel	0.52**	0.20*
HSoc	0.60**	0.41**

Note
* Significant at the .01 level
** Significant at the .001 level

Table 18   Correlation of Hebrew skills and time in Israel (all pupils)

Self–assessment measure	Time living in Israel	Visits to Israel
HSpk	0.26**	0.25**
HUnd	0.24**	0.28**
HRd	0.17	0.08
HProf	0.24**	0.22*
HAcad	0.23**	0.25**
HRel	0.10	0.02
HSoc	0.22*	0.28**

Note
* Significant at the .01 level
** Significant at the .001 level

Table 19   Correlation of Hebrew skills and time in Israel (excluding native speakers and long–term residents)

Bibliography and citation index

Abdulaziz, M.H. 1986. 'Factors in the development of modern Arabic usage.' *International Journal of the Sociology of Language* 62:11–25. [42]

ACTFL Provisional Proficiency Guidelines 1982. Hastings-on-Hudson, NY: American Council on the Teaching of Foreign Languages. [70(n 11)]

Adjémian, C. 1976. 'On the nature of interlanguage systems.' *Language Learning* 26:297–320. [33, 39]

Amara, M. and **B. Spolsky.** 1986. 'The diffusion and integration of Hebrew and English lexical items in the spoken Arabic of an Israeli village.' *Anthropological Linguistics* 28:43–54. [146(n 4)]

Anderson, J.R. 1980. *Cognitive Psychology and its Implications.* San Francisco: Freeman. [170]

Anisfeld, M. and **W.E. Lambert.** 1961. 'Social and psychological variables in learning Hebrew.' *Journal of Abnormal and Social Psychology* 63:524–9. [210]

Asher, J.J. 1964. 'Towards a neo-field theory of behavior.' *Journal of Humanistic Psychology* 4:85–94. [191]

Asher, J.J. 1981. 'The total physical response (TPR): theory and practice' in H. Winitz (ed.): *Native and Foreign Language Acquisition.* New York:The New York Academy of Sciences. 379:324–31. [191]

Asher, J.J. 1984. MS. 'Comprehension training: the "outrageous" hypothesis that works.' Paper prepared for the Thirteenth Annual University of Wisconsin-Milwaukee Linguistics Symposium, 29–31 March, 1984. [191]

Asher, J.J. and **R. Garcia.** 1960. 'The optimal age to learn a foreign language.' *Modern Language Journal* 53:334–41. [95]

Ashworth, M. 1985. *Beyond Methodology: Second-Language Teaching and the Community.* Cambridge: Cambridge University Press. [29(n 8)]

Atkinson, P. 1985. *Language, Structure, and Reproduction: An Introduction to the Sociology of Basil Bernstein.* London: Methuen. [45(n 19)]

Bach, K. and **R.M. Harnish.** 1979. *Linguistic Communication and Speech Acts.* Cambridge, Mass.: The MIT Press. [77]

Bachman, L.F. forthcoming. *Fundamental Considerations in Language Testing.* Oxford: Oxford University Press. [234(n 3)]

Baetens Beardsmore, H. and **M. Swain.** 1985. 'Designing bilingual education: aspects of immersion and "European Schools" models.' *Journal of Multilingual and Multicultural Development* 6:1–15. [190, 211]

Beebe, L. 1980. 'Sociolinguistic variation and style shifting in second language acquisition.' *Language Learning* 30:433–47. [39]

Beebe, L. and **H. Giles.** 1984. 'Speech-accommodation theories: a discussion in terms of second-language acquisition.' *International Journal of the Sociology of Language* 46:1–32. [139, 141]

Bell, A. 1984. 'Language style as audience design.' *Language in Society* 13:145–204. [137–8, 140–1, 45(n 16)]

Bernstein, B. 1964. 'Elaborated and restricted codes: their social origins and some consequences' in J.J. Gumperz and D. Hymes (eds.): *The Ethnography of Communication. American Anthropologist* 66 (6)/2. [45(n 19)]

Bialystok, E. 1978. 'A theoretical model of second language learning.' *Language Learning* 28:69–84. [2, 47, 62]

Bialystok, E. 1979. 'Explicit and implicit judgements of L2 grammaticality.' *Language Learning* 29:81–104. [47]

Bialystok, E. 1981. 'The role of linguistic knowledge in second language use.' *Studies in Second Language Acquisition* 4:31–45. [41, 48]

Bialystok, E. 1982. 'On the relationship between knowing and using linguistic forms.' *Applied Linguistics* 3:181–206. [48–9, 62]

Bialystok, E. 1984. 'Strategies in interlanguage learning and performance' in A. Davies, C. Criper, and A.P.R. Howatt (eds.): *Interlanguage*. Edinburgh: Edinburgh University Press. [48]

Bialystok, E. 1985. 'The compatibility of teaching and learning strategies.' *Applied Linguistics* 6:255–62. [108, 201(n 8)]

Bialystok, E. and **E. B. Ryan.** 1985. 'A metacognitive framework for the development of first and second language skills' in D. L. Forrest-Pressley, G. E. MacKinnon, and T. G. Waller (eds.): *Metacognition, Cognition, and Human Performance*. New York: Academic Press. [48]

Bialystok, E. and **M. Sharwood Smith.** 1985. 'Interlanguage is not a state of mind: an evaluation of the construct for second-language acquisition.' *Applied Linguistics* 6:101–17. [33, 44(n 3), 48–9]

Bickerton, D. 1973. 'The nature of a creole continuum.' *Language* 49:641–69. [176]

Bickerton, D. 1975. *Dynamics of a Creole System*. Cambridge: Cambridge University Press. [176]

Bickerton, D. 1977. 'Pidginization and creolization: language acquisition and languages universals' in A. Valdman (ed.): *Pidgin and Creole Linguistics*. Bloomington: Indiana University Press. [176, 178, 186(n 11)]

Bickerton, D. and **C. Odo.** 1976. *Change and Variation in Hawaiian English*. Final Report of NSF Project No. GS–39748. [177]

Birdsong, D. 1987. MS. 'A role for negative evidence in second-language acquisition.' Paper read at the Annual Meeting of the American Association for Applied Linguistics, 1987. [200(n 2)]

Blanc, H. 1964. *Communal Dialects in Baghdad*. Harvard Middle Eastern Monographs, X. Cambridge, Mass.: Harvard University Press. [132]

Bley-Vroman, R. 1983. 'The comparative fallacy in interlanguage studies: the case of systematicity.' *Language Learning* 33:1–18. [33]

Blickenstaff, C.C. 1963. 'Musical talents and foreign language learning ability.' *Modern Language Journal* 47:359–63. [106]

Blom, J-P. and **J.J. Gumperz.** 1972. 'Social meaning in linguistic structure: code-switching in Norway' in J.J. Gumperz and D. Hymes (eds.): *Directions in Sociolinguistics*. New York: Holt Rinehart and Winston. [147(n 12)]

Blum-Kulka, S. 1982. 'Learning to say what you mean in a second language: a study of the speech act performance of learners of Hebrew as a second language.' *Applied Linguistics* 3:29–59. [54]

Bowerman, M. 1982. 'Starting to talk worse. Clues to language acquisition from children's late speech errors' in S. Strauss (ed.): *U-shaped Behavior Growth*. New York: Academic Press. [108]

Breitborde, L.B. 1983. 'Levels of analysis in sociolinguistic explanation.' *International Journal of the Sociology of Language* 39:5–43. [140, 162]

Brière, E. 1968. *A Psycholinguistic Study of Phonological Interference*. The Hague: Mouton. [120–1]

Brière, E. 1978. 'Variables affecting native Mexican children's learning Spanish as a second language.' *Language Learning* 28:159–74. [195]

Brown, P. and **S.C. Levinson.** (1978), 1987. *Politeness: Some Universals in Language Use*. Cambridge: Cambridge University Press. [55]

Bruck, M. 1978. 'The suitability of early French immersion programs for the language-disabled.' *Canadian Journal of Education* 3:45–72. [88]

Bruck, M. 1982. 'Language-impaired children's performance in an additive bilingual education program.' *Applied Psycholinguistics* 3:45–61. [88]

Bruner, J. 1981. 'The social context of language acquisition.' *Language and Communication* 1:155–78. [131]

Brutten, S.R., P.J. Angelis, and K. Perkins. 1985. 'Music and memory: predictors for attained ESL oral proficiency.' *Language Learning* 35:299–313. [106]

Campbell R. and R. Wales. 1970. 'The study of language acquisition' in J. Lyons (ed.): *New Horizons in Linguistics.* Harmondsworth: Penguin Books. [52]

Canale, M. and M. Swain. 1980. 'Theoretical bases of communicative approaches to second language teaching and testing.' *Applied Linguistics* 1:1–47. [52–3, 62]

Carroll, J.B. 1961. 'Fundamental considerations in testing for English language proficiency of foreign students.' *Testing.* Washington, DC: Center for Applied Linguistics. [60–1, 74]

Carroll, J.B. 1962. 'The prediction of success in intensive foreign language training' in R. Glazer (ed.): *Training Research and Education.* Pittsburgh, Pa.: The University of Pittsburgh Press. [29(n 5), 71, 148]

Carroll, J.B. 1963. 'Research on teaching foreign languages' in N.L. Gage (ed.): *Handbook of Research on Teaching.* Chicago: Rand McNally. [105]

Carroll, J.B. 1967. 'The foreign language proficiency levels attained by language majors near graduation from college.' *Foreign Language Annals* 1:131–51. [64, 195]

Carroll, J.B. 1973. 'Implications of aptitude test research and psycholinguistic theory for foreign language teaching.' *International Journal of Psycholinguistics* 2:5–14. [107]

Carroll, J.B. 1981. 'Conscious and automatic processes in language learning.' *Canadian Modern Language Review* 37:462–74. [2, 7]

Carroll, J.B. and S.M. Sapon. 1957. *Modern Language Aptitude Test.* New York: Psychological Corporation. [104]

Carroll, J.B. and S.M. Sapon. 1967. *Modern Language Aptitude Test—Elementary.* New York: Psychological Corporation. [104]

Carter, R. 1987. 'Is there a core vocabulary? Some implications for language teaching.' *Applied Linguistics* 8:178–93. [81]

Cazden, C.B., H. Cancino, E. Rosansky, and J.H. Schumann. 1975. 'Second language acquisition in children, adolescents and adults.' Final Report. US Department of Health, Education, and Welfare. [10(n 15), 176–7]

Chastain, K. 1975. 'Affective and ability factors in second language acquisition.' *Language Learning* 25:153–61. [113]

Chaudron, C. 1985. 'Intake: on models and methods for discovering learners' processing of input.' *Studies in Second Language Acquisition* 7:1–14. [192]

Chihara, T. and J.W. Oller Jr. 1978. 'Attitudes and attained proficiency in EFL: a sociolinguistic study of adult Japanese learners.' *Language Learning* 28: 55–68. [195]

Chomsky, N. 1980. *Rules and Representations.* Oxford: Blackwell. [90, 99(n 6), 125]

Chomsky, N. 1981. *Lectures on Government and Binding.* Dordrecht, Holland: Foris Publications. [90, 125]

Chomsky, N. 1982. *Some Concepts and Consequences of the Theory of Government and Binding.* Cambridge, Mass.: MIT Press. [89–90, 125]

Chomsky, N. 1986. *Knowledge of Language: its Nature, Origin, and Use.* New York: Praeger Publishers. [186(n 12)]

Clark, E. 1973. 'What's in a word?' in T. Moore (ed.): *Cognitive Development and the Acquisition of Language*. New York: Academic Press. [108]

Clark, H. and E. Clark. 1978. 'Universals, relativity, and language processing' in J. Greenberg (ed.): *Method and Theory: Universals of Human Language*. Volume 1. Stanford University Press. [123]

Clark, J.L.D. (ed.) 1978. *Direct Testing of Speaking Proficiency: Theory and Practice*. Princeton, NJ: Educational Testing Service. [64]

Clarke, M.A. 1976. 'Second language acquisition as a clash of consciousness.' *Language Learning* 26:377–90. [112]

Clément, R., R.C. Gardner, and P.C. Smythe. 1977. 'Motivational variables in second language acquisition: a study of francophones learning English.' *Canadian Journal of Behavioral Science* 9:205–15. Cited in Gardner 1985. [114]

Clément, R. and B.G. Kruidenier. 1983. 'Orientations in second language acquisition: I. The effects of ethnicity, milieu and target language on their emergence.' *Language Learning* 33:273–94. [155–6]

Clyne, M. (ed.) 1986. *An Early Start: Second Language at Primary School*. Melbourne: River Seine Publications. [99(n 7)]

Cohen, A.D. 1982. 'Neurolinguistics and second language acquisition.' *TESOL Quarterly* 16:305–6. [6, 87]

Cohen, P.R. 1985. *Heuristic Reasoning about Uncertainty: An Artificial Intelligence Approach*. London: Pitman. [231(n 2)]

Cook, V.J. 1985. 'Chomsky's universal grammar and second language learning.' *Applied Linguistics* 6:2–18. [89–90, 101, 115(n 1), 125, 126–7]

Cooper, R.L. and S. Carpenter. 1976. 'Language in the market' in M.L. Bender, J.D. Bowen, R.L. Cooper, and C.A. Ferguson (eds.): *Language in Ethiopia*. Oxford: Oxford University Press. [165(n 9)]

Cooper, R.L. and C.W. Greenbaum. 1987. MS. 'Accommodation as a framework for the study of simplified registers.' [179]

Coppieters, R. 1987. 'Competence differences between native and near-native speakers.' *Language* 63:544–73. [45(ns 5, 7]

Corder, S.P. 1967. 'The significance of learners' errors.' *IRAL-International Review of Applied Linguistics* 5:161–70. [32]

Corder, S.P. 1975. '"Simple Codes" and the source of a second language learner's initial heuristic hypothesis.' *Studies in Second Language Acquisition* 1:1–11. [10(n 15)]

Corder, S.P. 1978. 'Language distance and the magnitude of the language learning task.' *Studies in Second Language Acquisition* 2. Reprinted in Corder (1981).

Corder, S.P. 1981. *Error Analysis and Interlanguage*. Oxford: Oxford University Press. [32]

Coupland, N. 1980. 'Style-shifting in a Cardiff work-setting.' *Language in Society* 9:1–12. [139]

Coupland, N. 1984. 'Accommodation at work: some phonological data and their implications.' *International Journal of the Sociology of Language* 46:49–70. [139]

Cross T. 1978. 'Mothers' speech and its acquisition with rate of linguistic development in young children' in N. Waterson and C. Snow (eds.): *The Development of Communication*. New York: John Wiley and Sons. [181, 190]

Cummins, J. 1979. 'Cognitive academic language proficiency, linguistic interdependence, the optimum age question, and some other matters.' *Working Papers on Bilingualism* 19:197–205. [45(n 21)]

Cummins, J. 1980. 'The cross-lingual dimensions of language proficiency: implications for bilingual education and the optimal age issue.' *TESOL Quarterly* 14:175–87. [102]

Cummins, J. 1984. 'Wanted: a theoretical framework for relating language proficiency to academic achievement among bilingual students' in C. Rivera (ed.): *Language Proficiency and Academic Achievement.* Clevedon: Multilingual Matters. [45(n 21)]

Cziko, G. 1984. 'Some problems with empirically-based models of communicative competence.' *Applied Linguistics* 5:23–38. [73–4]

Danesi, M. 1988. 'Neurological bimodality and theories of language teaching.' *Studies in Second Language Acquisition* 10:13–31. [99(n 5)]

Davies, A. 1984. 'Introduction' in A. Davies, C. Criper, and A.P.R. Howatt (eds.) 1984:ix-xv. [36, 44(n 3)]

Davies, A., C. Criper, and **A.P.R. Howatt,** (eds.) 1984. *Interlanguage.* Edinburgh: Edinburgh University Press. [36, 44(n 3)]

Davies, E.E. 1987. 'A contrastive approach to the analysis of politeness formulas.' *Applied Linguistics* 8:75–88. [58(n 12)]

Davis, J.A. 1985. *The Logic of Causal Order.* Sage University Paper series on Quantitative Applications in the Social Sciences, series no. 07–055. Beverly Hills, Calif.: Sage Publications. [213]

Dickerson, L.J. 1974. 'The learner's interlanguage as a system of variable rules.' *TESOL Quarterly* 9:401–8 [33, 36]

Dickerson, L.J. and **W.B. Dickerson.** 1977. 'Interlanguage phonology: current research and future directions' in S.P. Corder and E. Roulet (eds.): *The Notions of Simplification, Interlanguages, and Pidgins: Actes du 5ème Colloque de Linguistique Appliquée de Neuchâtel.* [38]

Dickerson, W.B. 1976. 'The psycholinguistic unity of language learning and language change.' *Language Learning* 26:215–32.

Di Pietro, R. 1987. *Strategic Interaction: Learning Languages through Scenarios.* Cambridge: Cambridge University Press. [172]

Dodson, C.J. 1985. 'Second-language acquisition and bilingual development: a theoretical framework.' *Journal of Multilingual and Multicultural Development* 6:325–46. [9(n 9), 45(n 12)]

Dulay, H. and **M. Burt.** 1974. 'A new perspective on the creative construction processes in child second language acquisition.' *Language Learning* 24:253–78. [93, 120]

Dulay H., M. Burt, and **S. Krashen.** 1982. *Language Two.* New York: Oxford University Press. [56, 95]

Eckman, F. 1977. 'Markedness and the contrastive analysis hypothesis.' *Language Learning* 27:315–30. [121–2]

Eckman, F. 1981a. 'On the naturalness of interlanguage phonological rules.' *Language Learning* 31:195–216. [123]

Eckman, F. 1981b. 'On predicting phonological difficulty in second language acquisition.' *Studies in Second Language Acquisition* 4:18–30. [123]

Eckman, F. 1984. MS. 'The markedness differential.' Paper prepared for the Thirteenth Annual University of Wisconsin-Milwaukee Linguistics Symposium, 29–31 March 1984.

Edelsky, C., B. Altwerger, F. Barkin, B. Flores, S. Hudelson, and **K. Jilbert.** 1983. 'Semilingualism and language deficit.' *Applied Linguistics* 4:1–22. [43, 45(n 21)]

Edmondson W., J. House, G. Kasper, and **B. Stemmer.** 1984. 'Learning the pragmatics of discourse: a project report.' *Applied Linguistics* 5:113–27. [55]

Eisenstein, M. and **J. Bodman.** 1986. '"I very appreciate": expressions of gratitude by native and non-native speakers of American English.' *Applied Linguistics* 7:166–85. [55]

Ellis, R. 1981. 'The role of input in language acquisition: some implications for second language teaching.' *Applied Linguistics* 2:70–82. [190]

Ellis, R. 1982. 'The origins of interlanguage.' *Applied Linguistics* 3:207–23. [33]

Ellis, R. 1985. *Understanding Second Language Acquisition.* Oxford: Oxford University Press. [6, 10(ns 14, 17), 29(n 4), 30–1, 35–6, 44(n 2)]

Ellis, R. and G. Wells. 1980. 'Enabling factors in adult-child discourse.' *First Language* 1:46–82. [190]

Ely, C.M. 1986a. 'An analysis of discomfort, risktaking, sociability, and motivation in the L2 classroom.' *Language Learning* 36:1–26. [115]

Ely, C.M. 1986b. 'Language learning motivation: a descriptive and causal analysis.' *Modern Language Journal* 70:28–35. [156, 164]

Ervin-Tripp, S. 1974. 'Is second language learning like the first?' *TESOL Quarterly* 8:111–27. [94, 99(n 9)]

Færch, C. and G. Kasper. 1986. 'Cognitive dimensions of language transfer' in E. Kellerman and M. Sharwood Smith (eds.) 1986:49–65. [49]

Færch, C. and G. Kasper. 1987. 'Perspectives on language transfer.' *Applied Linguistics* 8:111–36. [129]

Fairbanks, K. 1982. MS. 'Variability in interlanguage.' [38]

Fathman, A. 1975. 'The relationship between age and second language productive ability.' *Language Learning* 25:245–53. [92, 194–5]

Felix, S.W. 1981. 'The effect of formal instruction on second language acquisition.' *Language Learning* 31:87–112. [93–4, 194]

Ferguson, C.A. 1959. 'Diglossia.' *Word* 14:47–56. [42]

Ferguson, C.A. 1964. 'Baby talk in six languages' in J.J. Gumperz and D. Hymes (eds.): *The Ethnography of Communication. American Anthropologist* 66(6)/2. [179]

Ferguson, C.A. 1971. 'Absence of copula and the notion of simplicity: a study of normal speech, baby talk, foreigner talk, and pidgins' in D. Hymes (ed.): *Pidginization and Creolization of Language.* New York: Cambridge University Press. [173, 179]

Ferguson, C.A. 1975. 'Toward a characterization of foreigner talk.' *Anthropological Linguistics* 17:1–14. [179]

Ferguson, C.A. 1976. 'The structure and use of politeness formulas.' *Language in Society* 5:137–51. [55]

Ferguson, C.A. 1981. '"Foreigner talk" as the name of a simplified register.' *International Journal of the Sociology of Language* 29:9–11. [179]

Fishman, J.A. 1970. *Sociolinguistics: a Brief Introduction.* Rowley, Mass.: Newbury House. [133]

Fishman, J.A. 1972. 'Domains and the relationship between micro- and macrosociolinguistics' in John J. Gumperz and Dell Hymes (eds.): *Directions in Sociolinguistics.* New York: Holt Rinehart and Winston. [140]

Fishman, J.A., R.L. Cooper, R. Ma, *et al.* 1971. *Bilingualism in the Barrio.* Language Science Monographs, Volume 7. Bloomington, Ind.: Indiana University Publications.

Fisiak, J. 1983. 'Present trends in contrastive linguistics' in K. Sajavaara (ed.): *Cross-language Analysis and Second Language Acquisition.* Volume 1. [118–9]

Fisiak, J., M. Lipinska-Grzegorek, and T. Zabrocki. 1978. *An Introductory English-Polish Contrastive Grammar.* Warsaw: Panstwowe Wydawnictwo Naukowe. [119]

Flege, J.E. 1987. 'A critical period for learning to pronounce foreign languages?' *Applied Linguistics* 8:162–77. [99(n 8)]

Flick, W. and G. Gilbert. 1976. 'Second language learning versus pidginization.'

Journal of Creole Studies. Cited in Schumann 1978b. [175]

Freed, B.F. 1980. 'Talking to foreigners versus talking to children: similarities and differences' in R.C. Scarcella and S.D. Krashen (eds.): *Research in Second Language Acquisition.* Rowley, Mass.: Newbury House. [179]

Freed, B.F. 1981. 'Foreigner talk, baby talk, native talk.' *International Journal of the Sociology of Language.* 28:29–39. [179]

Fries, C.C. 1945. *Teaching and Learning English as a Foreign Language.* Ann Arbor, Mich.: University of Michigan Press. [117]

Fromkin, V.A. 1987. 'The lexicon: evidence from acquired dyslexia.' *Language* 63:1–22. [86]

Galloway, L.M. 1981. 'The convolutions of second language: a theoretical article with a critical review and some new hypotheses towards a neuropsychological model of bilingualism and second language performance.' *Language Learning* 31:439–64. [6, 86]

Gardner R.C. 1979. 'Social psychological aspects of second language acquisition' in H. Giles and R. St Clair (eds.): *Language and Social Psychology.* Oxford: Basil Blackwell. [26, 154]

Gardner, R.C. 1983. 'Learning another language: a true social psychological experiment.' *Journal of Language and Social Psychology* 2:219–39. [5, 158]

Gardner, R.C. 1985. *Social Psychology and Second Language Learning: the Role of Attitudes and Motivation.* London: Edward Arnold. [5, 105, 112, 114, 116(n 7), 149, 151, 154–5, 159, 214]

Gardner, R.C., R. Clément, P.C. Smythe, and C.L. Smythe. 1979. 'The Attitude/ motivation test battery—revised manual.' Research Bulletin No. 15, Language Research group, University of Western Ontario. [105]

Gardner, R.C., R.N. Lalonde, and R. Pierson. 1983. 'The socio-educational model of second language acquisition: an investigation using LISREL causal modeling.' *Journal of Language and Social Psychology* 2:1–16. [26, 154]

Gardner, R.C. and W.E. Lambert. 1959. 'Motivational variables in second language acquisition.' *Canadian Journal of Psychology* 13:266–72. [113, 137, 149, 151]

Gardner, R.C. and W.E. Lambert. 1972. *Attitudes and Motivation in Second Language Learning.* Rowley, Mass.:Newbury House. [150]

Gardner, R.C. and P.C. Smythe. 1975. 'Second language acquisition: a social psychological approach.' Research Bulletin No. 332, Department of Psychology, University of Western Ontario. Cited in Gardner 1985. [114]

Gardner, R.C., P.C. Smythe, and G.R. Brunet. 1977. 'Intensive second language study: effects on attitudes, motivation, and French achievement.' *Language Learning* 27:243–62. [150–2]

Gardner, R.C., P.C. Smythe, and R. Clément. 1979. 'Intensive second language study in a bicultural milieu—an investigation of attitudes, motivation and language proficiency.' *Language Learning* 29:305–20. [153]

Gardner, R.C., P.C. Smythe, R. Clément, and L. Gliksman. 1976. 'Second language acquisition: a social psychological perspective.' *Canadian Modern Language Review* 32:198–213. [114]

Gass, S.M. 1979. 'Language transfer and universal grammatical relations.' *Language Learning* 29:327–44. [124]

Gass, S.M. 1982. 'From theory to practice' in M. Hynes and W. Rutherford (eds.): *On TESOL '81.* Washington, DC: TESOL. [196]

Gass, S.M. 1986. 'An interactionist approach to L2 sentence interpretation.' *Studies in Second Language Acquisition* 8:19–37. [30]

Gass, S.M. and E.M. Varonis. 1985. 'Variation in native speaker speech modification to non-native speakers.' *Studies in Second Language Acquisition* 7:37–58. [184]

Genesee, F. 1976. 'The role of intelligence in second language learning.' *Language Learning* 26:267–80. [102–3]

Genesee, F. 1982. 'Experimental neuropsychological research on second language processing.' *TESOL Quarterly* 16:315–22. [6, 87]

Genesee, F. 1983. 'Bilingual education of majority-language children: the immersion experiments in review.' *Applied Psycholinguistics* 4:1–46. [88, 162]

Genesee, F. 1987. *Learning through Two Languages: Studies of Immersion and Bilingual Education.* Rowley, Mass.: Newbury House. [99(n 4), 103, 212]

Genesee, F. and R.Y. Bourhis. 1983. 'The social psychological significance of code switching in cross-cultural communication.' *Journal of Language and Social Psychology* 1: 1–25. [163]

Genesee, F., P. Rogers, and N. Holobow. 1983. 'The social psychology of second language learning: another point of view.' *Language Learning* 33:209–24. [156]

George, H.V. 1972. *Common Errors in Language Learning.* Rowley, Mass.: Newbury House. [123]

Geschwind, N. 1979. 'Specializations of the human brain.' *Scientific American* 241/3:180–201. [98(n 1)]

Gibbons, J. 1985. 'The silent period: an examination.' *Language Learning* 35:255–68. [191]

Giles, H. 1979. 'Accommodation theory: some new directions.' *York Papers in Linguistics.* [138]

Ginsberg, R. G. 1986. 'Issues in the analysis of language loss: methodology of the Language Skills Attrition Project' in B. Weltens, K. de Bot, and T. van Els (eds.) 1986. [231(n 7)]

Givón, T. 1979. 'From discourse to syntax. Grammar as a processing strategy' in T. Givón (ed.): *Discourse and Syntax.* New York: Academic Press. [185(n 3)]

Gliksman, L. 1976. 'Second Language Acquisition: the Effects of Students' Attitudes on Classroom Behavior.' Unpublished MA thesis, University of Western Ontario. Cited in Gardner 1983. [159]

Gould, S.J. 1981. *The Mismeasure of Man.* Hamondsworth: Penguin Books. [75]

Greenberg, J. 1966. 'Language universals' in T.A. Sebeok *et al.*(eds.): *Current Trends in Linguistics*, Volume 3. The Hague: Mouton. [123]

Gregg, K.R. 1984. 'Krashen's monitor and Occam's razor.' *Applied Linguistics* 5:79–100. [9(n 2), 57(n 2), 192]

Grice, H.P. 1975. 'Logic and conversation' in P. Cole and J. Morgan (eds.): *Syntax and Semantics. 3. Speech Acts.* New York:Academic Press. [183]

Guiora, A.Z. 1972 . 'Construct validity and transpositional research: Toward an empirical study of psychoanalytic concepts.' *Comprehensive Psychiatry* 13. [111]

Guiora, A.Z. 1982. 'Language, personality and culture: or the Whorfian hypothesis revised' in M. Hynes and W. Rutherford (eds.): *On TESOL '81.* Washington, DC: TESOL. [111]

Guiora, A.Z. 1983. 'The dialectic of language acquisition.' *Language Learning* (Special Issue) 33/5:3–12. [111]

Guiora, A.Z. and W.R. Acton. 1979. 'Personality and language: a restatement.' *Language Learning* 29:193–204. [110]

Guiora, A.Z., H. Lane, and L.A. Bosworth. 1968. 'An exploration of some personality variables in authentic pronunciation of a second language' in E. Zale (ed.): *Proceedings of the Conference on Language Behavior.* New York: Appleton-Century-Crofts. [110]

Hale, T. and E. Budar. 1970. 'Are TESOL classes the only answer?' *Modern Language Journal* 54:487–92. [194]

Hamayan, E., F. Genesee, and G.R. Tucker. 1977. 'Affective factors and language exposure in second language learning.' *Language Learning* 27:225–42.

Harley, B. 1986. *Age in Second Language Acquisition*. Clevedon: Multilingual Matters. [96–7, 103]

Hatch, E.M. 1983. *Psycholinguistics: a Second Language Perspective*. Rowley, Mass.: Newbury House. [6, 84]

Heath, S. Brice. 1982. 'Questioning at home and at school: a comparative study' in G. Spindler (ed.): *Doing the Ethnography of Schooling*. New York: Holt Rinehart and Winston. [189]

Hidalgo, M. 1986. 'Language contact, language loyalty, and language prejudice on the Mexican border.' *Language in Society* 15:193–220. [156]

Holtzman, P. 1967. 'English language testing and the individual.' *Selected Conference Papers of the Association of Teachers of English as a Second Language*. Washington, DC: NAFSA. [74]

Horwitz, E.K. 1986. 'Preliminary evidence for the reliability and validity of a foreign language anxiety scale.' *TESOL Quarterly* 20:559–62. [115]

Horwitz, E.K., M. Horwitz, and **J. Cope.** 1986. 'Foreign language classroom anxiety.' *Modern Language Journal* 70:125–32. [114]

Huebner, T. 1985. 'System and variability in interlanguage syntax.' *Language Learning* 35:141–64. [35, 45(n 10)]

Hughes, A. 1983. 'Second language learning and communicative language teaching' in K. Johnson and D. Porter (eds.): *Perspectives in Communicative Language Teaching*. London: Academic Press. [6]

Hughes, A. and **D. Porter** (eds.). 1983. *Current Developments in Language Testing*. London: Academic Press. [81(n 3)]

Hymes, D. 1972. 'On communicative competence' in J.B. Pride and J. Holmes (eds.): *Sociolinguistics*. Harmondsworth: Penguin Books. [52, 131]

Hymes, D. 1985. 'Toward linguistic competence.' *Revue de l'AILA: AILA Review* 2:9–23. [57(ns 7, 8), 131]

Jackendoff, R. 1983. *Semantics and Cognition*. Cambridge, Mass.: MIT Press. [4, 12–13, 53, 81(n 9), 84, 100]

Jakobson, R. 1941. *Kindersprache, Aphasie und allgemeine Lautgesetze*. Uppsala: Almquist and Wiksell. [228]

Jakobson, R. 1960. 'Closing statement: linguistics and poetics' in T.A. Sebeok (ed.): *Style in Language*. New York: The Technology Press of MIT and John Wiley and Sons. [57(n 8)]

Johnson, K. 1986. MS. 'Language teaching as skill training.' Paper read at the Centre for Applied Language Studies Colloquium, University of Reading, May 1986. [170]

Johnson, K. 1988. 'Mistake correction.' *English Language Teaching Journal* 42:89–96. [51]

Jordens, P. 1986. 'Production rules in interlanguage: evidence from case errors in L2 German' in E. Kellerman and M. Sharwood Smith (eds.) 1986:91–109. [50, 77]

Joreskog, K.G. and **D. Sorbom.** 1978. *LISREL: Analysis of Linear Structural Relationships by the Method of Maximum Likelihood*. Chicago: International Educational Services. [155]

Kachru, B.B. 1986. *The Alchemy of English: the Spread, Models and Functions of Non-Native Englishes*. Oxford: Pergamon. [45(n 17)]

Kean, M.L. 1986. 'Core issues in transfer' in E. Kellerman and M. Sharwood Smith (eds.) 1986:80–90. [128]

Keefe, J.W. (ed.). 1979. *Student Learning Styles: Diagnosing and Prescribing Programs*. Reston, Va.: National Association of Secondary School Principals. [109]

Kellerman, E. 1979. 'The problem with difficulty.' *Interlanguage Studies Bulletin* 4:27–48. [123]

Kellerman, E. 1984. MS. 'Two constraints on transfer.' Paper prepared for the Thirteenth Annual University of Wisconsin-Milwaukee Linguistics Symposium, 29–31 March 1984.

Kellerman, E. 1986. 'An eye for an eye: crosslinguistic constraints on the development of the L2 lexicon' in E. Kellerman and M. Sharwood Smith (eds.) 1986:35–48.

Kellerman, E., and M. Sharwood Smith (eds.). 1986. *Crosslinguistic Influence in Second Language Acquisition*. New York: Simon and Schuster. [79, 128]

Kelley, J.P. 1982. 'Interlanguage Variation and Social/Psychological Influences within a Developmental Stage.' Unpublished MA thesis. University of California at Los Angeles. Cited in Schumann 1985. [145]

Kelly, R. 1981. 'Aspects of communicative performance.' *Applied Linguistics* 2:169–79. [53]

Kennedy, G. D. 1987. 'Expressing temporal frequency in academic English.' *TESOL Quarterly* 21:69–86. [70(n 9)]

Kitch, K.A. 1982. 'A Description of a Mexican-American's Interlanguage and his Socio-psychological Profile.' Unpublished MA thesis, San Diego State University. Cited in Schumann 1986. [145]

Klein, W. 1986. *Second Language Acquisition*. Cambridge: Cambridge University Press. [6, 9(ns 2, 9), 35–6, 41, 166–8, 171, 185(n 3)]

Klein-Braley, C. 1981. 'Empirical Investigation of Cloze Tests.' PhD dissertation, University of Duisburg. [75]

Kloss, H. 1968. 'Notes concerning a language-nation typology' in J.A. Fishman, C.A. Ferguson, and J. Das Gupta (eds.): *Language Problems of Developing Nations*. New York: John Wiley and Sons. [135, 144]

Kohn, K. 1982. 'Beyond output: the analysis of interlanguage development.' *Studies in Second Language Acquisition* 4:137–52. [32–3]

Kohn, K. 1986. 'The analysis of transfer' in E. Kellerman and M. Sharwood Smith (eds.) 1986:21–34. [129]

Krahnke, K.J. 1985. Review of *The Natural Approach: Language Acquisition in the Classroom*, by S.D. Krashen and T.D. Terrell. *TESOL Quarterly* 19:591–603. [9(n 1)]

Kramsch, C.J. 1985. 'Classroom interaction and discourse options.' *Studies in Second Language Acquisition* 7:169–83. [185(n 7)]

Krashen, S.D. 1980. 'The theoretical and practical relevance of simple codes in second language acquisition' in R.C. Scarcella and S.D. Krashen (eds.): *Research in Second Language Acquisition*. Rowley, Mass.: Newbury House. [188, 190]

Krashen, S.D. 1982. *Principles and Practice in Second Language Acquisition*. Oxford: Pergamon. [62]

Krashen, S.D. 1985. *The Input Hypothesis*. London: Longman. [201(n 7)]

Krashen, S.D., C. Jones, S. Zelinski, and C. Usprich. 1978. 'How important is instruction?' *English Language Teaching Journal* 32:257–61. [201(ns 6, 7)]

Krashen, S.D. and H.W. Seliger. 1976. 'The role of formal and informal linguistic environments in adult second language learning.' *International Journal of Psycholinguistics* 3:15–21. [201(n 6)]

Krashen, S.D., H.W. Seliger, and D. Hartnett. 1974. 'Two studies in second language learning.' *Kritikon Litterarum* 3:220–8. [201(n 6)]

Krashen, S.D. and T.D. Terrell. 1983. *The Natural Approach: Language Acquisition in the Classroom*. Hayward, Calif.: The Hayward Press. [9(n 1), 191]

Kuhn, T.S. 1970. *The Structure of Scientific Revolutions*. 2nd edn. Chicago: University of Chicago Press. [219(n3)]

Kuno, S. 1974. 'The position of relative clauses and conjunctions.' *Linguistic Inquiry* 5:117–36. [177]

Labov, W. 1969. 'The study of language in its social context.' *Studium Generale* 23:30–87. [37, 73]

Labov, W. 1972. *Sociolinguistic Patterns*. Philadelphia, Pa.: The University of Pennsylvania Press. [137]

Lado, R. 1957. *Linguistics across Cultures*. Ann Arbor, Mich.: The University of Michigan Press. [117, 121]

Lado, R. 1961. *Language Testing: The Construction and Use of Foreign Language Tests*. London: Longman. [60]

Lado, R. 1985. '"Total" approach to second language learning and teaching' in B. Wheatley *et al.* (eds.): *Current Approaches to Second Language Acquisition*. Bloomington, Ind.: Indiana University Linguistics Club. [7]

Lalonde, R.N. 1982. 'Second Language Acquisition: a Causal Analysis.' Unpublished MA thesis, University of Western Ontario, London, Ontario. Cited in Gardner 1985. [151]

Lalonde, R.N. and R.C. Gardner. 1984. 'Investigating a causal model of second language acquisition: where does personality fit?' *Canadian Journal of Behavioural Science* 15:224–37. Cited in Gardner 1985. [156]

Lambert, R.D. and B.F. Freed. 1982. *The Loss of Language Skills*. Rowley, Mass.: Newbury House. [231(n 6)]

Lambert, R.D. and S. Moore. 1986. 'Problem areas in the study of language attrition' in B. Weltens, K. de Bot, and T. van Els (eds.) 1986. [231(n 6)]

Lambert, W.E. 1967. 'A social psychology of bilingualism.' *Journal of Social Issues* 23:91–109. [150]

Lambert, W.E., R.C. Gardner, H.C. Barik, and K. Tunstall. 1963. 'Attitudinal and cognitive aspects of intensive study of second language.' *Journal of Abnormal and Social Psychology* 66: 358–68. [156]

Lamendella, J.T. 1977. 'General principles of neurofunctional organization and their manifestation in primary and nonprimary language acquisition.' *Language Learning* 27:155–98. [6, 86]

Landes, J.E. 1975. 'Speech addressed to children: issues and characteristics of parental input.' *Language Learning* 25/2:355–79. [187–8]

Langacker, R.W. 1968. 'Review of Stockwell and Bowen, *The Sounds of English and Spanish*.' *Foundations of Language* 4:211–18. [118]

LeBlanc, R. and G. Painchaud. 1985. 'Self-assessment as a second language placement instrument.' *TESOL Quarterly* 19:673–87. [234(n 2)]

Lehtonen, J., and K. Sajavaara. 1983. 'From traditional contrastive linguistics towards a communicative approach: theory and applications within the Finnish-English cross-language project' in K. Sajavaara (ed.): *Cross-Language Analysis and Second Language Acquisition*. 1:81–94. [119]

Lenneberg, E. 1967. *Biological Foundations of Language*. New York: John Wiley and Sons. [90, 187]

Lerdahl, F. and R. Jackendoff. 1983. *A Generative Theory of Tonal Music*. Cambridge, Mass.: The MIT Press. [12–13]

Levin, L. 1972. *Comparative Studies in Foreign-Language Teaching: The GUME Project*. Stockholm: Almquist and Wiksell. [57(n 3)]

Lewis, E.G. 1980. *Bilingualism and Bilingual Education: A Comparative Study*. Albuquerque: University of New Mexico Press. [70(n 23)]

Lightbown, P. 1983. 'Exploring relationships between developmental and instructional sequences in second language acquisition' in H.W. Seliger and M. H. Long (eds.): *Classroom Oriented Research in Second Language Acquisition*. Rowley, Mass.: Newbury House. [196]

Lightbown, P. 1985. 'Great expectations: second-language acquisition research and classroom teaching.' *Applied Linguistics* 6:173–89. [10(n 13)]

Liskin-Gasparro, J.E. 1984. 'The ACTFL Proficiency Guidelines: an historical perspective' in T.V. Higgs (ed.): *Teaching for Proficiency, the Organizing Principle.* ACTFL Foreign Language Education Series, No. 15. Lincolnwood, Ill.: National Textbook Co. [70(n 11)]

Littlewood, W.T. 1981. 'Language variation and second language acquisition theory.' *Applied Linguistics* 2:150–68. [37]

Long, M.H. 1980. 'Input, Interaction, and Second Language Acquisition.' Unpublished doctoral dissertation, University of California at Los Angeles. [181]

Long, M.H. 1981. 'Questions in foreigner talk discourse.' *Language Learning* 31:135–57. [181–2]

Long, M.H. 1983a. 'Native speaker/non-native speaker conversation and the negotiation of comprehensible input.' *Applied Linguistics* 4:126–41. [57(n 2), 181]

Long, M.H. 1983b. 'Does second language instruction make a difference? A review of research.' *TESOL Quarterly* 17:359–82. [193–5]

Long, M.H. 1983c. 'Linguistic and conversational adjustments to native speakers.' *Studies in Second Language Acquisition* 5:177–93. [181, 184]

Long, M.H. 1988. 'Instructed interlanguage development' in L. Beebe (ed.): *Issues in Second Language Acquisition: Multiple Perspectives.* New York: Newbury House. Pages 115–41. [171, 196–7]

Lowenberg, P.H. 1986. 'Non-native varieties of English: nativization, norms and implications.' *Studies in Second Language Acquisition* 8:1–18. [44(n 4)]

Mackey, W. 1965. *Language Teaching Analysis.* London: Longman. [79]

McLaughlin, B. 1978. 'The monitor model: some methodological considerations.' *Language Learning* 28:309–32. [9(n 2)]

McLaughlin, B. 1987. *Theories of Second-Language Learning.* London: Edward Arnold. [9(n 2), 11, 57(n 2), 230]

McLeod, B. and B. McLaughlin. 1986. 'Restructuring or automaticity? Reading in a second language.' *Language Learning* 36:109–23. [185(n 5)]

Macnamara, J. 1973. 'The cognitive strategies of language learning' in J.W. Oller, Jr and J.C. Richards (eds.): *Focus on the Learner: Pragmatic Perspectives for the Language Teacher.* Rowley, Mass.: Newbury House. [97, 108]

McNeill, D. 1966. 'Developmental psycholinguistics' in F. Smith and G. Miller (eds.): *The Genesis of language.* Cambridge, Mass.: MIT Press. [32]

McNeill, D. 1970. *The Acquisition of Language.* London: Harper and Row. [187]

Mandelbrot, B. 1974. *The Fractal Geometry of Nature.* New York: W.H. Freeman. [226]

Maple, R.F. 1982. 'Social Distance and the Acquisition of English as a Second Language: A Study of Spanish-speaking Adult Learners.' Unpublished doctoral dissertation, The University of Texas at Austin. Cited in Schumann 1986. [145]

Martin-Jones, M. and S. Romaine. 1986. 'Semilingualism: a half-baked theory of communicative competence.' *Applied Linguistics* 7:26–38. [43, 45(n 21)]

Mason, C. 1971. 'The relevance of intensive training in English as a foreign language for university students.' *Language Learning* 21:197–204. [194]

Mazurkewich, I. 1984. 'The acquisition of dative alternation by second language learners and linguistic theory.' *Language Learning* 34:91–109. [127]

Mazurkewich, I. 1985. 'Syntactic markedness and language acquisition.' *Studies in Second Language Acquisition* 7:15–33. [127]

Meisel, J.M. 1976. 'Linguistic simplification. A study of immigrant workers' speech and foreigner talk' in S. P. Corder and E. Roulet (eds.): *The Notions of Simplification, Interlanguages and Pidgins and their Relations to Second Language Pedagogy.* Geneva: Droz. [175]

Miller, G.A. and S. Isard. 1963. 'Some perceptual consequences of linguistic rules.' *Journal of Verbal Learning and Verbal Behavior* 2:217–28. [75]

Milroy, J. and L. Milroy. 1985. *Authority in Language: Investigating Language Prescription and Standardization.* London: Routledge and Kegan Paul. [45(n 18)]

Morris, B.S.K. and L. Gerstman. 1986. 'Age contrasts in the learning of language-relevant materials: some challenges to the critical period hypothesis.' *Language Learning* 36:311–52. [99(n 9)]

Munby, J. 1978. *Communicative Syllabus Design.* Cambridge: Cambridge University Press. [70(ns 8, 21)]

Naiman, N., M. Fröhlich, H.H. Stern, and A. Todesco. 1978. 'The good language learner.' Research in Education Series No. 7. Toronto: Ontario Institute for Studies in Education. [159]

Nemser, W. 1971. 'Approximative systems of foreign language learners.' *IRAL—International Review of Applied Linguistics* 9:115–23 [32]

Neufeld, G.G. 1974. 'A theoretical perspective on the nature of language aptitude.' Proceedings of the Fifth Symposium of the Canadian Association of Applied Linguistics. Cited in Gardner 1985. [105]

Newmeyer, F.J. 1982. 'On the applicability of transformational generative grammar.' *Applied Linguistics* 3:89–120.

Nikolic, T. 1986. 'Teaching a foreign language to visually impaired children in school.' *Language Teaching* 19:218–31. [99(n 5)]

Obler, L. K. 1983. 'Knowledge in neurolinguistics: the case of bilingualism.' *Language Learning* (Special Issue) 33/5:159–91. [85, 87, 99(n 2)]

Ochs, E. 1982. 'Talking to children in Western Samoa.' *Language in Society* 11:77–104. [189]

Odmark, J. 1979. MS. 'Communicative competence, markedness, and second language acquisition.' Paper read at the 54th annual meeting of the Linguistic Society of America. [123]

Oller, J.W. Jr. 1979. *Language Tests at School.* London: Longman. [105]

Oller, J.W. Jr. 1981. 'Language as intelligence.' *Language Learning* 31:465–92. [102]

Oller, J.W. Jr. (ed.) 1983. *Issues in Language Testing Research.* Rowley, Mass.: Newbury House. [72]

Oller, J.W. Jr. 1984. '"g", what is it?' in A. Hughes and D. Porter (eds.): *Current Developments in Language Testing.* London: Academic Press. [75]

Oller, J.W. Jr. and P.A. Richard-Amato. (eds.) 1983. *Methods that Work: A Smorgasbord of Ideas for Language Teachers.* Rowley, Mass.: Newbury House. [1]

Ong, W.J. 1982. *Orality and Literacy: the Technologizing of the Word.* London: Methuen. [45(n 20)]

Oscarson, M. 1988. MS. 'Self-assessment of communicative proficiency.' Paper read at the Language Testing Research Colloquium, University of Illinois at Urbana-Champaign, 5–7 March 1988. [234(n 2)]

Oskarsson, M. 1984. *Self-Assessment of Foreign Language Skills: A Survey of Research and Development Work.* Strasbourg: Council of Europe. [234(n 2)]

Oxford, R.L. 1986. 'Second language learning strategies: current research and implications for practice.' Technical Report, Center for Language Education and Research, University of California, Los Angeles. [116(n 4)]

Oyama, S. 1982a. 'The sensitive period for the acquisition of a non-native phonological system' in S.D. Krashen, R.C. Scarcella, and M. Long (eds.): *Child-Adult Differences in Second Language Acquisition.* Rowley, Mass.: Newbury House. [95]

Oyama, S. 1982b. 'The sensitive period and comprehension' in S.D Krashen, R.C. Scarcella, and M. Long (eds.): *Child-Adult Differences in Second Language Acquisition.* Rowley, Mass.: Newbury House. [96]

Paribakht, T. 1985. 'Strategic competence and language proficiency.' *Applied Linguistics* 6: 132–46. [58(n 10)]

Parkinson, B. and **J. Higham.** 1987. MS. 'Are there discrete learner types?' Institute for Applied Language Studies, University of Edinburgh. [116(n 5)]

Patkowski, M.S. 1980. 'The sensitive period for the acquisition of syntax in a second language.' *Language Learning* 30:449–72. [96]

Patkowski, M.S. 1987. MS. 'Age and accent in a second language; a reply to James Emil Flege.' Paper read at the 1987 Annual Meeting of the Linguistic Society of America. [99(n 8)]

Philipsen, G. and **D. Carbaugh.** 1986. 'A bibliography of fieldwork in the ethnography of speaking.' *Language in Society* 15:387–97. [58(n 11)]

Pica, T. 1985. 'The selective impact of classroom instruction on second language acquisition.' *Applied Linguistics* 6:214–22. [196]

Pica, T. 1987. 'Second-language acquisition, social interaction, and the classroom.' *Applied Linguistics* 8:2–21. [186(n 8)]

Pimsleur, P. 1963. 'Predicting success in high school foreign language courses.' *Educational and Psychological Measurement* 23:349–57. [105]

Pimsleur, P. 1966. *The Pimsleur Language Aptitude Battery.* New York: Harcourt Brace Jovanovitch. [104–5]

Prabhu, N.S. 1987. *Second Language Pedagogy.* Oxford: Oxford University Press. [201(n 9)]

Prator, C. 1978. 'The British heresy in TESL' in J.A. Fishman, C.A. Ferguson, and J. Das Gupta (eds.): *Language Problems of Developing Nations.* New York: John Wiley and Sons. [45(n 17)]

Quirk, R. 1987. 'The question of standards in the international use of English' in P.H Lowenberg (ed.): *Georgetown University Round Table on Languages and Linguistics 1987.* Washington, DC: Georgetown University Press. [146(n 7), 45(n 17)]

Quirk, R. and **H.G. Widdowson.** (eds.) 1985. *English in the World: Teaching and Learning the Language and Literatures.* Cambridge: Cambridge University Press. [45(n 17)]

Raatz, U. and **C. Klein-Braley.** 1982. 'The C-test: a modification of cloze procedures' in *Practice and Principles in Language Testing 4.* Colchester: University of Essex. [76]

Reid, J. M. 1987. 'The learning style preferences of ESL students.' *TESOL Quarterly* 21:87–111. [109]

Ritchie, W. 1978. 'The right-roof constraint in adult acquired language' in W. Ritchie (ed.): *Second Language Acquisition Research: Issues and Implications.* New York: Academic Press. [127]

Rivera, C. (ed.) 1984a. *Language Proficiency and Academic Achievement.* Clevedon: Multilingual Matters. [45(n 21)]

Rogers, M. 1987. 'Learners' difficulties with grammatical gender in German as a foreign language.' *Applied Linguistics* 8:48–74. [130(n 4)]

Rumelhart D.E., J.L. McClelland, and the **PDP Research Group.** 1986. *Parallel Distributed Processing: Explorations in the Microstructures of Cognition.* Volume I, *Foundations*; Volume II, *Psychological and Biological models.* Cambridge, Mass.: The MIT Press. [57(n 9), 226]

Rutherford, W.E. 1982. 'Markedness in second language acquisition.' *Language Learning* 32:85–108. [123]

Sampson, G. 1987. Review article. *Language*, 63:871–86. [57(n 9), 226]

Sampson, G.P. 1982. 'Converging evidence for a dialectical model of function and form in second language learning.' *Applied Linguistics* 3:1–28. [7]

Schachter, J. 1983. 'Nutritional needs of language learners' in M.A. Clark and J. Handscombe (eds.): *On TESOL '82: Pacific Perspectives on Language Learning and Teaching*. Washington, DC: TESOL. [188, 190]

Schauber, E. and E. Spolsky. 1986. *The Bounds of Interpretation: Linguistic Theory and Literary Text*. Stanford, Calif.: Stanford University Press. [12, 25, 29(n 3), 82]

Scherer, G.A.C. and M. Wertheimer. 1964. *A Psycholinguistic Experiment in Foreign-Language Teaching*. New York: McGraw-Hill. [30]

Schieffelin, B. 1979. 'How Kaluli Children Learn What to Say, What to Do, and How to Feel.' Unpublished doctoral dissertation, Columbia University. [189]

Schmidt, M. 1980. 'Coordinate structures and language universals in interlanguage.' *Language Learning* 26:397–416. [38, 127]

Schmidt, R. 1977. 'Sociolinguistic variation and language transfer in phonology.' *Working Papers in Bilingualism* 12:79–95. [39]

Schmidt, R. 1983. 'Interaction, acculturation, and the acquisition of communication competence. A case study of an adult' in N. Wolfson and E. Judd (eds.): *Sociolinguistics and Language Acquisition*. Rowley, Mass.: Newbury House. [144]

Schmidt, R.W. and J.C. Richards. 1980. 'Speech acts and language learning.' *Applied Linguistics* 1:129–57. [54]

Schumann, J.H. 1974a. 'The implications of interlanguage, pidginization and creolization for the study of adult second language acquisition.' *TESOL Quarterly* 8:145–52.

Schumann, J.H. 1974b. 'The implications of pidginization and creolization for the study of adult second language acquisition' in J.H. Schumann and N. Stenson (eds.): *New Frontiers in Second Language Learning*. Rowley, Mass.: Newbury House. [176]

Schumann, J.H. 1975a. 'Affective factors and the problem of age in second language acquisition.' *Language Learning* 25:209–36. [97]

Schumann, J.H. 1975b. 'Second Language Acquisition: the Pidginization Hypothesis.' Unpublished doctoral dissertation, Harvard University. [69(n 3)]

Schumann, J.H. 1976a. 'Social distance as a factor in second language acquisition.' *Language Learning* 26:135–44. [174]

Schumann, J.H. 1976b. 'Second language acquisition: the pidginization hypothesis.' *Language Learning* 26:391–408. [69(n 3)]

Schumann, J.H. 1978a. *The Pidginization Process: A Model for Second Language Acquisition*. Rowley, Mass.: Newbury House. [10(n 15), 69(n 3), 173, 178]

Schumann, J.H. 1978b. 'The relationship of pidginization, creolization and decreolization to second language acquisition.' *Language Learning* 28:367–80. [10(n 15), 175–7]

Schumann, J.H. 1980. 'The acquisition of English relative clauses by second language learners' in R.C. Scarcella and S.D. Krashen (eds.): *Research in Second Language Acquisition: Selected Papers of the Los Angeles Second Language Acquisition Research Forum*. Rowley, Mass.: Newbury House. [177]

Schumann, J.H. 1982. 'Simplification, transfer, and relexification as aspects of pidginization and early second language acquisition.' *Language Learning* 32:337–66. [177–8]

Schumann, J.H. 1984. MS. 'The acculturation model: the evidence.' Paper prepared for the Thirteenth Annual University of Wisconsin-Milwaukee Linguistics Symposium, 29–31 March 1984. [145]

Schumann, J.H. 1986. 'Research on the acculturation model for second language acquisition.' *Journal of Multilingual and Multicultural Development* 7:379–92. [142, 144, 165(n 7)]

Schumann, J.H., J. Holroyd, R.N. Campbell, and F.A. Ward. 1978. 'Improvement of foreign language pronunciation under hypnosis: a preliminary study.' *Language Learning* 28:143–8. [112]

Scotton, C.M. 1983. 'The negotiation of identities in conversation: a theory of markedness and code choice.' *International Journal of the Sociology of Language* 44:116–36. [163]

Scovel, T. 1978. 'The effect of affect on foreign language learning: a review of the anxiety literature.' *Language Learning* 28:129–42. [113]

Scovel, T. 1982. 'Questions concerning the applicability of neurolinguistic research to second language learning/teaching.' *TESOL Quarterly* 16:323–32. [6, 87]

Searle, J.R. 1969. *Speech Acts: an Essay in the Philosophy of Language*. Cambridge: Cambridge University Press. [54]

Sebeok, T.A. (ed.) 1960. *Style in Language*. New York: The Technology Press of MIT and John Wiley and Sons. [57(n 8)]

Seliger, H.W. 1982. 'On the possible role of the right hemisphere in second language acquisition.' *TESOL Quarterly* 16:307–14. [6, 87]

Seliger, H.W. 1983. 'The language learner as linguist: of metaphors or realities.' *Applied Linguistics* 4:179–91.

Seliger, H.W., S.D. Krashen, and P. Ladefoged. 1975. 'Maturational constraints in the acquisition of second language.' *Language Sciences* 38:20–2. [95]

Selinker, L. 1969. 'Language transfer.' *General Linguistics* 9:67–92. [32]

Selinker, L. 1971. 'Interlanguage.' *IRAL—International Review of Applied Linguistics* 10:209–31. [32–3]

Selinker, L. and D. Douglas. 1985. 'Wrestling with "context" in interlanguage theory.' *Applied Linguistics* 6:190–204. [40, 44(n 2), 45(n 16)]

Selinker, L., M. Swain, and G. Dumas. 1975. 'The interlanguage hypothesis extended to children.' *Language Learning* 25:139–52. [35]

Seright, L. 1985. 'Age and aural comprehension achievement in Francophone adults.' *TESOL Quarterly* 19:455–73. [96]

Sharwood Smith, M. 1983. 'Cross-linguistic aspects of second language acquisition.' *Applied Linguistics* 4:192–99. [50]

Sharwood Smith, M. 1985. 'Preface'. *Applied Linguistics* 6:211–13. [201(n 8)]

Sharwood Smith, M. 1986. 'The competence/control model, crosslinguistic influence and the creation of new grammars' in E. Kellerman and M. Sharwood Smith (eds.) 1986. [49]

Sharwood Smith, M. and E. Kellerman. 1986. 'Crosslinguistic influence in second language acquisition: an introduction' in E. Kellerman and M. Sharwood Smith (eds.) 1986:1–9. [49]

Shohamy, E. 1983. 'The stability of the oral proficiency trait on the oral interview speaking test.' *Language Learning* 33:161–71. [64]

Shohamy, E. and T. Reves. 1985. 'Authentic language tests: where from and where to?' *Language Testing* 2:48–59. [64]

Sinclair, J. 1985. 'Selected issues' in R. Quirk and H.G. Widdowson (eds.) 1985:248–54. [45(n 18)]

Skehan, P. 1980. 'Language aptitude: a review.' *English Language Research Journal* 1, University of Birmingham. [107]

Skehan, P. 1986a. 'Cluster analysis and identification of learner types' in V.J. Cook (ed.): *Experimental Approaches to Second Language Acquisition*. Oxford: Pergamon. [107]

Skehan, P. 1986b. 'The role of foreign language aptitude in a model of school learning.' *Language Testing* 3:188–221. [105]

Sledd, J. 1969. 'Bi-dialectalism: the linguistics of white supremacy.' *The English Journal* 1307–16. [132]

Smith, D.M. 1972. 'Some implications for the social status of pidgin languages' in D.M. Smith and R. Shuy (eds.): *Sociolinguistics in Cross-Cultural Analyses.* Washington, DC: Georgetown University Press. [175]

Snow, C.E., R. van Eeden, and **P. Muysken.** 1981. 'The interactional origins of foreigner talk: municipal employees and foreign workers.' *International Journal of the Sociology of Language.* 28:411–30. [179]

Sollenberger, H.E. 1978. 'Development and current use of the FSI oral interview test' in J.L.D. Clark (ed.) 1978. [63]

Spada, N.M. 1987. 'Relationships between instructional differences and learning outcomes: a process-product study of communicative language teaching.' *Applied Linguistics* 8:137–61. [198]

Spolsky, B. 1967. 'Do they know enough English?' in *Selected Conference Papers of the Association of Teachers of English as a Second Language.* English Language Series 13, NAFSA Studies and Papers. Washington, DC: National Association for Foreign Student Affairs. [74]

Spolsky, B. 1968. 'Language testing—the problem of validation.' *TESOL Quarterly* 2:88–94. [53, 75]

Spolsky, B. 1969a. 'Attitudinal aspects of second language learning.' *Language Learning* 19:271–85. [147(n 16)]

Spolsky, B. 1969b. 'Linguistics and language pedagogy—applications or implications?' in J. Alatis (ed.): *Twentieth Annual Round Table on Languages and Linguistics.* Washington, DC: Georgetown University Press. [10(n 13)]

Spolsky, B. 1971. 'Reduced redundancy as a language testing tool' in G.E. Perren and J.L. Trim (eds.): *Applications of Linguistics.* Cambridge: Cambridge University Press.

Spolsky, B. 1973. 'What does it mean to know a language, or how do you get someone to perform his competence?' in J.W. Oller Jr. and J.C. Richards (eds.): *Focus on the Learner: Pragmatic Perspectives for the Language Teacher.* Rowley, Mass.: Newbury House. [73]

Spolsky, B. 1974. 'Speech communities and schools.' *TESOL Quarterly* 8:17–26. [146(n 2)]

Spolsky, B. 1977. 'Language testing: art or science' in G. Nickel (ed.): *Proceedings of the Fourth International Congress of Applied Linguistics.* Volume 3. Stuttgart: Hochschulverlag. [60]

Spolsky, B. 1978b. 'A model for the evaluation of bilingual education.' *International Review of Education* 24:347–60. [146(ns 1, 9)]

Spolsky, B. 1979a. 'The comparative study of first and second language acquisition' in F.R. Eckman and A.J. Hastings (eds.): *Studies in First and Second Language Acquisition.* Rowley, Mass.: Newbury House.

Spolsky, B. 1979b. 'Contrastive analysis, error analysis, interlanguage and other useful fads.' *Modern Language Journal* 62:250–57. [130(n 1), 45(n 6)]

Spolsky, B. 1981. 'Bilingualism and biliteracy.' *Canadian Modern Language Review* 37:475–85 [146(n 6)]

Spolsky, B. 1984. MS. 'Authenticity and language testing.' Paper read at the AILA Congress, Brussels, August 1984. [81(n 2)]

Spolsky, B. 1985a. 'The limits of authenticity in language testing.' *Language Testing* 2:31–40. [70(n 15), 81]

Spolsky, B. 1985b. 'Theories of second language learning: spying out the Promised Land' in B. Wheatley *et al.* (eds.): *Current Approaches to Second Language Acquisition.* Bloomington, Ind.: Indiana University Linguistics Club. [9(n 2)]

Spolsky, B. 1985c. 'Formulating a theory of second language learning.' *Studies in Second Language Acquisition* 7:269–88. [5, 9(n 2), 57(n 2)]

Spolsky, B. 1985d. 'Some psycholinguistic conditions for second language learning.' *Per Linguam* 1:2–11. [70(n 22)]

Spolsky, B. 1986a. 'Avoiding the tyranny of the written word: the development of the mediated mode of Jewish literacy from the first to tenth centuries.' *Australian Review of Applied Linguistics* 9/2: 23–37. [136]

Spolsky, B. 1986b. 'Teaching Hebrew in the Diaspora: Rationales and goals.' *Jewish Education* (September): 11–20. [208]

Spolsky, B. and R.L. Cooper. 1986. 'The languages of Jerusalem: Arab-Jewish encounters in Jerusalem.' Final Report on Ford Foundation Grant No. 12 through the Israel Foundation Trustees. Bar-Ilan University Research Authority. [146(n 5), 165(n 9)]

Spolsky, B., J. Green, and J.A.S. Read. 1976. 'A model for the description, analysis and perhaps evaluation of bilingual education' in A. Verdoodt and R. Kjolseth (eds.): *Language and Society*. Louvain: Peeters. [146(n 9)]

Spolsky, B., B. Sigurd, M. Sato, E. Walker, and C. Aterburn. 1968. 'Preliminary studies in the development of techniques for testing overall language proficiency.' *Language Learning* (Special Issue) 18/3:79–101. [74]

Spolsky, E. 1985. 'Towards a cognitively responsible theory of inference: or, what can synapses tell us about ambiguity?' *Theoretical Linguistics* 12:197–203. [13]

Sridhar, S.N. 1976. 'Contrastive analysis, error analysis and interlanguage: three phases of one goal?' *Indian Linguistics* 37:258–81. [118]

Stauble, A. 1978. 'The process of decreolization: a model for second language development.' *Language Learning* 28:29–54. [10(n 15), 176]

Stauble, A. 1981. 'A comparative study of a Spanish-English and Japanese-English second language continuum.' Unpublished doctoral dissertation, University of California at Los Angeles. Cited in Schumann 1986. [145]

Stauble, A.E. and J.H. Schumann. (in press) 'Toward a description of the Spanish-English basilang' in K. Bailey, M. Long, and S. Peck (eds.): *Selected Papers from the Third Los Angeles Second Language Research Forum*. Rowley, Mass.: Newbury House. [177]

Stern, H.H. 1983. *Fundamental Concepts of Language Teaching*. Oxford: Oxford University Press. [5, 9(n 6), 69(n 1), 84, 104]

Stern, H.H. 1985. Review of J.W. Oller Jr. and P.A. Richard-Amato (ed.) 1983. *Methods that Work: A Smorgasbord of Ideas for Language Teachers. Studies in Second Language Acquisition* 7: 249–51. [1]

Sternberg, F.S. and E.K. Horwitz. 1986. 'The effect of induced anxiety on the denotative and interpretive content of second language speech.' *TESOL Quarterly* 20:131–5. [115]

Stevenson, D.K. 1981. 'Beyond faith and face validity: the multitrait multimethod matrix and construct and discriminant validity of oral proficiency testing' in A.S. Palmer, P.J.M. Groot, and G.A. Trosper (eds.): *The Construct Validation of Tests of Communicative Competence*. Washington, DC: TESOL. [74]

Stevenson, D.K. 1985. 'Authenticity, validity, and a tea party.' *Language Testing* 2:41–7. [70(n 2), 81(n 7)]

Stevick, E.W. 1986. *Images and Options in the Language Classroom*. Cambridge: Cambridge University Press. [169, 199–200]

Stewart, W. 1968. 'A sociolinguistic typology for describing national multi-lingualism' in J.A. Fishman (ed.): *Readings in the Sociology of Language*. The Hague: Mouton. [133, 135, 146(n 3)]

Street, R.R. Jr. and H. Giles. 1982. 'Speech accommodation theory: a social cognitive approach to language and speech behavior' in M. Roloff and C. Berger (eds.): *Social Cognition and Communication*. Beverly Hills, Calif.: Sage. [139]

Strevens, P.D. 1978. 'The nature of language teaching' in J. Richards (ed.): *Understanding Second and Foreign Language Learning*. Rowley, Mass.: Newbury House. Pages 179–203. [113, 116(n 7)]

Strevens, P.D. 1985. 'Language learning and language teaching: towards an integrated theory.' Forum lecture, LSA-TESOL Institute. [1, 6]

Strevens, P.D. 1987. 'English as an international language.' *English Teaching Forum* (Special Issue). [45(n 17)]

Strevens, P.D. 1988. 'Learning English better through more effective teaching. Six postulates for a model of language learning/teaching.' *World Englishes* 7/1: 51–61. [194]

Swain, M. 1981. 'Time and timing in bilingual education.' *Language Learning* 31:1–16. [94–5]

Symonds, P.M. 1930. *Foreign Language Prognosis Test*. New York: Columbia University Teachers College. [115(n 3)]

Tarallo, F. and J. Myhill. 1983. 'Interference and natural language processing in second language acquisition.' *Language Learning* 33:55–76. [124]

Tarampi, A.S., W.E. Lambert, and G.R. Tucker. 1968. 'Audience sensitivity and oral skill in a second language.' *Philippine Journal for Language Teaching* 6:27–33. Cited in Gardner 1985. [113]

Tarone, E. 1979. 'Interlanguage as chameleon.' *Language Learning* 29:181–92. [33, 37]

Tarone, E. 1982. 'Systematicity and attention in interlanguage.' *Language Learning* 32:69–84. [37]

Tarone, E. 1983. 'On the variability of interlanguage systems.' *Applied Linguistics* 4:142–64. [38, 41]

Tarone, E. 1984. MS. 'The interlanguage continuum.' Paper prepared for the Thirteenth Annual University of Wisconsin-Milwaukee Linguistics Symposium, 29–31 March 1984.

Tarone, E. 1985. 'Variability in interlanguage: a study of style-shifting in morphology and syntax.' *Language Learning* 35:373–95. [38]

Taylor, B. 1974. 'Towards a theory of language acquisition.' *Language Learning* 24:23–36. [157]

Thomas, J. 1983. 'Cross-cultural pragmatic failure.' *Applied Linguistics* 4:91–112. [55]

Titone, R. 1982. 'Second-language learning: an integrated psycholinguistic model' in B. Bain (ed.): *The Sociogenesis of Language and Human Conduct*. New York: Plenum. Pages 273–85. [9(n 11)]

Titone, R. 1985. 'The four basic language skills—myth or reality' in K.R. Jankowsky (ed.): *Scientific and Humanistic Dimensions of Language: Festschrift for Robert Lado*. Amsterdam/Philadelphia: John Benjamins Publishing Co. [57(n1), 70(n 7)]

Titone, R. and M. Danesi. 1985. *Applied Psycholinguistics: An Introduction to the Psychology of Language Learning and Teaching*. Toronto: University of Toronto Press. [9(n 11), 10(n 13)]

Trites, R. 1981. *Primary French Immersion: Disabilities and Prediction of Success*. Toronto, Ont.: Ontario Institute for Studies in Education Press. [88]

Trosset, C.S. 1986. 'The social identity of Welsh learners.' *Language in Society* 15:165–91. [166]

Tucker, G.R., E. Hamayan, and F. Genesee. 1976. 'Affective, cognitive, and social factors in second language acquisition.' *Canadian Modern Language Review* 23:214–26. [103]

Upshur, J. 1968. 'Four experiments on the relation between foreign language learning and teaching.' *Language Learning* 18:111–24. [193–4]

van Ek, J.A. 1975. *The Threshold Level*. Strasbourg: Council of Europe. [70(n 19)]

van Els, T. 1986. 'An overview of European research on language attrition' in B. Weltens, K. de Bot, and T. van Els (eds.) 1986. [231(n 6)]

Varonis, E.M. and **S. Gass.** 1985. 'Non-native/non-native conversations: a model for negotiation of meaning.' *Applied Linguistics* 6:71–90. [171]

Vigil, N. and **J.W. Oller Jr.** 1976. 'Rule fossilization: a tentative model.' *Language Learning* 26:281–95. [189]

von Elek, T. 1982. 'Test of Swedish as a second language: an experiment in self-assessment.' Work papers from the Language Testing Research Center, No. 31. Göteborg University. [234(n 2)]

Wagner, D. A. and **A. Lotfi.** 1983. 'Learning to read by "rote".' *International Journal of the Sociology of Language* 42:111–21. [70(n 18)]

Wagner-Gough, J. and **E. Hatch.** 1975. 'The importance of input data in second language acquisition studies.' *Language Learning* 25:297–308. [188]

Wardhaugh, R. 1974. *Topics in Applied Linguistics*. Rowley, Mass.: Newbury House. [121]

Washabaugh, W. and **F. Eckman.** 1980. Review of J.H. Schumann, *The Pidginization Process*. *Language* 56:453–6. [178]

Waterson, N. and **C. Snow** (eds.) 1978. *The Development of Communication*. New York: John Wiley and Sons. [179]

Wells, C.G. 1985. *Language Development in the Pre-School Years*. Cambridge: Cambridge University Press. [105]

Weltens, B., K. de Bot, and **T. van Els.** 1986. *Language Attrition in Progress*. Dordrecht, Holland: Foris Publications. [231(n 6)]

Wertheimer, Max. 1923. 'Laws of organization in perceptual forms' in W.D.Ellis (ed): 1938. *A Source Book of Gestalt Psychology*, London: Routledge, Kegan and Paul. [13]

Wesche, M.B. 1981. 'Language aptitude measures in streaming, matching students with methods, and diagnoses of learning problems' in K.C. Diller (ed.): *Individual Differences and Universals in Language Learning Aptitude*. Rowley, Mass.: Newbury House. [107]

Weslander, D. and **G.V. Stephany.** 1983. 'Evaluation of an English as a foreign language program for Southeast Asian students.' *TESOL Quarterly* 17:473–80. [196]

Whinnom, K. 1971. 'Linguistic hybridization and the "special case" of pidgins and creoles' in D. Hymes (ed.): *Pidginization and creolization of languages*. Cambridge: Cambridge University Press. [175]

White, L. 1985. 'Universal grammar as a source of explanation in second language acquisition' in B. Wheatley *et al.* (eds.): *Current Approaches to Second Language Acquisition*. Bloomington, Ind.: Indiana University Linguistics Club. [124]

White, L. 1987. 'Against comprehensible input: the input hypothesis and the development of second-language competence.' *Applied Linguistics* 8: 95–110. [192]

Widdowson, H.G. 1979. *Explorations in Applied Linguistics 1*. Oxford: Oxford University Press. [70(n 15)]

Widdowson, H.G. 1984a. *Explorations in Applied Linguistics 2*. Oxford: Oxford University Press. [10n 13), 225]

Widdowson, H.G. 1984b. 'Discussion' in A. Davies, C. Criper, and A.P.R Howatt (eds.): *Interlanguage*. Edinburgh: Edinburgh University Press. [36, 40]

Widdowson, H.G. and **C. Candlin.** 1987. 'Language teaching: a scheme for teacher education.' Series editors' Introduction (published in each book). Oxford: Oxford University Press. [200]

Wilds, C. 1975. 'The oral interview test' in R.L. Jones and B. Spolsky (eds.): *Testing Language Proficiency*. Arlington, Va.: Center for Applied Linguistics. [63]

Wode, H. 1981. *Learning a Second Language: I. An Integrated View of Language Acquisition.* Tübingen: Gunter Narr Verlag. [6]

Wolfson, N. 1986. 'Research methodology and the question of validity.' *TESOL Quarterly* 20:689–99. [81(n 1)]

Wolfson, N. and E. Judd. (eds.) 1983. *Sociolinguistics and Language Acquisition.* Rowley, Mass.: Newbury House. [58(n 12)]

Yule, G., J.L. Yanz, and A. Tsuda. 1985. 'Investigating aspects of the language learner's confidence: an application of the theory of signal detection.' *Language Learning* 35:473–88. [116(n 8), 169]

Zobl, H. 1983. 'Markedness and the projection problem.' *Language Learning* 33:293–314. [124]

Zobl, H. 1985. 'Grammars in search of input and intake' in S. Gass and C. Madden (eds.): *Input and Second Language Acquisition.* Rowley, Mass.: Newbury House. [196]

Index